Aboriginal Suicide
is Different

In memory of two friends and mentors—
Pastor Sir Douglas Nicholls, KCVO, OBE
and
Dr Charles Perkins, AO

Both had, and valued, purpose in life.

Aboriginal Suicide
is Different

A Portrait of Life and Self-Destruction

Colin Tatz

Aboriginal
Studies
Press

First published in 2001 by Aboriginal Studies Press
for the Australian Institute of Aboriginal and Torres Strait
Islander Studies, GPO Box 553, Canberra ACT 2601.
2nd Edition 2005.

The views expressed in this publication are those of the
author and not necessarily those of the Australian Institute
of Aboriginal and Torres Strait Islander Studies.

National Library of Australia Cataloguing-in-Publication
Data:

Tatz, Colin.
Aboriginal suicide is different : a portrait of life
and self-destruction.

2nd ed.
Bibliography.
Includes index.
ISBN 0 85575 498 2.

1. Aboriginal Australians — Suicidal behavior. 2.
Aboriginal Australians — Social conditions. I.
Australian Institute of Aboriginal and Torres Strait
Islander Studies. II. Title.

362.280899915

Design and layout by Aboriginal Studies Press
Printed in Australia by Union Offset Printing

COVER: Painting by Michael Mucci

Contents

Introduction to the Second Edition

In July 2005, the US Food and Drug Administration (FDA) at last issued a Public Health Advisory warning about the need to watch very closely the 'increased suicidal thinking or behavior' among those adults being treated with anti-depressant drugs.[1] A bitter irony, indeed. An army of drug-makers and health professionals have for long proclaimed that pharma-therapy relieves depression, a 'mental disorder' declared to be the major, if not the sole, cause of suicide. Now the salvation drugs, at least in the context of suicide, appear to be not only curative but causative.

This second edition of *Aboriginal Suicide is Different*, first published by Aboriginal Studies Press in its Report Series in 2001, is timely. Youth suicide escalates among the Aboriginal young in Australia, New Zealand, Canada, the United States, Scandinavia and in the Pacific island states. Suicide prevention agencies, and their strategies, proliferate. Biological psychiatry suggests that explanations are to be found in biochemistry and genetics. And sceptics like me continue to call for evermore attention to systemic social, cultural and political explanations — and paths to alleviation.

This edition retains the original text, but benefits from the addition of this preamble, an expanded bibliography, and a new index. My editor, Dr Peter Arnold, insists there is no such thing as good writing, only good re-writing. I agree. But this book does not include any recasting or rephrasing apart from the additions noted.

Here I have some space for reactions to those who have publicly disparaged my perspective on Aboriginal youth suicide; for some observations on later fieldwork experience in polar Canada; for some reflections on events since 2001; and for the expression of one regret.

Biomedicine

First, the regret. A major theme of this book is the inappropriateness of the public health or medical model for Australian Aboriginal, Maori and indigenous youth suicide generally. My sustained contention is that most, if not all, indigenous youth suicide has no basis in 'mental ill-health', in depression, let alone in genetics or biochemistry. In company with James Hillman (1997), my assertion is that we need *understanding* of the suiciders — rather than longer lists of 'at-risk' factors, more comparative statistics, more post-hoc diagnoses that assume, even insist, that mental ill-health/ depression is the only or inevitable cause. I argue for contextual study, including external factors such as 'Westernisation', the legacy of colonialism, enduring racism, chronic unemployment, the impoverishment of body and soul; and for internal factors such as parenting problems, sexual abuse, alcohol and drug overuse, perpetual grief cycles, an absence of adult mentors, illiteracy and deafness from chronic middle ear infections. I also argue that we should embrace these cultural and social factors in developing strategies for alleviating the problem — not their perfunctory acknowledgement as factors.

The text does get there, in plain language. But it would have done so in shorter time, more succinctly, and, perhaps, more provocatively, had I benefited from Dani Filc's paper on 'The medical text: between biomedicine and hegemony', admittedly published three years later (Filc 2004, 1275–85).

A fellow political scientist, Filc confronts 'biomedicine', that is, the dominant medical ideology which contends that illness and disease are located solely within the individual and that treatment is predominantly, if not exclusively, surgical and/or pharmacological. Such location 'exonorates society from any responsibility in the aetiology of the disease'. Biomedicine de-socialises and de-contextualises disease and explains *any* social phenomenon, where on the occasions it is considered relevant, in medical terms. The patient, not society, is the ultimate repository of responsibility (Filc 2004, 1276–9).

'Evidence-based medicine' is now the ruling ideology, the new medical religion or, rather, the new medical 'science'. Its task is to 'develop statistical techniques of analysis in order to determine "scientifically based" universal ways of treating conditions or diseases'. In short, Filc contends that biomedicine sees disease as always emanating from within the individual — never as a consequence of, or as a part of, a social problem. Even where the social context is self-evident in youth suicide, it is excluded, or deemed to be medical rather than social or political. *Aboriginal Suicide is Different* is the antithesis of this view: the social context is forever evident and medical factors can be excluded — unless unequivocally shown, in the individual case, to be relevant.

'Disorders'

In several critiques of my work, 'mental disorders' are invoked as given gospel, as self-evident 'facts' which need no further explanation or elaboration. There is a smugness of certainty that the defined disorders are 'scientific' and proven — even though 'disorders' are reversed, or re-defined, or changed at breathtaking pace. Not surprisingly, I have a jaundiced view — if you'll forgive the medical metaphor — of that bible of the American Psychiatric Association, the *Diagnostic and statistical manual for mental disorders*, known in short as DSM-IV-TR. It lists over 50 major categories of mental disorder, with new names for new disorders — biomedicine gone mad, so to speak. Thus, a Mathematical Deficit Syndrome is a definable 'disorder' — meaning that, if you can't do maths, you think about it and feel bad about it (DSM-IV-TR 2000, 531). In like vein, you apparently have a mental disorder if you smoke, drink a bit too much and ingest caffeine (2000, 231), have an aggressive nature, exhibit anti-social tendencies (2000, 740), have an erectile problem (2000, 545), a male orgasmic disorder (2000, 369), or exhibit hypochondria (2000, 504).

Some researchers view these 'syndromes' as controversial. Be that as it may, they stand out quite plainly on the pages of DSM-IV-TR as *disorders*. Reser (2004, 40) defends DSM when he invokes that volume's appendix on 'cultural formulation', one which addresses cultural context and cultural explanations. Yet these explanations and sensitivies are relevant only in so far as they *might* contribute to a patient's already medicalised problem.

Whatever happened to such normal social states of being as anxiety, dejection, dis-ease, disquiet, fear, glumness, joylessness, misery, pessimism, sadness, uneasiness, unhappiness?

Science and statistics

I confess to offering statistics (of my own and of others) throughout the text. Statistics, especially of the comparative variety, are the staple of suicid-ologists. I have succumbed, with reservations, to some of their language. Filc has helped me understand, in part, these reservations: 'there is a lack of awareness', he writes, 'that the construction and evaluation of "scientific data" are social processes' (2004, 1276–8); and that evidence-based medicine, as a consequence of an uncritical approach to statistics, relies on an ingenuous epistemology that considers 'facts' as absolute certainty, as 'true knowledge', as 'objective things' beyond inference, question or reproach.

Suicide statistics, the lifeblood of thousands of researchers and writers, are the 'data' exhumed from coronial records. Students of suicide rarely go into the field, assess the social (or cultural) climate of their own societies, let alone of indigenous societies, work with those who are 'dysfunctional' and have attempted or threatened suicide, and observe and analyse the life and times of those who succeed. In the text I note that the late Joseph Zubin, a renowned American psychopathologist and authority on the aetiology of schizophrenia, once said, 'in most behaviour disorders we have at least part of the process at hand for examination', but 'in suicide all we usually have is the end result, arrived at by a variety of paths'. 'Unravelling the causes after the fact', he declared, 'is well nigh impossible' (Tatz 2001, 95).

Most suicide specialists extrapolate, that is, they conjecture from what the 'records' say; the 'records' become 'hard data' and are regarded as inviolable facts. My text deals at length with coronial 'facts' — and their dubious recording, labeling and interpretation, especially in New South Wales. David Lester, among a few others, has discussed the perennial problem of the unreliability of suicide statistics (Lester 1987, 1993). To assert that sets of records in coroners' or statisticians' offices are demonstrable, verifiable 'truth' is naïve, to say the least.

Dudley (2004, 28) has stated that the 'golden standard' of psychiatry when seeking out depression or mental illness is to use 'standardised psychiatric diagnostic interviews with relatives and friends, workmates and medical attendants', even to the extent of translating them and using them in different cultural settings. We know only too well from social science research methodology and its problems that respondents most often tell questioners only what they are prepared to tell, or what the questioners want to hear. (A decade ago, American sociologists were calling for the administration of lie-detector tests to research respondents, lamenting that they weren't always telling their questioners 'the truth'.) When the collectivity of clipboard multiple-choice tick boxes, and when hearsay interview records become 'scientific' merely because of their arranged form and presentation, we are in deep trouble. As much as we may want to have a 'science of suicide', we can't.

The book as a 'polemic'?

One of the first reviews of this book was by Robert Goldney, Professor of Psychiatry at Adelaide University, in the form of an article in a professional journal[2] (Goldney 2001, 257–9). The book, he wrote, 'is a poignant and powerful reminder of Aboriginal suffering', but 'it rejects many hard won findings in the scientific study of suicidal behaviour and therefore does not advance our understanding of suicide...' In particular, he points to 'significant levels of mental disorder' in Andrew Cheng's study (1995) of two indigenous Taiwanese groups and the Han Chinese from mainland China 'where mental disorders were present in the majority' of the suicides. Another study in Chennai (Madras) 'reported on the universality of mental disorder in this population (Vijayakumar &

Rajkumar, 1999)'. Nowhere in these reports, of course, is 'mental disorder' defined, demonstrated, explained, analysed or questioned. Nor does Goldney explain why Taiwanese and Chennai findings are, by their very nature, evidence that such 'disorders' exist in Australian Aboriginal and Maori societies.

Goldney condemns my rejection of the genetic/biochemical search for answers. He states that twenty years of published data have highlighted such contributions, and they shouldn't be dismissed.[3] He concludes that 'Tatz's view is polemical and lacks scientific objectivity'.

Psychiatry, Psychology and Law invited my reply. It was short. I confessed to being a 'polemical scientist', engaging in controversial discussion and argument, attacking and refuting the opinions of others. I have spent a lifetime controverting the doctrines and belief systems of many, especially in the fields of race politics and genocide studies. Surely, I contend, disputing and opposing is a proper occupation for a scientist. I suspect that Goldney — along with other critics mentioned below — thinks that 'polemical' means something altogether else, and something pejorative.

Goldney conveys the message that psychiatry and suicidology are hard sciences, based on biomedical 'facts' and not on clinical intuition. He sees these 'sciences' as gathering objective information deductively and harvesting 'true knowledge', quantifiable with measuring rods and capable of producing replicable, precise results. He appears to suggest that the methods of the natural sciences should be used in all areas of investigation — including philosophy, the humanities and the social sciences. 'Scientific objectivity' is thus a higher order of truth, especially as its results are 'hard won'.

Goldney's view on objectivity in his own field was made abundantly clear in his expert testimony in a series of much publicised civil cases in Sydney, the 'Shakespearean saga' known collectively as *Moran v. Moran*. Kristina Moran sued Doug and Greta Moran, the parents, and Peter, the brother, of her deceased husband Brendan, claiming that their infliction of physical and emotional harm ultimately led to her husband's suicide. Several psychiatrists were called to ponder and to speculate on the nature of suicide, and Brendan's likely state of mind. My reply quoted from a book by Murray Waldren, who reported on the case (Waldren 2001, 192–202):

> After lunch Goldney agreed that as an expert witness it was important to give his evidence in an objective and dispassionate a manner as possible and not favour one side over the other.

> Was that what he had been doing?

Yes, he replied, he had paid particular attention to that. There was no way to test scientifically the issues that have been debated, and so one had to fall back on clinical evidence and case studies in the literature.

One cannot but help notice how the adamancy and certitude expressed in academic journals become either opinion or probability (or even mere possibility) under forensic cross-examination.[4] One cannot but note how little suicidologists read, or absorb, philosophic works on suicide by eminent thinkers like James Hillman and Carl Elliott; the peer-reviewed academic journal article alone becomes the gospel, the very citation of 'truth'.

Lessons from Nunavut

Following the publication of this book, I presented papers on Aboriginal youth suicide to several conferences in 2002. Audiences at Suicide Prevention Australia in Sydney, the Australasian Coroners' Association Conference in Manly, and the Royal Australian and New Zealand College of Psychiatrists Congress in Canberra, responded politely enough. There was no overt hostility or rejection. For the most part, indigenous youth suicide was greeted as an interesting, somewhat curious phenomenon which lay outside the boundaries of their knowledge or experience.

The executive summary of my original report to the Australian Institute of Criminology was published on-line in 1999.[5] Public servants involved in suicide prevention in the Canadian territory of Nunavut read this abbreviated report. 'You seemed to be talking about us', they said, and invited me to attend the Canadian Association for Suicide Prevention (CASP) Conference in Iqaluit in May–June 2003. I gave the keynote address in the capital to some 650 circumpolar delegates, mainly Inuit people. The conference was significant in so many ways, not the least the manner in which the Inuit people effectively hijacked the CASP Annual Congress and hauled it from the usual velvet lounges of Toronto or Montreal venues to a permafrost town of 6,000 people, some 1,500 frozen miles north of Ottawa. The agenda was also hijacked, focusing almost exclusively on Dene and Inuit suicide in the Northwest Territories, Alaska, Nunavut and Nunavik (northern Quebec).

The essence of my address was the essence of this book. It was later given as a paper to the Twenty-Eighth International Congress on Law and Mental Health Conference in Sydney in October 2003, and then revised, expanded and published in *Australian Aboriginal Studies* (Tatz 2004).

The Inuit response was unexpected: almost all of the plenary audience attended what was meant to be a small-group tutorial following. All who spoke in that unscheduled open session rejected Western medical terminology and 'branding', as they described it. There is no general term for mental health or illness in the very precise and word-rich Inuktitut language. They have two words, *Insumaluttuq*, which implies that one is thinking too much, and *Isumaqanngituq*, which means 'having no mind' or not thinking at all (Kirmayer et al. 2001, 4). They spoke of family violence, alcohol, drug and glue-sniffing abuse, and a few talked of demon- or spirit-possession. They were quite clear about the environmental and social contexts of violence, but demurred strongly about 'psychological disorders'. Inuit people appeared to me to be extremely tolerant of bizarre behaviour in others, unwilling to see what biomedicine insists that we see as illness. Two members of the audience — a psychologist and a social worker (both non-Inuit) — expressed their anxiety that my message might deprive them of their livelihoods. This was not, and is not, my intention.

Among Inuit, health and wellbeing are contingent on family and kinship relationships and activities, as well as on talking and communication. A third and essential ingredient of wellbeing is to be found in two letters of the alphabet, IQ — not the IQ that has been so signally abused and misused for a century in race politics, but IQ standing for *Inuit Qaujimatuqangit*, that is, traditional knowledge, including hunting, camping, tool- and clothes-making, in short, their cosmology and belief system (Kral 2003, executive summary).

I held workshops with young males, focusing in particular on the use of winter sport as a means of mitigating, deflecting or deferring suicide. I learned how valuable it is to have suicide placed so plainly in the open among primary and secondary pupils. In the Iqaluit conference venue, the middle school, each corridor and classroom was replete with student-created posters depicting suicide and talking about how to handle it and its alternatives. Teachers, pupils, the headmasters and the police are daily involved in aspects of suicide: it is not the taboo, the secret, the hush-hush and the no-no topic so often found in the Australian school system.

I learned what a Royal Commission can do when it puts its mind to suicide (RCAP, 1995). The self-destructive behaviour of Aboriginal people, it stated, 'cannot be analysed in terms of "mental disorders" but must be looked at in the context of historical colonial relations' (quoted by Coulthard 1999, 3). The noted risk factors and high suicide rates 'are a direct result of Canada's relations with the aboriginal population'. Here, at last, we have the polar opposite of biomedicine.

As to data, the rates for Nunavut for 1998 were 79 deaths per 100,000 overall, but an astonishing 207 per 100,000 for the 15–25 age group (Isaacs et al. 1998, 4–5). Hicks (2005) has confirmed these levels of suicide: of all the deaths in Nunavut from 1999 to 2003, 27 per cent were from suicide, and 74 per cent of these suicides were younger than 25 years of age. Noteworthy was a report by Tim Neily, the Chief Coroner in Nunavut, that there were 110 suicides between 1 April 1999, the date of Nunavut's grant of self-government and territory status, and June 2003, a remarkably high figure in a population of 26,000 people. The non-indigenous rates for the period 1995 to 2003 are edifying: Australia 26.6 deaths per 100,000; New Zealand, 44.1, and Canada, a range from 13 to 17.9 deaths (Isaacs et al 1998, Tatz 2004, 16, Hicks 2005).

The most emphatic lesson from Nunavut was the quality of the work by the Chief Coroner. I concede that Nunavut is Tim Neily's large but little territory, removed as it is from the maelstrom of large population centres. But the depth and breadth of his post-mortem social profiles of deceased could be a model for all. He doesn't have any more answers, but he certainly has many more questions than any other coronial system I know of. He inspects suicides by times of day, days of the week, weeks of the month, months of the year, by phases of the moon, by summer and winter suicides; he assesses social relations prior to the deed; he interviews all friends and relatives, over time, in depth, not with a one-off clipboard. In short, he does everything that my text says a good forensic anthropologist/suicide profiler ought to do.

Somewhat surprising is the prevalence of hanging among the Inuit. Kral (2003, 23) reported that hanging is more prevalent in eastern Canada, especially in Nunavut, while the Dene people in the west of the Northwest Territories tend to use firearms. In Nunavut, of the 110 suicides between April 1999 and June 2003, 93 were males, 17 female: 74 males used hanging, 8 used firearms, and 1 used a knife; 15 females used hanging and 2 used firearms. Hanging thus accounts for 80 per cent of Inuit deaths. Interestingly, this is in a society where every household would have at least three to four guns, used for hunting prey and food. (The issue of hanging is dealt with at some length in Chapter 5 of the text.)

Suicide is not a feature or a factor in traditional Inuit life. In certain circumstances they have a practice of 'sacrificial suicide': thus, an older woman may tell a camping and hunting party enduring bad weather to go ahead while she, and they, know that she is sacrificing herself for the survival of the group. Apart from a rash of suicides in the seventeenth century, Inuit suicide was not a major social problem before 1960. Nor were Aboriginal and Maori suicide on the statistical map before that date.

An important report on youth suicide — *Acting on What We Know* (AOWWK 2002) — is commendable. Its explanations could well cover many, if not most, of the Aboriginal and Maori situations, namely, colonisation and its aftermath, the introduction of some devastating social habits (tobacco, alcohol and gambling), residential schools (and the more serious practice of forcible removal of children in Australia), oil and gas exploration, mining, the establishment of Distant Early Warning systems in Arctic sites during the Cold War, tribal destruction, racism and endless bureaucratic controls. But despite these insights, the official Canadian conviction is writ clear: while saying that they aren't certain about causality, they think that suicide is a mental disorder and therefore that treatment/prevention lies exclusively in the medical/psychiatric domain.

In 2003, Australia's National Aboriginal Community Controlled Organisations (NACCHO) produced a significant paper, *A way through?*, that is, the way through the minefield of measuring Aboriginal mental health. The paper contests, as I do, the value and validity of the 'dominant epidemiological discourse'. It insists on defining the issues from 'Aboriginal community perspectives' and demands that 'measurement' of health has a more rigorous framework 'whereby the term "holisitic" becomes one of considerable substance'. It praises the Aboriginal initiatives these past 15 years in retrieving 'ownership' of their health. It is an impressive analysis, yet one marred, in my view, by remaining welded to some sort of instrument of measurement. Instruments can measure cholesterol, liver function, and diabetic glucose levels: they cannot and do not 'cure', or even alleviate, the illnesses or their causes. Having come so far down the track, why does NACCHO, as does AOWWK, still hold to medical/psychological/sociological measuring rods as ends in themselves?

In contrast, we now hear a call for 'a separate Aboriginal suicidology', something I deemed essential in the book. Elliott-Farrelly (2004) discusses the possibility of a suicidology separate from the mainstream. Even though the author appears not to have read this book, it is refreshing to see such a paper emanate from a major Aboriginal medical service (Illawarra, in Wollongong) in a mental health journal.

Australian Aboriginal Studies

In 2004 Graeme Ward, editor of the *Australian Aboriginal Studies* journal, and I discussed publication of the now well-exposed paper following my visit to Nunavut. The manuscript was sent to three anonymous external readers who provided considered responses, passed on to me anonymously. One didn't want it published, considering it was 'seriously flawed' in not giving balanced credence to the biomedical model. A second produced a long critique listing 'difficulties' and 'strengths' of the essay, concluding that I offered 'some compelling directions for further enquiry'. A third characterised the essay as provocative; but it was a rhetorical argument, an 'ideological position and challenge' rather than a research report and an evaluation of the evidence of others. This reviewer saw my position as offering 'unfortunate consequences with respect to prejudicial disciplinary and profession practice judgements, and the discounting of important and very necessary initiatives and programs at the level of preventive public health and individual and community intervention'. My paper is titled 'Aboriginal, Maori and Inuit youth suicide: avenues to alleviation?'. The question mark is evident and the abstract is plain enough: 'To generate discussion about the need for the separation of this growing problem from the mainstream medical approach to suicide, a case is made for the development of entirely different pathways to suicide alleviation (a less ambitious and less grandiose aim than prevention) in these three societies.'

Because Ward and I think that debate is crucial, we invited all three reviewers to revise their assessments and publish them as review articles alongside my original. Two accepted the challenge and their contributions appear in *Australian Aboriginal Studies*, 2004/2, following my article. Clearly we had had some success in achieving 'discussion'. Readers who have an abiding interest in this subject should consult this issue of the journal. I have carefully analysed what they have to say. I have also received a number of quite different responses — of the 'I agree with everything you say' variety — from cultural psychiatrists, suicide scholars, sociologists and social anthropologists in the United States, Canada and New Zealand. As important to me are the strongly expressed responses of approval from Aboriginal, Maori and Inuit peoples. At this point we are left with a curious quadrangle: the dead youth, whose numbers grow as I write; the families of the deceased, blighted and scarred by their losses; the governments and agencies that pour millions into suicide prevention; and the legions of interventionists and preventionists whose myriad papers weigh heavily, though hardly effectively, on library shelves.

Questions: Has indigenous youth suicide continued, and increased, in these three colonised societies? Has the public health/medical/ biomedicine approach significantly reduced, let alone prevented, actual and threatened suicidal behaviour? Have biological psychiatry, neurobiology, psycho-pharmacology and all manner of 'evidence-based' diagnoses and treatments solved the riddle of suicide?

There was no documented Aboriginal, Maori and Inuit youth suicide before the 1960s. Some scholars have posited a cultural tradition of Aboriginal suicide.[6] That is either correct or every official, coroner, statistician, missionary, anthropologist and native elder or writer in these three communities elected to omit the fact. The onus is on the biomedicalists to show what new suicide gene, cell, hormone or 'soul' surfaced in these physiologically diverse, intermarried, 'mixed-race' communities at that point in the last century. At what point did 'chemical imbalance of the brain' manifest in these populations? How, and why?

We all need a reminder about history — that diagnoses of 'suicide while of unsound mind', or 'suicide while the balance of the mind was disturbed', had nothing whatever to do with the medical profession until relatively recently. Until 1870 in England, under property and inheritance law, a suicide was deprived of both the right to bequeath and to a religious burial. The estate was forfeited to the Crown; thereupon, lawyers, not doctors, deliberately concocted a protection against such a silly law and got the suicide's estate, assets and inheritors 'off the hook' by declaring him not responsible for his actions. Did the lawyers really know something then which it has taken biomedical scientists another century and more to discover? We have moved from suicide as (religious) *badness*, criminalising the act for centuries, to *madness* as a conscious legal fiction, to *sadness as illness* as an iron law of biomedicine.

Hollywood films and the advertising industry have given us a seemingly simple philosophy: we have a *right* to be happy. Accordingly, we deserve alleviation of, and medication for, unhappiness. In my view, the late Viktor Frankl had the realistic measure of our being: 'to live is to suffer'.

Dudley (2004, 27) — one of the respondents to my journal article — sees my use of this notion as an attack on middle-class 'hedonism'. He is right, for the most part. Ethical hedonism is the belief — by both ancient Epicureans and modern utilitarians — that happiness is the sole or chief good in life. Psychological hedonism is more to my meaning, namely, the theory that all human behaviour is fundamentally motivated by the pursuit of pleasure or the avoidance of pain.

As this preamble was being completed, I chanced upon two relevant items in one edition of the *Weekend Sydney Morning Herald* (25 June 2005). In an opinion piece, social critic Hugh MacKay talked about 'the mad cult of perfectionism now sweeping the upper middle class' — ranging from perfect teeth to perfect lifestyles.[7] Life, he insists, is messy, relationships are complex, outcomes are uncertain and people are irrational.

In an extract from her new *Quarterly Essay*,[8] Gail Bell — drug educator and pharmacist — laments how 'misery-chic', the phrase of the 1990s, has become hard core 'depression' in the 2000s. In 2004, no less than 12 million prescriptions for antidepressants were dispensed in a population of 20 million people! This is 'despite the well-known risk of suicidal thoughts and attempts that occur in adults [and children] during early stages of antidepressant drug treatment'. Like Filc, she sees *angst* in ordinary life 'repackaged in a medical presentation'; she also condemns the bioreductionism which says that 'we are our hormones': 'We are our neurotransmitters. It silences other voices. Happiness, the message seems to say, is only possible as long as the neurotransmitters are flowing.'[9]And depression, though still a mystery to science, is deemed to be findable, there, 'in the synaptic cleft'.[10] Her conclusion is fitting:[11]

> We may have to discard some ideas: that life equates to entertainment; that a bad day is somehow a bad movie for which we are entitled to a refund from the video hire shop (with the added satisfaction of complaining to the management). We may have to take responsibility for our own happiness. We may have to consider, like Nietzsche, that 'the worst sickness of men has originated in the way they have combated their sickness. What seemed a cure has in the long run produced something worse than what it was supposed to overcome.'

We could well heed that — and then read Frankl's *Man's Search for Meaning* to learn something about purpose in life rather than 'the pursuit of happiness', let alone 'perfection'.

Among many criticisms, Reser — a highly critical responder to my journal piece — insists that I explain what I mean by 'alleviation'. My language is plain enough, both in the book and the article: to find strategies that lessen, reduce, moderate, relieve, divert, deflect or defer the current rates at which the young take their lives. My book lists several research directions and over a dozen strategies and programs. Most of them lie outside the domain of the suicide scholars and biomedical interventionists. Is that perhaps the problem?

I conclude that not only is Aboriginal suicide different from the depressive mainstream phenomenon, but it will remain different for as long as we dig our heels in and insist that there is only one 'hard won scientific way' to approach the problem of the young dead and want-to-be dead.

Notes

1. *FDA Talk Paper*: FDA Reviews Data for Antidepressant Use in Adults, http://www.fda.gov/cder/drug/advisory/SSR1200507.htm.
2. 'Is Aboriginal suicide different? A commentary on the work of Colin Tatz', *Psychiatry, Psychology and the Law*, 9, 2, 2002, 257–9.
3. Wittingly or unwittingly, in several fields (including suicide), the entire genetic/biochemical domain is part of the old racist discourse on biological determinism.
4. Of interest, and relevance, in this case was the application by the defendants to have the case heard without a jury, partly on the ground that the medical issues were too complex for a lay jury to resolve. Hidden J.

ruled that conflicting psychiatric evidence is common enough and 'there is no reason why a jury in the present case, guided by the burden of proof, could not make a realistic assessment of the conflicting expert opinions' (Supreme Court of New South Wales Common Law Division, 21360/95, 22, 27 August 1995, 29 September 1999, *Moran v. Moran & 4 Others* [1999] NSWSC 977).

5. 'Aboriginal suicide is different: Aboriginal youth suicide in New South Wales, the Australian Capital Territory and New Zealand: towards a model of explanation and alleviation', Criminology Research Council Grant 25/96–7, 1999, found in www.aic.gov.au/crc/reports/tatz/index.html, 14 July 1999.

6. Reser (2004, 38) concedes that suicide and self-destruction have been a ubiquitous theme and element in Aboriginal art and popular culture — but only 'for the past four decades', which supports my strong contention.

7. To get 'their thighs sculpted, their breasts or their backyards professionally redesigned. They hunt for perfect teacher at the perfect school, and bang on endlessly about the perfect lifestyle', *Weekend Sydney Morning Herald*, 25 June 2005, 28.

8. *Good Weekend, Sydney Morning Herald*, 25 June 2005; The Worried Well: the Depression Epidemic and the Medicalisation of our Sorrows, *Quarterly Essay*, # 18, 2005, Black Inc., Melbourne.

9. *Quarterly Essay*, 11.

10. Ibid. 40.

11. Ibid. 69.

Tables

Acknowledgements

The Criminology Research Council funded a three-year field study, 'Aboriginal Youth Suicide in New South Wales, the Australian Capital Territory and New Zealand: Towards a Model of Explanation and Alleviation'. This book is based on my report — CRC Project 25/96–7 — presented to the Council in Canberra in July 1999. Revised and expanded, the formality of the report has been removed, new events and thoughts since July 1999 have been included, and most of the material in the appendices has been omitted. My thanks to members of the Council and the staff for their support and their reception of the report.

The 'we' in the text includes my wife, Sandra: she was co-researcher, interviewer, recorder, manager of itineraries and accounts, processor of words, and presenter and editor (with others) of the final work. Sandra was much more than 'a research assistant'. The work owes much to her moral support when spirits flagged, when grief overwhelmed, when those interviewed needed both wisdom and warmth as they talked about death, and when the language of my anger and outrage threatened to distort.

My good friend Dr Peter Arnold, a medical man who likes editing for a living, worked tirelessly on the report and on this version. He gave freely of his time and incomparable skill as wordsmith and grammarian. My profound thanks to him. Dr Michael Diamond and Dr Michael Dudley, both Sydney psychiatrists, offered insights and advice, as did Associate Professor Joseph Reser of the Psychology Department, James Cook University in Cairns, and Professor Ernest Hunter, previously with the Department of Social and Preventive Medicine at the University of Queensland, Cairns. Paul Reser, of the Sociology Department at James Cook University in Townsville, helped with some statistics; Associate Professor Winton Higgins, late of the Politics Department at Macquarie University, put several important and difficult issues into perspective; and Michelle Webster, clinical psychologist, gave us good counsel and professional wisdom.

Dr Annette Beautrais, of the Canterbury Suicide Project in Christchurch, introduced me to her work, her colleagues and the literature on suicide in New Zealand. Annette Graham, youth suicide researcher in the Victorian State Coroner's Office, informed me of source materials and offered insights from Victoria. Graham O'Rourke, manager of the Office of State Coroner in New South Wales, facilitated introductions to country coroners and gave us working space in the Glebe head office. Jeff Jarratt, Deputy Commissioner of the New South Wales Police Service, arranged all the necessary avenues to local police stations and staff. Colleen Brown, custodian of paintings by clients of her health service in Nowra, arranged for permission to reproduce the illustration in Chapter 10. The cover painting was drawn by Michael Mucci to illustrate one of my articles on Aboriginal suicide in the *Sydney Morning Herald*.

Our thanks to the 396 people we interviewed — primarily in Australia and New Zealand — on the subject of suicide among Aboriginal, Islander and Maori peoples. They gave of their time, insights, feelings, enthusiasm, values and thoughts. Their names are listed in the original report, but have been omitted here. The text of the original report is to be found on the Criminology Research Council website, at <www.aic.gov.au>.

I have been a member of the Australian Institute of Aboriginal and Torres Strait Islander Studies since its inception in 1964. Only recently did I begin a publication relationship, beginning early in 1999 with a research monograph on genocide in Australia. Then, in 2000, there was the excellent production by the Aboriginal Studies Press of *Black Gold: The Aboriginal and Islander Sports Hall of Fame*, followed now by this volume. My sincere thanks to the Principal, Russ Taylor, to the managers of the Press, Penelope Lee and Karen Leary, to my in-house editor, Raylee Singh and to Rachel Ippoliti, the in-house designer for Aboriginal Studies Press.

Background and Explanation

This is a study of youth who have, or feel they have, no purpose in life
— or who may be 'seeking freedom in death'. It is a portrait of self-
destruction by young Aboriginal men and women. There is focus on
suicide by Maori, Pacific Islanders, Canadian and American Indians,
people who have endured similar, but not identical, histories as racial
minorities in colonial systems.

I have approached this study with caution, sensitivity and sensibility.
It must be read as a whole. Failure to do so could lead to data and the
accounts of individual tragedies being used out of context. Such misuse
of the information would aggravate the grief of the families of those
whose deaths I am trying to explain. To understand Aboriginal suicide,
one has to understand Aboriginal history: their way of life has been
destroyed, resulting in a loss of structure, cohesion and meaning. The
legacy for the present generation is a loss of basic communal values. The
continuing effects of that history on today's Aborigines contribute far
more, in my view, to an understanding of Aboriginal suicide than psychological, sociological or medical theories. To ignore or, worse, to deny that
history is to obscure the origins, causes and nature of a current problem
and to frustrate any alleviation.

I found no excitement or intellectual exhilaration in carrying out or
reporting on this research — only distress. The material is distressing for
the bereaved families, for those who work in and with Aboriginal communities, and even for those who have few or no feelings for anything
Aboriginal, but who see Aborigines as fellow human beings.

Clearly disquieting are the prevalence and nature of young death, the
seeming senselessness of youth failing to appeal for help, the agony of
their decisions, and the often painful manner of their deaths. Equally
disturbing, though less obvious to most Australians, are the many unpalat-
able aspects of contemporary Aboriginal life. After some 40 years of

working towards improvement in Aboriginal affairs — in education, health, housing, law, economics, politics, sport — I have been forced to recognise a deterioration in the daily conditions of Aboriginal life.

Aboriginal society has negated, or abrogated, its formerly precious social attributes — kinship, reciprocity, mutuality, sharing, care of young and old, incest taboos. A people with previously ordered lives now has lives which are disordered. The inevitable outward indicators of despair are evident — alcohol and drug abuse and the attention of the police. In attempting to explain the causes of these disorders, and of their outward manifestations, I have to describe characteristics and behaviours which could be read as reflecting poorly on a people who are, literally, struggling for survival.

Herein lies the danger: this material might be used by sensation-seeking media, or by those who, in denying Aboriginal aims, claims and history, seek to bolster their stereotypes of an inferior people, undeserving of currently available funding and services. Here I have in mind individuals like Mr Peter Howson, a former Liberal cabinet minister in the Holt federal government, and his publisher, P.P. McGuinness, editor of *Quadrant* and leader of a denialist movement, who quote my writings about Aboriginal violence as 'professorial' evidence of their diminished quality as a 'civilised' people. I hope that journalistic, academic and party-political integrity will prevail over sensationalist attitudes, spite, or wilful misuse of this material.

Suicide among Maori is as much of a problem in New Zealand as is Aboriginal suicide in Australia. 'Little is known about suicide and self-harm by Maori': this is the considered opinion of the Maori Suicide Review Group which explored ways of reducing Maori suicide in custody. Despite this belief, I learned much from the Maori experience, and from researchers dedicated to examining the alarming increase in Maori youth suicide. This information has been incorporated here.

Based on earlier experience of life in South Africa, I have a strong belief that alienation can, by contrast with its tendency to damage societies, be a spur to achievement. Today's crisis in Aboriginal societies is, indeed, producing immense strength, resolve and courage, especially among the women. It is also producing important responses from the non-Aboriginal world: above all, that Aborigines have a continuity in Australian society, a constitutional and social 'validity', a basis on and in land, the right to dignity as citizens, the right to an acknowledgment of past depredations and repression, and the right to be accorded a measure of reparation and restitution. They have a right to life, which most of us understand to include a healthy and happy life of some longevity, assisted by all the services of civilised society which facilitate that span. But this is not yet within their grasp. That so many young Aboriginal people prefer death to life implies a rejection of what we, in the broader Australian society, have to offer. It reflects our failure, as a nation, to offer sufficient incentives for young Aborigines to remain alive. The same holds true, I believe, for New Zealand.

As the year 2000 ended, Survival International presented a devastating report on Brazil's Indians to the United Nations Commission on Human Rights (*Sydney Morning Herald*, 21 November). The section on the 27,000-strong Guarani was called 'Nothing To Live For'. From 1.5 million, they are now less than 30,000, and matters are hardly helped by a suicide rate 40 times that of Brazil as a whole. Suicide in the context of fragmented reserve communities, amid a host of new illnesses, widespread alcoholism, a cessation of sacred rituals, and a breakdown of community structures and values may make some kind of perverse 'sense'. In which case, what can we say of Australia?

Many recommendations arise from this research. Several can be implemented as single issues, requiring small adjustments to existing programs or protocols. Others require a serious rethinking about major issues: the social and cultural versus the medical approaches to suicide; the concept of youth; the valid need to separate some aspects of Aboriginal life from mainstream society; and the enormous task for Aborigines, and for those who provide them with support, of trying to find ways of 'de-conditioning' Aboriginal youth who so readily regard suicide as inevitable.

My original application to the Criminology Research Council described this as a pilot study which, if informative and useful, could lead to an Australia-wide investigation on the same lines. I no longer contemplate any such wider study. As the North Queensland report by Hunter and others was also released in 1999, I am now convinced that, while the facts available from studies in other states and the Northern Territory might well add to the margins of the national picture, they would not substantially alter the broad conclusions reported in these two studies. This is not to say that suicide research is complete or conclusive, or that others should not replicate this work to determine its validity.

The Hunter and others work (1999) is a valuable public health model. Although my work falls within the domain of health, it is essentially a model for those outside of public and private health agencies, such as coroners, magistrates, police, corrective service and juvenile justice staff, teachers, educators, literacy specialists, lawyers, social workers, social scientists, those in political life at federal, state and municipal levels, and the media. If it assists those in the medical (especially psychiatric) and psychology professions, that will be a bonus. Above all, it is an attempt to assist Aboriginal and Torres Strait Islander people. They already have more than enough to cope with in their lives. They do not need the additional burden which suicide now imposes on their young and on their grieving families.

I regret that this book does not amount to an *understanding* of suicide from 'within', but is, rather, an explanation from 'without'. The available literature has *not* provided understanding, neither here nor abroad: masses of statistics and catalogues of 'at risk' factors provide neither insight nor comprehension. I have had to settle for outside or 'distant' explanations which rely on concepts, classifications, comparisons, descriptions, and on the devising of strategies — not for the individual, not for any personal therapy, but for the collective of suicides and would-be suicides. At best, this is a verbal, three-dimensional ultrasound rather than a two-dimensional photograph, or perhaps a searching portrait that tries to elicit and depict the soul rather than the appearance of the suicide.

1

The Social and Political Contexts

Violent behaviour, such as threats and physical assault, occurs in every society. It grows out of the social order and can therefore be understood only in a social context.

— Emanuel Marx[1]

There is no comparison

Suicide is suicide, but Aboriginal suicide is different.

In 1990–91, Australia had the world's fourth highest rate of male and female youth suicide.[2] New Zealand, after Finland, has the highest rates for young males; it has the highest rate for females, while Maori youth suicides doubled between 1984 and 1994.[3] If the Australian figures are even reasonably accurate, Aboriginal rates are probably between two and five times the non-Aboriginal. The study by Hunter and others (1999) for North Queensland shows that the suicide risk is much greater in the Aboriginal population.

Australia, as a nation, has a strong history (and sense) of assimilationism. However, after a long period of imposed segregation (rather than voluntary separatism), we have, in the past two decades, sought to 'mainstream' all, or most, things Aboriginal. But suicide is *not* a topic to be submerged within the national picture. To do so obfuscates the social realities which cause such high rates. Because Aboriginal suicide has unique social and political contexts, it must, instead, be seen as a distinct phenomenon.

That a problem exists is clear. An appreciation of its nature, causation and possible remedies requires the isolation and demarcation of the differences which distinguish the Aboriginal phenomenon. Very few Aborigines live 'non-Aboriginal' lives, divorced from their social and personal histories, origins, geographies, families, lifestyles, cultures and subcultural *mores*. This is as true of so-called 'urban part-Aborigines' as it is

1

of tradition-oriented groups in rural and remote Australia. In short, the overall context of Aboriginal life is determined both voluntarily by themselves, and, all too often, imposed gratuitously by non-Aborigines. Five or six factors or forces — such as poverty, unemployment, low esteem, low morale, ennui, drug or alcohol abuse — are common to Aboriginal and non-Aboriginal suicides (and, I suspect, to Maori and *pakeha* [white] suicides). But variations in the intensity of these coinciding features are not sufficient to explain the clearly higher Aboriginal propensity to commit suicide and to attempt suicide. Additional historical and social factors pertain only to Aborigines in contemporary Australian society. These same factors are also likely to affect Maori and Pacific Islander youth in New Zealand, Native American youth in Canada and the United States, the Inuit youth of Canada, and certainly the Guarani of Brazil.

Communities in crisis

There is a crisis in many Aboriginal communities. It is a legacy of past violations by a hostile and even genocidal settler society. Ironically, much of the 'new violence' has its origins in the attempts, by non-Aborigines and, on occasion, by Aborigines, to eliminate discrimination, stop segregation and bestow or gain civil rights. Some of the remedy rests with federal, state and municipal governments. Some rests with Aboriginal and Islander communities: the 352,970 people who comprise barely 2 per cent of the population.[4] My task is not to assemble statistical profiles and compare rates of youth suicide but, through analysis and diagnosis, to explain and so possibly mitigate some of that violence — the suicides and attempted suicides.

The Aboriginal crisis is remarkable because it arises in a materially rich, stable, liberal democracy which has embraced policies of anti-discrimination, affirmative action and social justice, and which unceasingly perceives itself as 'the land of the fair go', or more latterly in the land of Olympism, as 'the land of the level playing field'. What outside observers see is a chain of behaviour tearing communities apart: drug and alcohol abuse, child molestation, domestic violence, incest, rape, serious physical assault, homicide, self-mutilation, attempted suicide and suicide.

Suicide has become a particularly potent portent of the contemporary Aboriginal existence. Why this violence? Why this particular response to life's circumstances, when, on the face of it, things *appear* to be so much better than they were 30, certainly 40, years ago?

A catalogue of pluses

In 1997, the historian Geoffrey Blainey disparaged the 'black armband' interpretation of Australian history. He defined this as the way in which the interpretation of Aboriginal issues has allowed 'the minuses to virtually wipe out the pluses'. His balance-sheet did not define either of these categories. Nor have Prime Minister John Howard and the conservative politicians and journalists who have appropriated the term done so. Therefore, to appreciate the social order and social context of contemporary Aboriginal life, we need to look briefly at the 'positives' and the 'negatives'.

Much more public money than ever before is spent on Aboriginal and Torres Strait Islander people; more social service benefits are paid directly to Aboriginal recipients, and there is more actual Aboriginal employment.[5] The Community Development Employment Program (CDEP), by which people work for the number of hours which equate with their social service benefit, is well established. Some 32,000 Aboriginal people now work instead of 'getting sit-down money', as the Northern Territory Aborigines once described it. The scheme, albeit flawed in several respects, has brought some self-worth and dignity — a major achievement not recognised by those who have sought, lately, to attack the system.

There is more housing, through Aboriginal-run housing associations. In 2000, the army spent five months at Jumbun community, near Tully in North Queensland, installing a sewerage system, a project heralded as a fine example of 'practical reconciliation'. There is language salvation in several centres; there is language maintenance in several schools, and there are literacy centres. There are more and better educational facilities, and perhaps six to eight Aboriginal-run community schools. More and more youth are sitting for the NSW Higher School Certificate, or its state equivalents, leading to university study. Aboriginal Studies is an elective matriculation-level subject in high schools, and many states offer the subject from the first year of senior school.[6] Aboriginal Studies units and courses proliferate in universities and TAFE colleges. There are work-skills programs and Aboriginal-run and -owned enterprises. Mining royalties are paid in a handful of areas, notably for uranium in Arnhem Land, and for oil and gold in Central Australia.

Aboriginal legal aid and medical services function reasonably effectively. A few thousand Aboriginal associations are legally incorporated. Many of the outstations — to which Aborigines have moved from the earlier missions and settlements — have resource centres. There has been a virtual end to the 'old guard' of Native Affairs or Community Services

Departments: the 'hard men', the untrained men, ill-educated in Aboriginal administration, have, with a few exceptions, departed the scene.

Everywhere, except in Western Australia, land rights are a reality. Even in the west, several sheep and cattle station leases are held by Aborigines. The much-disparaged Queensland system of 'Deeds of Grant in Trust'— by which land is granted in batches of 50 years on stringent lease conditions — is working well. There are strong land councils in the Northern Territory and New South Wales.

Darwin Aborigines own a television station; an Aboriginal radio station broadcasts from Alice Springs. Aboriginal programs feature nation-wide on ABC and SBS radio and television. On occasion, even the commercial channels offer positive programs. Black artists, writers, theatre and dancing groups are not only recognised, but lauded. Aboriginal sporting achievement — the subject of four of my books — is outstanding and is recognised.[7] The presence of ten Aborigines in the national Olympic team in 2000 certainly 'lifted the profile'. There is growing Aboriginal participation in political and parliamentary life, and greater local decision-making than before. Most states have passed anti-discrimination legislation. Aborigines have discovered that they have a greater chance of recovering or establishing rights through the legal rather than through the political system, and have won 16 of their last 23 forays before the High Court. Aborigines are now part of the national agenda and are no longer relegated, as over the last 150 years, to being 'merely' a welfare problem.

In practical, physical and legal terms, major changes have occurred since the 1960s: the repressive legislation has all but gone, albeit leaving scars that will take generations to fade; the system by which Aborigines were minors in law, seemingly in perpetuity, has ended, albeit with administrative remnants and relics still intact; the so-called 'dinosaurs'— the old boss superintendents and managers of institutions called settlements, reserves and missions, replete with powers of physical punishment and imprisonment — have gone; the old prohibitions on freedom of movement, religious and cultural practices have ended. Not least, Aboriginal issues have become a major concern for reputable international bodies — United Nations committees, Amnesty International and the Save the Children Fund, among others. The spotlight on ill-health, life expectancy, the stolen generations, mandatory sentencing laws, incarceration rates and deaths in custody has been at the initiative of these agencies and has been increasingly utilised by an Aboriginal leadership willing to go abroad for a hearing.

An inventory of minuses

Despite these manifold improvements and advances, Aborigines remain the least healthy sector of Australian society. Infant mortality is high, notwithstanding claims of 'huge' reductions over the past 20–30 years. From a figure of 100 to 150 deaths per 1000 live (Aboriginal) births in the 1960s, the 1990 figure is about 23 in 1000 not surviving one year, compared with the national figure of 8 (Horton 1994, 1278–85). Life expectancy is not consonant with that enjoyed by the rest of our essentially affluent society. The highest life expectancy for an Aboriginal male is 58 (in Western Australia) and the lowest is 53 (in the Northern Territory). Most men do not live beyond 50 — some 25 to 28 years less than white Australian males. The Durri Aboriginal Medical Service at Kempsey states that male life expectancy is 40. A most telling example of these realities is the Australian (Rules) football team, the Rovers, which won the Far West premiership in Ceduna, South Australia, in 1958. By 1987, less than 30 years later, all but one of the 18 young men were dead, reaching neither 50 nor 55.

At the Booroongen Djugun Aboriginal Corporation, which operates a nursing home and community care centre near Kempsey, Aboriginal persons are defined, for the purpose of aged care, as 42 if male and 53 if female. In Narooma, the Koorie Aged Care facility admits anyone over 45. Trachoma and malnutrition are prevalent. Obesity, heart disease and diabetes loom large. Renal failure occurs at a young age, often before 10 in towns in the far west of New South Wales. The second largest single cause of death, after 'circulatory diseases', is 'non-natural causes'.

The Jumbun army sewerage installation is presented as a special bonus, as a practical example of positive discrimination. One has to ask two questions about this innovation. First, why is the provision of a basic utility regarded as a bonus? Second, why is there no comment on the civic authorities' longstanding and deep-seated abdication of responsibility for such an essential service, a failure of local civic will and action which requires peacetime army units to remedy?

Aborigines are the poorest group in society. The 1996 census shows an unemployment rate of 22.7 per cent, compared with the national figure of 8.1 per cent; Aboriginal weekly income is $135 per person, compared with the national average of $273, and an Aboriginal adult's take-home pay packet is 25 per cent less than the average for a non-Aborigine.

Proportionately, Aborigines are the most arrested, the most imprisoned and the most convicted group in our society. The Criminology Research Council publishes statistics which regularly show the disproportionate

Aboriginal rates of arrest, conviction and incarceration — often for minor offences. The Royal Commission into Aboriginal Deaths in Custody (RCIADIC) addressed this matter at length: it found that Aboriginal representation in police custody was 29 times that of non-Aborigines: 'Too many Aboriginal people are in custody too often' (1991, vol. 1, 6).

Chronic housing shortages, appalling sanitation and garbage disposal facilities in many remote communities, poor roads and difficult access to facilities, increasingly short terms of service by support staff, constant budget cuts, and the almost total absence of sport, leisure and recreational facilities in many communities add up to a social index which places Aborigines at the bottom in all areas of action and endeavour.

Confusion and ambiguity

Much in Aboriginal policy and practice is confusing, contradictory and ambiguous. Ambiguity can be a useful tool, especially in a democracy, when used as a controlling device, as a means of asserting power, regulating crises or handling or appeasing competing claims. In essence, it creates (sometimes unconsciously and without malice) *uncertainty, unease, ambivalence and a confusing diffusion of responsibility*. There is, however, a limit to how much ambiguity people can endure. Ambiguity in the Aboriginal context is not so much a contrivance as an *unintended* outcome of governmental insecurity and uncertainty about what to do or how to do it, about avoiding obvious breaches of human rights while remaining unwilling to commit Australian society to equality and to an acceptance of our native peoples. Ambiguity has serious consequences when a people are told that they live in an egalitarian society but find that their every action or feeling, indeed their very being, is highlighted as inferior, different, and of less importance.

The ambiguities and, often, their inherent contradictions, bewilder not only the Aboriginal and Islander peoples but also those responsible for bringing government policies to fruition. Dozens of examples can be cited and elaborated upon. I want to mention seven areas which illustrate ambiguity and which impinge directly on the daily lives of most communities: land rights; the question of a treaty or compact; Aboriginal participation in decisions affecting them; Aboriginal and Islander identity; the meaning of policy slogans like 'reconciliation'; removed children and a national apology; and the 'One Australia' philosophy that brooks no special treatment for any one group.

Land rights

There is much confusion about land rights.

Is it a political or social movement? Is it a philosophy, a political umbrella under which Aborigines and Islanders can cohere (as with Black Power in the United States several decades ago)? Is it a quintessential ownership without which Aboriginal life cannot be sustained, an embryonic or developing land-based nationalism? Or is it a means of reparation and restitution for the depredations and dispossessions of the past? For all Aborigines, the phrase signifies at least two things: first, the giving back of something, as opposed to two centuries of 'things' being taken away; second, and inherent in the first, a signal recognition that they exist and have some legitimate claims on the nation-state.

What a Labor government initiated in 1973, a Liberal government concluded with the passing of the *Aboriginal Land Rights (Northern Territory) Act 1976*. The then Prime Minister, Malcolm Fraser, displayed a reformist outlook, neither emulated nor respected by federal or state Liberal governments since. This was the first statute in Australian history which sought only to give rights, not to diminish or restrict them, even though one can criticise the very narrow concept it espoused, namely, that land could only be granted if people demonstrated religious and spiritual attachment to it. For a brief moment, we beheld acceptance of some valued conventions, as James Tully calls them: first, a recognition that Aborigines existed and had some legitimate rights; second, that any interference with, or change to, any people's rights had to receive the consent of all parties; and, third, that Aborigines as an identifiable, self-determining group would survive (1995, 119–27).

Since that landmark Act, land rights in all jurisdictions but Western Australia have been achieved with varying degrees of rejection, reluctance and legal challenge. In 1984, the federal government promised uniform land rights legislation. By 1986, that notion was dead, and the two major political parties fought the West Australian state election on a platform based on the extent to which each would *restrict* land rights. At century's end, there was a costly campaign to enact legislation to establish state and territory regimes by which native title can be permanently extinguished and the right of the Aboriginal people to negotiate access to traditional land can be seriously restricted. The Coalition's 1998 Wik legislation is a defining moment: it sees a recently 'encitizened' community 'uncitizened' in land law. This is not, as the protagonists claim, because of racial discrimination, which is assuredly what it is, but in the cause of 'equal citizenship' and 'good property law'. Earlier, the High Court had ruled that where Aboriginal rights and those of pastoral *lease*holders (not owners) conflicted, the latter's interests should prevail. Nevertheless, the Wik judges made the sensible decision that Aboriginal and pastoral rights could, and should, coexist. The present Coalition government's view is that

Aboriginal rights should not in any way impinge on what is believed to be a solely white domain. Accordingly, Aboriginal rights should be extinguished because they are unable even to coexist with white property interests.

In 1998, the Coalition government appointed John Reeves QC to review the 1976 Land Rights Act. The object, according to political journalist Alan Ramsey, is 'to shred the integrity' of the Act by breaking down the powers of the Central and Northern Land Councils, and by giving the essentially anti-land rights — and essentially anti-Aboriginal — Northern Territory government greater control over Aboriginal land.[8] It is hard to disagree with this analysis. In Aboriginal eyes, there has been a serious turning back of hard-won achievements since the Mabo 2 High Court judgement.

The matter of a treaty

There is confusion, uncertainty and unease about a proposed 'treaty'.

For nearly two decades, discussion, debate and continuing argument about a treaty — a compact or a settlement of some kind — has occurred.[9] In November 2000, a member of the executive of the Council for Aboriginal Reconciliation stated: 'The whole question of an agreement, without using words that are loaded, is something that the Council has for over the past 10 years discussed, and everyone is of the common view that it is something that has to be achieved — whether it be called treaty, compact or agreement'.[10] Chapter 10 of the *Reconciliation — Australia's Challenge* report[11] insists that, after ten years of deliberation and consultation, there must be some formal settlement of the issues presented. Most Aborigines are not demanding an equal voice as a 'nation', but they do seek the credence and credibility of being able to sit at a negotiating table to discuss 'reconciliation', land use, and levels of autonomy. The ink was not yet dry on the report before the Prime Minister rejected any such formal compact, and several major newspapers inveighed against the idea (as blocking the path to reconciliation).[12]

Other countries have such treaties, compacts or agreements. New Zealand has recognised the Maori as a 'first people', worthy of negotiation. The 1840 Treaty of Waitangi has been ruled a legally enforceable instrument, resulting in a special Waitangi Tribunal that listens to Maori claims and makes substantial compensations.[13] South Africa has faced the past from 1960 — the somewhat strange date set by the government — through its Truth and Reconciliation Commission, and there is ongoing discussion about the size and nature of reparation. In 1996, Canada's Royal Commission on Aboriginal Peoples concluded that 'there must be an acknowledgement that great wrongs have been done to Aboriginal 'people', the 506,000 Amerindian and Inuktitut who now form 1.7 per cent of the population. The new Territory of Nunavut is one major outcome of their 'first nation' status.

Prime Minister John Howard has rejected any movements towards a national reparation, or a treaty: *that*, he claims, implies two nations, a notion he 'will never accept' (Tatz 1999, 46–7). In December 2000, the Prime Minister rejected the treaty notion, then declared 'reconciliation is and should be an unstoppable force', thereby signalling some change in his hitherto hard-line stance. In the same month, he awarded the Aboriginal Affairs portfolio to the Minister for Immigration as an adjunct, not primary, responsibility. For the first time since 1973, there is no longer a minister responsible solely for Aboriginal Affairs. The very first utterance of the new minister, Philip Ruddock, was a rejection of any treaty consideration because such would imply two nations — and that is deemed divisive.[14] Whatever the federal government's rationale, the result is ambiguity.

'Aboriginalisation'

There is uncertainty about Aboriginal control over their own affairs.

From the 1960s, Aborigines were told by Aboriginal advancement organisations and political parties that Aboriginal control over their own affairs was a universal goal. By the early 1970s, most advancement leagues and progress associations had 'Aboriginalised'. But, as of 1973, they all began to be dismantled as a result of federal Labor's policy and practice of recruiting as many Aborigines of talent as possible into its own government bureaucracy. Thereafter, all federal governments adopted 'Aboriginalisation' as a matter of course.

For several years, the newly created federal Department of Aboriginal Affairs (DAA) had an Aboriginal permanent head in (the late) Charles Perkins. In 1990, the Aboriginal and Torres Strait Islander Commission (ATSIC) replaced DAA. It is an elected body of commissioners who believe that they are intended to be the policy makers.

For a year (1998–99), ATSIC maintained a vote of no confidence in the then Minister for Aboriginal Affairs, Senator John Herron. He turned elsewhere for advice, yet, by June 1999, he had only one Aboriginal person in his immediate group of some 30 advisers. Ambiguity enveloped this minister, more so than any of his predecessors in this difficult portfolio. Aborigines perceived him as always subordinating their interests to the Coalition's interests in mining, tourism and development. In 2000, his views on the stolen generations, and the number so taken, further alienated any Aboriginal support he may have had. He was, in effect, sacked by the Prime Minister at the end of 2000.

The growth in the employment rate of Aborigines in the public service since 1973 has been enormous, including a handful of appointments at the most senior levels. There is, however, no doubt that Aboriginal affairs agencies rank low in the public service hierarchy, and that, within specific Aboriginal agencies, non-Aborigines hold much or all of the power.

Identity

There has been a battle over Aboriginal and Islander identity.

Until the repeal of the special Acts and ordinances which applied solely to Aborigines and Islanders, mainly between 1958 and 1984, Aborigines were defined on the basis of their 'degree of blood'. In 1969, when W.C. Wentworth was the minister responsible for Aboriginal Affairs, self-definition was adopted: any person, descended from Aborigines, who says he or she is Aboriginal, and who is accepted as such by the group, is Aboriginal. Aborigines applauded this rational approach. While the racist and eugenicist element in society lamented the disappearance of 'blood-ness', and all the controls which went with it, this was a major advance.

However, in the almost 30 years since, there has been an artificial dichotomy between two 'races'—'Kakadu Man', tribally rich and tribally pure, and 'Redfern Man', urban, poor, and pretending to be what he is not. At various times in the past 20 years, branches of Liberal and National parties have called for a 'tightening' of definitions, mostly centred on 'darkness' of colour or on 'real Aborigines', those people 'who dance corroborees' and 'hunt kangaroos'.

Aborigines have engaged in a long struggle for the right to name themselves, culminating in the 1980s and 1990s in the now common usage of *Koori* in New South Wales and Victoria, *Nunga* in South Australia, *Nyungar* in the West, *Murri* in Queensland and *Yolgnu* in the Northern Territory. Torres Strait Islanders were officially accorded a distinct status in 1990 and South Sea Islanders were formally granted their separate identity by the Queensland government in 2000.

These distinctions are of importance to the people concerned. Yet they are currently universalised as 'indigenous Australians', a term neither sought nor endorsed by the majority of the people. It has become cute and fashion-able shorthand for the media, governmental agencies and academics: it is less clumsy than referring to 'Aborigines and Torres Strait Islanders'. However, the term is producing unnecessary heat and debate about who is indigenous, that is, born *in* or native *to* Australia. Despite the super-ficial attractions of the term, the next census cannot possibly ask: 'Is the

person of indigenous origin?' Nor, in 40 years of research in these communities, have I heard anyone refer to him or herself as an 'indigene', or as
someone who has an 'indigenist' approach to life.

It should be noted that New Zealand is not free of this identity issue
either. There are some 40 'methods' of defining Maori, and there is much
inconsistency in their applications. ('Maori' and '*pakeha*' are used in this
book in deference to current preference.) Identity bedevils police reporting,
coronial findings, and even the generally excellent suicide research by
academics.

Policy slogans

Few people can claim to understand and appreciate Aboriginal policy.

Policy slogans disappear soon after they are born. Little time is given
to their implementation before another new (and temporary) broom
sweeps in, producing yet more confusion. Since the discredited assimilationist philosophy was meant to end in the mid-1960s, there has been
a series of terms: self-determination, self-management, Aboriginalisation,
land rights (as a mantra covering all things), and now, reconciliation.
All have had their share of problems — problems of universal understanding, acceptance of the values which underpin them, communication
of these ideas and their practical significance to the people they are
intended to advance, and in the training and education of staff who
implement them.

The current policy slogan is 'reconciliation', exemplified by the statutory
Aboriginal Reconciliation Council and a week in May set aside as
National Reconciliation Week. It appeals as a sane approach, ethical and
moral. It offers hope, harmony and 'humane-ness'. It suggests an end to
enmity and a settling of differences. Reconciliation is, however, never
defined: it is simply parroted, leaving ambiguous assumptions and a
struggle to discern meaning or purpose. Reconciliation began as a non-
Aboriginal concept at the start of the 1990s, conceived by Robert
Tickner (then Labor's Aboriginal Affairs minister). It was to be a ten-year
program aimed at improving race relations through an increased understanding of Aboriginal and Islander culture and history, and then
through an appreciation of the causes of continued Aboriginal disadvantage in health, housing, education and employment.

For some proponents and believers, it means a moratorium — that is,
each party desisting from causing injury to the other. For many, it can
only mean the national Australian government bringing itself to use the
'sorry' word for the forcible removal of children, to articulate atonement
and to find a means of restitution or reparation for these practices. For

the authors of the final Reconciliation report, it means a people's move-ment and capitalising on the new-found broad public good will in order to complete the nation's 'unfinished business'. For others, it means 'a place in the sun' for 'indigenous Australians'; or an end to the bickering and the meanness; or it means not the history or the causes of poor health, housing, education and employment but their alleviation and improvement; or, for a number of concerned Australians, it means 'walking together' and/or 'forging a new relationship'.[15] A glance at the book, *Reconciliation*, edited by Michelle Grattan and published in May 2000 to coincide with the presentation of the Aboriginal Reconciliation Council working documents, shows just how divergent is the understanding of this word — which remains, in essence, little more than a slogan.

The stolen generations

The forcible removal of the children known as the 'stolen generations' has caused a great deal of unease, frustration and anger in both Aboriginal and mainstream societies.

My research overlapped with the inquiry into the 'Separation of Aboriginal and Torres Strait Islanders from Their Families' and the publication of its report, *Bringing Them Home* (HREOC 1997). Of the 120 judicial inquiries, parliamentary committee reports and royal commissions into aspects of Aboriginal affairs in the twentieth century, this is by far the starkest and strongest indictment. It concluded that Australia has wittingly committed genocide through the forcible transfer of children — not just yesteryear but as recently as the 1980s.

The Howard Coalition, succeeding Labor in March 1996, declared 'the Government can see no equitable or practical way of paying special compensation to these persons, if compensation were considered to be warranted'.[16] An array of defences has since been offered for the Commonwealth's 'no compensation, no apology' policy. Restitution will 'produce new injustices and inequities', 'create serious difficulties', cause 'adverse social and economic effects'. It will be 'very difficult to identify persons', it is all 'problematic', and, rather ominously for existing programs, it will 'divert resources in mounting or defending cases'. The govern-ment's conclusion is that 'there is no existing objective methodology for attaching a monetary value to the loss suffered by victims'. The govern-ment also takes the view that, in judging these practices, 'it is appropriate to have regard to the standards and values prevailing at the time of their enactment and implementation, rather than to the standards and values prevailing today'.

The Coalition government regularly expresses irritation and anger at the continued rejection of these 'principles'; it insists that the many vociferous critics are merely peddling 'political correctness' and, in so doing, are harming the reconciliation process, which it sees as *burying* the 'mistakes' of the past.

The 'assimilation factories' ceased very recently: the Retta Dixon Home in Darwin in 1980; Sister Kate's Home in Perth in 1987; St Francis' Home and Colebrook in South Australia in 1957 and 1978, respectively; and Bomaderry in New South Wales in 1988. The problem is not one which affected only past generations: it goes on affecting many people living now, including many of the suicide victims in this study. The Coalition talks about these events as being removed from our time and values, yet the repeal of the 'removal' laws began only as late as 1964 and continued, one state at a time, through to 1984. The last child removed was in Perth in 1970, when the authorities defied a judge's order to restore a child to its natural parent. Children continued to be removed well beyond 1970.

The Howard government has steadfastly refused to make a public apology on this matter. On Anzac Day 2000, the Prime Minister announced in Paris that he saw no inconsistency between his and the Turkish government's spoken 'sorryness' over events in 1917 and his refusal to say 'sorry' about Aboriginal child removals here so much later. Aboriginal family organisations state that there can be no reconciliation unless that matter is fully addressed, and then redressed, legally and politically. They note the Canadian and New Zealand apologies, as well as England's public regret at sending Liverpool children to Australia during World War II. They also note the formal state (but not Northern Territory) government apologies, and they point to former Prime Minister Paul Keating's 1992 'Redfern speech' in which he acknowledged, *inter alia*, that 'we' brought the diseases, the alcohol, 'we committed the murders', and 'we took the children from their mothers' (Tatz 1999, 41).

The low-water mark of the Coalition government's intransigence was Senator John Herron's support for, and endorsement of, a paper written by bureaucrats to a Senate inquiry in April 2000, one which, in effect, denigrated and diminished the stolen generations issue, much in the vein of the Commonwealth's submission to the *Bringing Them Home* inquiry (discussed above). Senator Herron contended that since an entire generation was not removed but perhaps only one in ten children, one could not use the phrase 'stolen generation(s)'. This sophistry produced a national outcry which further fuelled Aboriginal (and non-Aboriginal) determination about this matter.

In November 2000, a Senate inquiry reported on the federal government's implementation (or rather, non-implementation) of the *Bringing Them Home* recommendations.[17] It recommended, among other things, a motion for a national apology, a formal apology to members of the stolen generations by the Northern Territory government, a national memorial and a reparations tribunal. This painstaking report was hardly the work of 'vociferous black armband critics' or of those dedicated solely to 'political correctness'.

More confusion has arisen with the growth of a small, but busy, 'industry' of denialism. At one end of that endeavour, the Prime Minister has asked that school texts reflect glorious achievement rather than the unpleasant past. At the other end, a coterie of journalists — Paddy McGuinness, Piers Akerman, Andrew Bolt, Christopher Pearson, Michael Duffy and Frank Devine, among others — has joined with former cabinet minister Peter Howson, former bureaucrat Reg Marsh, former Governor-General Bill Hayden and barrister Douglas Meagher in denying that children were ever removed — except at parental request or agreement, or for the child's welfare. McGuinness has gone so far as to say that the entire body of evidence in the *Bringing Them Home* report is a hoax and an anthology of 'false memory'.[18]

The level playing fields

The 'level playing field' philosophy is possibly the most confusing and irreconcilable point of all.

John Howard, when leader of the federal Liberal opposition in 1989, declared that, in the name of the just society, there can be no special favours, no positive discrimination for any one group, especially not for Aborigines. He pledged repeal of existing land rights legislation, because no other group has such special benefits. The Liberal and National parties also proclaimed, in the 1990s, that none should be advantaged over another, expressing the philosophy that we are One Australia. The then Queensland Premier Rob Borbidge gave a practical example: he insisted that there can only be one Australian law, one that prevents non-Aborigines and Aborigines alike from taking crocodiles for food on Aboriginal reserves.[19]

The ideological implication of the 'level playing field' is the withdrawal, or elimination, of all special pleaders, so creating equality of treatment for individuals. It is a populist 'philosophy' which ignores the presence on the playing field of those who are already powerful. It is also a perspective lacking any appreciation of history. Canada rejects this and has adopted an antithetical view: the premises of the philosophy that 'all

Canadians are equal are very wrong'; that the 'equality approach', which ignores inequalities, 'is the modern equivalent of the mind-set that led to the Indian Act, the residential schools, the forced relocations — and the other nineteenth-century instruments of assimilation'.[20]

Conservative politics in Australia does not discuss or acknowledge the original reasons for legislation which attempts to protect, advantage or compensate Aborigines and Islanders. Nor does it acknowledge that no other group has had as disadvantaged a past as Aborigines. One could be tempted to dismiss much of the political rhetoric as mere election talk, but, in proclaiming such a 'just society', Howard obliterated — as did Canadian Prime Minister Pierre Trudeau in the 1960s — all Aboriginal and Islander personal, social, political, economic, cultural and legal history. The Howard–Trudeau proposition infers that, as of a given date, previous histories and legacies of injustice and inequality are expunged to make way for, at best, a clean slate or, at worst, a reconciliation slate.

The implications of this philosophy have devastating consequences. It is as if Aborigines, like new immigrants, have 'just arrived'; and, to share in the 'just' and 'equal' society, they must compete on equal terms. The Aboriginal question is thus merged into a 'multicultural society', one in which Aborigines are no different from recent immigrants. (It is significant that Aboriginal Affairs is now, in 2001, conjoined with Immigration and Multicultural Affairs under Minister Ruddock.) Past violations are disregarded, thereby absolving anyone from atonement or compensation.

On election, Howard began a systematic campaign against the 'black armband' interpretation of Australian history. Priority, he said, should be given to health, literacy and other practical programs. Although he has no jurisdiction over state school systems, he requests that syllabuses be rewritten to accommodate his view. Howard sympathises with those 'Australians who are insulted when they are told we have a racist, bigoted past'. Of note was Australia Day 1997. Prime Minister Howard declaimed that Australia should not be 'perpetually apologising for sins of the past'. In contrast, the Governor-General, Sir William Deane, said 'the past is never fully gone'; 'it is absorbed into the present and future' and it shapes 'what we are and what we do'—and, unless Australia achieves reconciliation by 2001, 'we'll enter the second century of our nation as a diminished people'.

The violence syndrome

There is a causal link between ambiguity and patterns of behaviour in many Aboriginal societies. The stages are: a feeling of *frustration*; followed by a sense of *alienation* from society, of not belonging, of foreignness; then *withdrawal* from society, no longer caring about membership, about loyalty, or about law-abiding behaviour; and then the threat of, or actual, *violence*.

The anthropologist Emanuel Marx (1976) talks of 'appealing violence' and 'coercive violence'. The former, discussed in the next chapter, is essentially about harm to self or to others, a cry for help when one is at the end of one's road. The latter is where a person uses violence in a premeditated and controlled manner, 'as an extreme but often effective means towards achieving a social objective'. At present, the harm in Aboriginal life is confined to self, to kin and, at times, to those who work with and for communities. At no point in Australia in this century have Aborigines resorted to coercive violence.

Earlier, I stated that things appear to be better now than two or three decades ago. Yet several key aspects of the present and prevailing socio-economic and living conditions are worse than when I first began looking at Aboriginal administration in the early 1960s. Then, there were virtually no human or civil rights, but the highly respected values of kinship, family reciprocity, child-rearing practices, care of the aged, incest prohibition, and punishment for offences against a strong moral code were relatively intact. While Aboriginal society was politically disadvantaged in, and removed from, the broader Australia, it had retained, within itself, many elements of social cohesion.

Today, by contrast, the agenda is external, concerned with relations with the broader Australia: land as property, land councils, High Court actions, cultural representation, Aboriginal participation in political and economic arenas, artistic recognition, sporting adulation and an enormous public consciousness about Aboriginality. Meanwhile, in many groups, the internal values of what once were ordered societies, even if that order was maintained by settlement and mission discipline, have disappeared, leaving rampant the values of disorder.

Notes

1. Marx, *The Social Context of Violent Behaviour*, 1.
2. Commonwealth Department of Human Services and Health, *Youth Suicide*, 22–3. The document cited Australian youth figures, aged 15–24, as 26.6 per 100,000 for males and 6.2 per 100,000 for females. The New Zealand figures were 38.7 and 6.7, respectively. By 1995, the New Zealand rates in the youth category were 44.1 for males and 12.8 for females (Ministry of Health, Youth Suicide Statistics).
3. Ministry of Health, *Suicide Trends in New Zealand*, 23–4.

4. The 1996 census shows a figure of 314,120 Aborigines, 28,744 Torres Strait Islanders, and 10,106 who are either of the above, or both, or South Sea Islanders.

5. For elaboration of what follows, see my article, 'Race Relations in the 21st Century', and my chapter, 'A Question of Rights and Wrongs'.

6. In the past two years the number of students undertaking Aboriginal Studies in New South Wales has declined: students, teachers and parents tend to shy away from 2-unit subjects in the Higher School Certificate. Strong efforts are being made to recruit students.

7. Particularly, *Obstacle Race*, and, with Paul Tatz, *Black Gold*.

8. *Sydney Morning Herald*, 1 May 1999.

9. Tatz, 'Aborigines and the Age of Atonement'. My view of the treaty idea, the 'Makarrata proposal' as it was known, was published in 1983. I opposed the notion, for reasons which were and which remain cogent. My opposition to the notion, and its workability, does not mean that the present Aboriginal insistence on a treaty is wrong. Their reasons may be as valid as mine.

10. *Australian*, 9 November 2000.

11. Commonwealth of Australia (2000).

12. For example, *Australian*, 8 December 2000.

13. The *Press*, Christchurch, 24 September 1997. In 1997 the Crown apologised to the South Island Ngai Tahu peoples and restored Maori authority over lakes, mountains and other property, providing at least $170 million in compensation. Two years earlier the Tainui Federation of Tribes of the North Island won compensation of $170 million and restoration of 15,400 hectares.

14. ABC News, 22 December 2000.

15. Australians for Native Title & Reconciliation, ANTaR, is the latest of several suburban groups seeking a fresh approach to Aboriginal matters.

16. The material following is from Tatz, *Genocide in Australia*, 43–50.

17. Senate Legal and Constitutional References Committee, *Healing: A Legacy of Generations*.

18. See *Quadrant*, vol. XLIV, no. 11, November 2000, for the views of McGuinness, Kenneth Maddock, Keith Windschuttle, and Douglas Meagher; see also Manne, *In Denial*.

19. '7.30 Report', ABC television, 12 March 1998.

20. *Royal Commission on Aboriginal Peoples, People to People, Nation to Nation*, highlights from Report of the Royal Commission on Aboriginal Peoples, Minister of Supply and Services, Canada, 1996, 9.

2

The Origins of the 'New Violence'

A person whose dependence on officials is so permanent and complete that he cannot even stage a public appeal may be driven to assault members of his family, and try to make them at least share his burden ... He repeatedly attempts to commit suicide, as a desperate means to regain the support of members of his family.

— Emanuel Marx[1]

Deaths in custody

My interest in Aboriginal suicide began when I was examining the relationship between Aboriginal juvenile delinquency and the availability of sport to young people. That research project, funded by the Criminology Research Council, was reported in the mid-1990s (Tatz 1994b; 1995). At the time of the delinquency–sport project, 1989–94, the major issue in Aboriginal life, and a political issue of magnitude in Australian public life, was an epidemic of young male suicides in custody.

John Pat's life had ended in custody in Roebourne, Western Australia, in 1983. Aged 16, he died, after his arrest outside a Roebourne hotel, of a fractured skull, haemorrhage, swelling and bruising to the brain, broken ribs and a torn aorta. A year after the acquittal of police charged over his death, Helen Corbett, of Perth, organised the Committee to Defend Black Rights. In 1986, members of the committee toured Australia, presenting talks by relatives of those who had died in custody. In 1987, it launched the Deaths in Custody Watch Committee (DCWC), incorporating Aboriginal, Torres Strait Islander and civil rights groups concerned about the deaths. Both organisations lobbied strongly for a royal commission into custody deaths. Lloyd Boney's death at Brewarrina, New South Wales, on 6 August 1987, the sixteenth during the first seven months of that year, was the catalyst. Five days later, Prime Minister Bob Hawke announced the Royal Commission into Aboriginal

Deaths in Custody, supported by the federal and all state governments. (Despite the findings of this royal commission, the DCWC still has reason to exist, in particular because of the disproportionate numbers of Aboriginal deaths in custody in Western Australia.)

My fieldwork crossed paths with RCIADIC staff as they investigated the deaths of 99 Aboriginal men and women who died in Australian police, prison and juvenile detention custody between 1 January 1980 and 31 May 1989. The most widely reported cases were those of Lloyd Boney, David Gundy and Eddie Murray in New South Wales; Kingsley Dixon in South Australia; John Pat and Robert Walker in Western Australia; and Muriel Binks in Queensland. As the Commission progressed, it published its findings on individual cases and then presented its final five-volume report (1991). Before these publications, many had believed that there was either an element of 'assistance' in some of these deaths and/or that the suicides were a result of factors inherent in the small spaces of incarceration.

In New Zealand, 47 Maori prison inmates committed suicide between 1971 and 1995. The Maori rate of suicide in prison was higher than that of the non-Maori.[2] There was no royal commission, but the Department of Corrective Services joined with the Maori organisation, Te Puni Kokiri, to report on ways of reducing suicide in custody. As in Australia, deaths while in custody appeared to be the most pressing issue. American Indian suicide in detention is described as 'dramatic, shocking, frustrating — and embarrassing to corrective services'.[3] Although 0.6 per cent of the population, Indian suicides are 5 per cent of all jail suicides.

Suicide in Aboriginal societies

Why this widespread belief that deaths while in custody were the most serious issue, a belief which I, myself, shared? Briefly, because suicide had been an alien concept in Aboriginal life. In my long involvement in Aboriginal affairs, especially in the Northern Territory, Queensland and Victoria, suicide had not been an issue. It was never mentioned by Aborigines, anthropologists, linguists, government officials, missionaries, magistrates, pastoralists or police. In 1968, Kidson and Jones found an absence of 'classical neuroses, psychosomatic illness and suicide' among Western Desert people. John Cawte's medico-sociological expedition to Arnhem Land in 1968 found 'nothing alarming' about Aboriginal suicide rates. In 1973, Ivor Jones, in his study of psychiatric disorders among Kimberley and desert people, reported that there was 'no incidence of suicide or homosexuality among full blood tribal Aborigines'. In 1975, Burvill reported higher Aboriginal than non-Aboriginal rates of parasuicide in Perth, but he had strong reservations about the 'validity of Aboriginal rates'. In the late 1980s, Harry Eastwell confirmed the 'low risk of suicide among the Yolgnu of the Northern Territory' (1988, 338).

Hunter and others state that 'some three decades ago the suicide of an Indigenous Australian was a rare occurrence' (1999, 91). Richard Kimber told the RCIADIC, in Central Australia, 'there is no hard evidence that in traditional society Aborigines committed suicide'. He recalled one report of a captured man who broke his chains and threw himself off a Murray River cliff in the 1840s.[4] Dr Lester Hiatt, former reader in anthropology at Sydney University, who has worked at Maningrida (in the Liverpool River region of Arnhem Land) for more than 40 years, cannot recall a single case of, or reference to, suicide — before mid-1998, when the first occurred.

Associate Professor Colin Yallop of Macquarie University told me that no Aboriginal language or dialect has a noun corresponding to suicide, although he conceded that the grammars may well have a reflexive concept that accords or corresponds with killing oneself. According to Hiatt, the local Burrara language at Maningrida uses the same word for hit as for kill, and that it is possible that someone who says he hit himself may well mean that he attempted to kill himself. Associate Professor Vivien Johnson, formerly of Macquarie University, confirms that she has never seen any representation of suicide, or self-destruction, in Aboriginal art.[5] (Recently such representation has emerged strongly in North Queensland and in Nowra, New South Wales: a graphic example from the latter is reproduced in this book.)

Many 'indigenous' societies have suicide mythology. For example, in the Bimin-Kuskumsin culture in Papua New Guinea, the ancestral goddess divided her staff into three, planting each as a tree: one of life, one of death, and one a 'hanging tree'. Those who travel to that tree are always forlorn, slovenly, depressed adult men, stumbling along the rocky, twisting path. During my research, we encountered one example of suicide embedded in culture. We were told of the myth of the Three Brothers, as represented in the three hills between Port Macquarie and Taree: South Brother, Middle Brother and North Brother. The Biripi legend is that an evil spirit killed two of the brothers and then the third brother killed the spirit, whereupon he committed suicide. The souls of the brothers reside in these hills. However, very few of our informants were aware of this story or saw it as in any way related to the present episodes of parasuicide or threatened suicides by youth in the region. By contrast, *whakamomori* (suicide) is a known concept and phenomenon in Maori culture. At one level, families seek to hush up a suicide, and show the same sense of stigma as is found in Western societies. At another level, there may be no dishonour: in Maori tradition, suicide is an honourable way out of shame or disgrace, or frustrated love, an exit with dignity.

I observed, through the work of one of my students, the unravelling of the circumstances of the death of Eddie Murray in the cells at Wee Waa, New South Wales, on 12 June 1981. Christine Stafford (then McIlvanie) was interested in Murray's death as a topic for her BA Honours dissertation at the University of New England (1982). She had lived in Wee Waa, where her then husband had been the ambulance officer and she a primary school teacher. She examined, in the broad sociopolitical sense, *what* rather than *who* had killed Eddie Murray. Sergeant 'K' of the Scientific Investigation Section of the Police Force in Sydney informed her that, in the period 1971–81, there had been one Aboriginal death in custody and five parasuicides in New South Wales. Police figures for Queensland in this period appear to have been nine suicides and eight parasuicides; for the Northern Territory, it is likely that there were five completed Aboriginal suicides in custody in that decade.

In short, while these figures were relatively high in a population whose culture seemed not to encompass suicide, in whose languages there were no obvious words for it, and in whose art there were no depictions of self-destruction, 1981 was not a crisis year — except for the Murray case, still fraught with suspicion of foul play.[6] In 1981, neither McIlvanie nor I had any reason to suspect that there was any significant prevalence of suicidal behaviour in, let alone outside of, custody. In short, while we were all aware of a growing violence in Aboriginal communities, its forms appeared, at that time, not to include suicide.

By the end of 1986–87, it became obvious that something was seriously amiss in custody. The prevailing belief was in foul play, violence by police and warders or, at 'best', inadequate care and supervision. To my knowledge, suicide outside of custody aroused no comment before the mid-1980s. Aboriginal suicide is a specific topic in the bibliography of the Australian Institute of Aboriginal and Torres Strait Islander Studies (AIATSIS). About 83 per cent of the items published or reported between 1968 and 1997 were for the cluster years of 1987–95, the period in which deaths in custody were the focus of attention.

Suicidal behaviour outside custody

On 23 October 1989, I gave a public lecture to a largely Nunga audience at Flinders University in Adelaide. During the previous week, the (then) Department of Aboriginal Affairs had become aware of eight non-custodial suicide attempts by Aborigines in Adelaide between 16 and 22 October. Audience members raised the youth suicide question, in the context of widespread diffidence and despair. Now more aware, I visited the Mildura Aboriginal legal aid office soon afterwards and asked if suicide was occurring in the town. 'No, absolutely not', replied the male administrator, whereupon a female staff member called out, 'What about my two daughters?' The girls had swallowed liquid paper and thumbtacks. The administrator explained that this was merely 'playing silly buggers', 'girls looking for attention'. Stories of this kind emerged in subsequent communities I visited and in several I revisited: generally, a concern by women about young girls, and dismissal, deflection or denial by older men.

After completing the sport–delinquency study, I published a paper on Aboriginal violence.[7] The 1980–90 decade, I wrote, had seen a marked increase in 'internal breakdown' within communities. There was, I explained, abundant evidence of worsening or increased

- personal violence within Aboriginal groups, even within families;
- child neglect, as in hunger and lack of general care;
- violence and damage committed while sober;
- Aboriginal deaths from non-natural causes;
- destruction of property, both white-supplied and own-acquired;
- attacks, often violent, on white staff working with the groups;
- suicide and parasuicide among the youth;
- consumption of alcohol, commonly and generally (but not always correctly) offered as the sole and total explanation of the violence; and
- constancy with which Aborigines externalised cause, blame and responsibility for all of the above.

A matter of history

To understand the onset of this 'disorder', perhaps a plague of disorders, it is essential to look, however briefly, at the history that gave rise to it.

Legislation to protect Aborigines began in an elementary way in the 1840s: by 1843, five of the colonies had appointed Protectors. Protection, in earnest and in great legislative detail, began in Victoria in 1869 and 1886, in Western Australia in 1886, in New South Wales in 1909, in South Australia in 1911, in the Northern Territory in 1910 and 1911, and in Tasmania in 1912. Most of these laws were predicated on the philosophy of 'soothing the dying pillow' of a race near extinction. Given that there was a widespread assumption that Aborigines were dying out, settlers fulfilled the prophecy by acting to ensure that such was indeed the outcome. The Myall Creek massacres of 1838, on the Gwydir River (in northern New South Wales), testified to settler attitudes.

There were to be two protective fences against genocide in most of Australia: the legal one, which was soon found to be insufficient, followed by the geographic one of sometimes extreme isolation, the additional barrier against white predators. Law would keep whites out, and Aborigines in protective custodianship. Geographic location would see to it that no one could get in, or out. Government-run settlements and Christian-run missions were established in inaccessible places to protect the people from their predators; to encourage, sometime to coerce, Aborigines away from the 'centres of evil'; to allow for the Christianising and civilising process in private and away from temptations; to enable better ministration to a doomed, remnant people.

Catherine deMayo has explained why 'mission' Aborigines came to be where many still are (see Tatz 1995, 36). One missionary concluded that 'the Christian Church and the Government can but play the part of physicians and nurses in a hospital for incurables'. These 'children of darkness' needed places like Yarrabah, near Cairns, described as 'splendidly secluded'. In New South Wales, the mission places were not as geographically isolated but were nevertheless institutions designed to separate and 'protect': Bomaderry, Bowraville, Erambie, Lake Macquarie, Maloga School, Parramatta, Warangesda, Wellington Valley, as well as the 'assimilation' homes at Kinchela and Cootamundra.

The missionaries did not simply supply a nursing service for 'incurables', and a burial service: they became active agents of various governmental policies, such as protection–segregation, assimilation, so-called integration, and some of the latter-day notions like self-determination and self-management. They were additionally delegated an astonishing array of unchallengeable powers. Uniquely, in terms of modern missionary activity in colonised societies, mission boards became the sole civil authority in their domains. They ran schools, infirmaries, farms and gardens, provided water, sewerage and similar public utility services, established dormitories, built jails, prosecuted 'wrongdoers', jailed them, counselled them, controlled their income, forbade their customs, and acted as sole legal guardians of every adult and every child. They also tried, with little success, to Christianise the inmates according to their varying dogmas and doctrines. The eighteenth-century English radical philosopher, Jeremy Bentham, has bequeathed us succinct phrasing for such 'penitentiary-homes'—ones in which the objectives are *safe custody, confinement, solitude, forced labour and instructions* (Tatz 1999, 22).

The special laws show that the 'protections' which parliaments had in mind were as much from outside intruders as from the Aborigines themselves. In Queensland, protection in theory became discrimination in practice. Stopping predators from entering necessitated the incarceration of Aborigines for life, even for generations, in the most inaccessible of places, places as remote as Yarrabah, Palm Island, Mornington Island, Doomadgee, Bamaga, Edward River, Weipa, Bloomfield River and Woorabinda. Protection of Aboriginal morality came to mean control of their movement, labour, marriages, private lives, reading matter, leisure and sports activities, even their cultural and religious rituals. Protection of their income came to mean control by police constables — as official Protectors of Aborigines — of wages, of withdrawals from compulsory savings bank accounts, of rights to enter contracts of labour, and of purchase and sale.

In the Northern Territory, from 1911 to 1957 and again from 1957 to 1964, when all 'full-blood' Aborigines were declared 'wards', protection included permits to leave the reserves and the Territory, prohibition on alcohol, prohibition of interracial sex, prohibition of interracial marriage unless with official permission, inability to vote or to receive social service benefits, employment at specified, statutory Aboriginal rates of pay (well below the basic wage, invented by Australia in 1907), exclusion from industrial awards, and so on.

In New South Wales, Governor Macquarie's Proclamation of 1816 declared that Aborigines were subject to the protection of white law, and in 1835 a Vagrancy Act made it punishable for anyone to be found lodging or 'wandering in company with any of the black natives of this Colony'. In 1838, Aborigines were prohibited from having access to alcohol. In 1839, a bill to preclude them as competent witnesses in criminal cases, on the grounds that they did not have 'any distinct idea of religion or fixed belief in a future state of rewards and punishments', was denied. The very attempt to introduce legislation of this kind is indicative of the way in which Aborigines were perceived and regarded.

The *Aborigines Protection Act 1909* became the primary statute that governed Aboriginal lives until 1969. The Aborigines Protection Board was given a number of general duties, including the distribution of blankets and clothing; the 'custody, maintenance and children of Aborigines'; management and regulation of premises; the exercise of 'a general supervision and care over all matters affecting the interests and welfare of Aborigines, to protect them against injustice, imposition and fraud'. Board officers had power to 'maintain discipline and good order on any reserve'; apportionment 'among Aborigines, of the earnings of any Aborigines living upon a reserve'; and 'the control of Aborigines residing upon a reserve'.

In 1915, the Act was amended to allow any youth who refused to go to the person to whom he was apprenticed to be removed to an institution and, if under 18, to be dealt with as 'a neglected child'. The Board also had power to control the child of any Aborigine if it was satisfied that this was 'in the interest of the moral or physical welfare of such child'. In 1940, the Act was again amended to further enable Aborigines 'to become assimilated into the general life of the community', but, in the same breath, it empowered the Board to establish homes for 'the maintenance, education and training of wards', defined as anyone under 18 admitted to the control of the Board or committed to an institution. All wages of such wards were made payable to the Board.

New South Wales Aborigines experienced an especial brand of discrimination that has haunted people to this day: the policy of 'exclusion on demand' in the public school system. The *Public Instruction Act 1880* laid down the framework for primary and secondary schooling. What happened thereafter is a landmark in the history of racism in this country. At the turn of the century, white parents began making complaints to schools about their children having to sit next to 'niggers'. Some teachers agreed to accept Aborigines, provided they were 'clean, clad and courteous'. Others would not have any. In 1900, John Perry, the Minister for Education, endorsed one teacher's stance not to accept Aboriginal children; this action became officially justified as 'the will of the people with the Minister's sanction' (Tatz 1995, 189–90). This practice of 'exclusion on demand' could be initiated by teachers or white parents. In 1902, Perry ordered teachers in all 2800 government schools to exclude Aboriginal children the moment white parents voiced an objection.

'Exclusion on demand' became standard practice throughout the state. When Aboriginal parents sought relief or objected, they were told to send their children to the special Aboriginal schools on reserves (the last of which disappeared in the 1980s), schools not staffed by the Education Department and commonly not run by qualified teachers. On arrival there, they were told that these special schools were for 'full-bloods' only, since those of 'admixture' were to be assimilated. This policy was still active in the northern tablelands in the mid-1970s. From the very rough statistics we have of those periods, it is likely that at least 50,000 Aborigines were denied access to either the white or the special Aboriginal schools for the first 70 years of the twentieth century. Here, then, is 'assimilation' practised either by way of total segregation or total exclusion from state systems. Here, too, is another source of a legacy of bitterness and hostility towards government agencies.

In 1983, the historian, Peter Read, published a short monograph on the 'stolen generations' in New South Wales. The annual reports of the Aborigines Protection (later Welfare) Board were always explicit: 'This policy of dissociating the children from [native] camp life must eventually solve the Aboriginal problem'. By placing children in 'first-class private homes', the superior standard of life would 'pave the way for the absorption of these people into the general population'. Further, 'to allow these children to remain on the reserve to grow up in comparative idleness in the midst of more or less vicious surroundings would be, to say the least, an injustice to the children themselves, and a positive menace to the State'. The committal notices prescribed by law required a column to be completed under the heading 'Reason for Board taking control of the child'. The great majority of responses were penned in one standard phrase: 'For being Aboriginal'! (Read 1983, esp. 8–9).

Read's estimate of the number of children removed in New South Wales between 1883 and 1969 is 5625, allowing (as he notes) for the distinct 'lack of records'. My assessment is much higher. I have not examined the remaining Board or child welfare records. I base my figure on an extrapolation of the numbers of forced removals and institutional-isation among the 1200 Aboriginal sportspeople recorded in my 1995 book on the Aboriginal experience as seen through the metaphor of sport. To cite one example: of the 172 men and women in the (revised) Aboriginal and Islander Sports Hall of Fame, 16 were removed, another 6 or 7 were adopted by white families, while another 22 grew up in institutions. In short, one in four was raised by persons other than their natural parents. In line with my own observations, Read's figure of perhaps 100,000 removals across the whole of Australia during a span of 100 years rings truer than his estimate for New South Wales. The national inquiry into the 'Separation of Aboriginal and Torres Strait Islander Children from Their Families', published as *Bringing Them Home*, summarises the situation thus: 'We can conclude with confidence that between one in three and one in ten indigenous children were forcibly removed from their families and communities in the period from approximately 1910 until 1970' (HREOC 1997, 37).

Of the 208 Aboriginal people interviewed in this study, every one had a connection, often a close one, with removal. Most often, those interviewed were the children of removed parents and, equally often, the youth engaged in aggressive or reckless or near-suicidal behaviour were, in turn, their children.

The era of protection–segregation did not end with the formal adoption of assimilation policies by the national conferences of officials in 1937, and again in 1951 and 1961. Despite proclamations of equality in those two latter decades, the old policies and practices persisted. The lay and clerical bureaucrats who remained as guardians could not or would not accept the 'elevation' of 'their' wards to the status (of power, goodness, correctness, civility) they themselves enjoyed. The settlements and missions continued as before, with total power vested in officials who maintained a regimen of work, instruction, discipline, good order and hygiene. These 'bogey men' were real enough. Draconian laws, wardship status, exclusion from schools and forcible removal of children became the indelible scars and memories of this century's Aboriginal population in New South Wales: 'the Welfare', to use the Aboriginal idiom, remains indelible in the contemporary Aboriginal psyche. There is, plainly, no other comparable experience in Western society, not even in South Africa in its darkest days.

The 'new violence'

Decolonisation

In another context, I have tried to explain the contemporary violence (Tatz 1999). Briefly, my contention is that it is *de*colonisation, rather than colonisation, which is a root cause. It was only after the Labor Party won federal office at the end of 1972 that these segregated institutions began to be dismantled: the 'inmates' stayed and became citizens (in legal theory), but the 'inspectors' of the harsh rules 'for the good order and discipline of the settlements'—the guards and the gatekeepers — disappeared, at least in the flesh. Their spectres lingered. What has also endured is the myth, and the euphemism, that all of this treatment — lasting nearly three-quarters of a century — was simply and mundanely nothing more than 'the era of handouts', the period of benevolent 'welfare'.

In an ironic sense, it was the removal of these often draconian structures that initiated the evolution of the present climate of violence and disorder. Almost all commentators, analysts and scholars attribute the present breakdowns, including the propensity for suicide, to past and continuing colonialism, racism, oppression, landlessness, population relocations, and the destruction of cultures and environments. The RCIADIC, in elucidating the underlying causes of the disproportionate numbers of Aborigines in custody, contains an excellent summary of these factors.[8]

The observations of the RCIADIC are all true, in the broad sense and sweep. Yet, apart from the broad impact of 100 years of discriminatory policy, there are specific decisions by governments which were largely responsible for the present turmoil. These 'asylums' or 'total institutions'[9] were forced to become 'communities' in name, regardless of whether or not there was an actual *communitas*. In the eras of protection–segregation and wardship, settlements and missions were designed as *institutions*, and the residents were termed *inmates*. There were legal and administrative locks and keys, as well as the physical kind. With the changes which came shortly before and after 1972, these nineteenth- and early twentieth-century institutions were euphemistically renamed 'communities', and the superintendents and managers transformed by administrative pen into 'community development officers'. No one tried to understand or define the characteristics of a community, no one trained the officers in 'development', and no one ever consulted the black populations about their notions of a civil order, an organised society, a polity, a commonwealth in miniature.

Born out of sheer political expedience, and out of a laziness about doing any homework concerning these groupings and their common or uncommon characteristics, bureaucrats eventually gave these prison-like institutions 'freedom', a budget and autonomy of a limited kind. Nobody considered how to de-institutionalise the institutions and to remove their penitentiary flavour. No one provided training in autonomy. Nobody remembered, or wanted to remember, that the inmates-turned-citizens were often people who had been involuntarily moved or exiled to these places, people who had had to be disciplined or punished, or people who had been rounded up by desert patrols and simply placed there for the 'social engineering' experiment of assimilation in the deserts and monsoon lands. Most places were *not* peopled by a *communis* or *communitas*. These people were not a voluntary association, with common tribal or linguistic membership and fellowship, or with common historical, political or cultural heritages. They were not communitarian in their membership and were neither cohesive nor socially coherent. Such cohesiveness as many such places had was institutional and imposed, not cultural, spiritual or linguistic.

The infrastructure in these institutions was artificial. The omnipresence of the 'inspector' (usually the director of the relevant Aboriginal Affairs department), the authoritarian laws and regulations under special legislation, and the associated powers, together with mission evangelism, gave these institutions 'viability' of a kind. Only in the 1970s, and in Queensland even later, did the struts and pillars propping up these institutions begin to be removed. Thus, there is now, in effect, a structural vacuum in many places, an absence of an overarching or binding philosophy (however bad or misguided), a lack of system, without goals beyond mere survival. The rallying call for land rights, especially since 1969, and the protracted legal hearings which resulted, have filled only a small part of that vacuum. Lacking structure, many 'communities' lacked order and have become *disordered*. The much-respected Aboriginal values of affection, reverence for family and kin, reciprocity, care of the young and aged, and veneration for law, lore and religion are floundering or have been displaced. What began as protection from physical genocide in the last century has resulted, at present, in *a widespread legacy of acute distress*.

Prior to undertaking this study, I had read Dr Ernest Hunter's published papers on suicides in the Kimberleys.[10] His concern about the rapidly increasing rates of youth suicide, self-mutilation and other violent behaviours impressed me. He has described self-mutilation, particularly among young males, including self-tattooing, often of their own name. Hunter says that this is usually done by alienated adolescents whose social networks are fragile and who need to claim and publicly proclaim their very identity. Dr Joseph Reser in Townsville was also reporting alarming suicide rates, at very young ages, in North Queensland. Suicide, I began to see, was but one manifestation of that legacy of acute distress.

RCIADIC findings

The RCIADIC findings in 1991 were: 37 per cent of deaths from natural causes; 34 per cent self-inflicted; 15 per cent from injuries (fights or falls occasioned by other than custody officers); 9 per cent related to 'substance abuse'; and 5 per cent from custodians' actions (vol. 1, 4–7). Of interest in the context of my study is that 27 deaths were of people aged between 14 and 24, 43 of the deceased were in custody for alcohol-related matters, and 12 were in custody for 'non-offences'. There was general relief that the shadow of murder had been removed by this scrupulous and Aboriginal-sympathetic inquiry. There were some who sought to show that the suicide figure was consonant with the Australian 'norm' for deaths in custody; others saw the suicide figure of 30 out of 99 as inconsistent with the (believed) Aboriginal propensity *not* to self-destruct.

By 1991, however, I was aware that Aboriginal youth suicide occurred much more commonly in freedom than it did in custody.

Suicide as a social indicator

Suicide, although the ultimate act of the distressed, is not the sole indicator of societal ills but is generally accepted as a very strong signal that something is seriously awry. Teenage suicide, especially teenage male suicide, has reached horrifying proportions in most Western societies in the past 30 years. But the leap in Aboriginal rates of suicide and attempted suicide is even more staggering, both statistically and as unspoken commentary about the value young Aborigines now place on life. The need to understand why so many young Aboriginal people prefer death to life gives impetus to my research. By contrast with the approach taken by the noted scholar, David Lester, who has published books on *Suicide from a Psychological Perspective* (1988) and *Suicide from a Sociological Perspective* (1989), my approach is anthropological and political, trying to discover if this form of violent behaviour has all or some of its origins in the social and political contexts in which it occurs.

Notes

1. Marx, *The Social Context of Violent Behaviour*, 5–6.
2. Maori Suicide Review Group, 'Reducing Suicide by Maori Prison Inmates', 1.
3. Duclos, Le Beau and Elias, in American and Alaska Native Mental Health Research, *Calling from the Rim*, 189–214.
4. Personal communication.
5. Personal communications from these three colleagues.
6. In November 1997, after years of agitation by Eddie's father, Arthur, the NSW State Coroner granted an order for an exhumation and further post-mortem. The forensic finding was that the deceased had a fractured sternum, possibly occasioned a day or two before his alleged self-hanging. The family's barrister, Robert Cavanagh, has maintained, on an SBS documentary shown in February 1998, that with such an injury he would have been incapable of carrying out the physical actions involved in his death. As at this time, no further action has taken place in the matter. An important document on the matter is *Too Much Wrong* by Cavanagh, Pitty and Woods.
7. Tatz, 'Aboriginal Violence'; Tatz, *Obstacle Race*, ch. 13, 297–340.
8. RCIADIC, *National Report*, vol. 2, ch. 10, 'The Legacy of History', 3–47.
9. The Canadian sociologist Erving Goffman coined these terms for North American mental institutions. He called them 'places of residence and work where a large number of like-situated individuals cut off from the wider society for an appreciable period of time, together lead an enclosed, formally administered round of life'. Prisons, he wrote, serve as a clear example, providing we 'appreciate that what is prison-like about prisons is found in institutions whose members have broken no laws' (1961, 11).
10. Hunter, 'Aboriginal Suicides in Custody', 'On Gordian Knots and Nooses', 'Changing Aboriginal Mortality Patterns', 'A Question of Power', and *Aboriginal Health and History*.

3
An Anthropology of Suicide

Thus even the author of the entry on suicide in the Encyclopaedia of Religion and Ethics writes, with unconcealed relief: 'Perhaps the greatest contribution of modern times to the rational treatment of the matter is the consideration ... that many suicides are non-moral and entirely the affair of the specialist in mental diseases.' The implication is clear: modern suicide has been removed from the vulnerable, volatile world of human beings and hidden safely away in the isolation wards of science.

— A. Alvarez[1]

Man's ability to kill himself has been a source of fascination since the beginning of human society. Philosophers from Marcus Aurelius and Seneca to Camus, writers (especially poets) from Virgil to Sylvia Plath, and sociologists from the beginning of the nineteenth century to the present day, have all contributed voluminously to its study. This widespread preoccupation has, if anything, obstructed the scientific investigation of suicide...

— Norman Kreitman[2]

Professor Tatz notes that he has 'approached this report with caution and sensibility', but the majority of [his] work is a polemical view based on qualitative research rather than any objective quantitative analysis of data.

— Robert Goldney[3]

Science and suicide

Methodology has always been a problem for the humanities and social sciences: their practitioners feel that they miss out, or are inadequate, in the face of the 'scientific method' of the natural and biological disciplines. While not perceiving their work as illegitimate or invalid, they wish it were more amenable to demonstrable proof. If they could quantify, preferably mathematically and statistically, they seem to say, they would then have validity — and thence legitimacy, the essential quality of physics, chemistry, geology and some branches of medicine. Even that doyen of American political science, Harold Lasswell, tried to reduce the study of politics to a 'science' of 'decision-making', believing that if each decision could somehow be reduced to an atomistic, measurable reality, then, with appropriate tags, we could watch the process of a decision — its formulation, adoption, implementation and consequences. He neglected the many decisions which, not being publicly stated, remain withdrawn, abandoned, hidden or unreported, and therefore not amenable to such analysis. For example, my decision on what material to omit from this book is known only to me and therefore cannot be 'tagged'. Acts of commission may be able to be ascertained — but acts of omission not so easily, if at all.

Most suicide studies are preoccupied with numbers, with percentages or rates, as if this kind of quantification established 'scientific veracity'. Professor Robert Goldney's review of my original report laments the polemical, qualitative research and the lack of 'any objective quantitative analysis of data'. If my sense and use of language is correct, qualitative analysis means detection of the nature of the constituents of a subject, as in the components of a chemical — as opposed to the mere measurement of those constituents. My intent is quite clear: to elucidate, discover, isolate, examine and analyse the ingredients of Aboriginal youth suicide — at the risk of controversy. I reject the 'safe' way, the path of so-called 'objectivity' that is mistakenly believed to underlie measurement. As to the term 'polemics', as used by Goldney and others, it is often used pejoratively: quantitative scientific research abhors controversy, confrontation and, surprisingly in the context of suicide, critical interrogation of both the literature and the phenomenon. They imply a safety in numbers.

The best scientific studies are 'double blind' or, at least, controlled. Several Aboriginal projects have been rejected by grant-giving bodies because the applicants were not able to design a study using a non-Aboriginal control group. Again, Goldney points to my failure 'to attempt to control for other confounding variables', such as the 'high degree of prevalence of mental disorders in those who have suicided in indigenous groups in Taiwan and also, more recently, in a diverse population in India' (2000, 443). I address mental disorders and the whole vexed question of 'mental illness' at some length later, but here I must note that *there are simply no other groups whose backgrounds and circumstances so match the Aboriginal experience that the effects of any single causative factor can be studied in isolation from other confounders.* Mentally ill or mentally healthy Taiwanese don't help, and nor do Indian. Aboriginal birth, life and death differ so much in quality and circumstance from the non-Aboriginal that attempts at explanation through quantification and comparison, or by the use of control groups, are futile. To insist on 'science' in this context, as Kreitman would have it, is to obstruct meaning and understanding. The pursuit of meaning may well be 'polemical', but I will always prefer the search for explanation and understanding above the striving for measurement.

Suicide and the royal commission

Suicide is often the province of statisticians. In Australia, it has also largely remained in what Alvarez calls 'isolation wards'. The RCIADIC was the first major exercise to begin to identify Aboriginal suicide in a context beyond confinement. Of the report's 2277 pages, 569 traverse 'the under-lying issues which explain the disproportionate number of Aboriginal people in custody'. The Commission summarises, in one excellent volume, all there is to be said about Aboriginal incarceration, but says very little indeed about suicide outside of custody. It examines

- 'the legacy of history';
- aspects of contemporary Aboriginal life, including the status of Aborigines;
- demographic and social indicators of health, income, housing;
- indigenous mechanisms of social control;
- Aboriginal identity;
- relations with the non-Aboriginal community;
- Aborigines in the criminal justice system and relations with the police;
- young Aboriginal people in the criminal justice system;
- the harmful use of drugs and alcohol;
- schooling;
- employment and poverty;
- land needs; and
- the issue of self-determination.

Only 13 pages are devoted to 'Pretended Suicide' (a term I find unacceptable), 'Reasons for Suicide' and 'Epidemic and Multiple Self-Inflicted Deaths'.[4] Even so, much of the material, admittedly summarised from lengthy submissions, deals with factors relevant to each individual deceased who came within the terms of reference. There is little discussion of youth suicide outside of custody, or about its possible causation. While the Commission was, admittedly, confined to suicide in custody, its discussion of suicide outside of custody is peripheral and almost perfunctory.

The section begins with what can be called the classic 'silly buggers' explanation (1991, ch. 2, p. xxx). The 1987 *Report on Yarrabah Suicides* by A.F. Wattridge, a public servant, was a RCIADIC exhibit. In part, Wattridge wrote,

> the usual purpose of the suicide attempt is to seek and/or regain the attention and affection of a boyfriend or girlfriend after a quarrel ... It is fairly common on communities for men to shoot themselves through the fleshy part of the upper arm with a .22 rifle. This action gains maximum sympathy from girlfriends ... Stabbing or slashing of the arm, leg or chest are common methods of 'attempting suicide'. Again there is usually no major damage unless an artery is accidentally severed.[5]

For not entirely clear reasons, the Commission called this form of ambivalent suicide, 'pretended suicide' — that is, there was 'no intention of killing oneself and ... it occurs under an impulse of strong emotion, such as helplessness or desperation'. The word 'pretend' is hardly consonant with so strong an emotion as 'desperation'.

The RCIADIC then moves from 'pretended' suicide to the reasons for successful suicide. Admitting that the psychiatric and psychological evidence given encompassed a 'range of causal factors, underlying issues, and contextual phenomena', there was clearly an acceptance that suicide relates to 'multiple psychological stresses', 'long term stresses' and 'short term stresses'. Heavy-drinking syndromes, 'lack of self-esteem', 'the sense of failing oneself, one's family or one's community' were suggested. Dr Joseph Reser's theory of 'reactance' was postulated, 'the human tendency to attempt to restore freedom of action when it is taken away'. In Chapter 6, I elaborate on this reason, which Reser defines as follows: 'To imitate the style of suicide of one's kin, friends or Aboriginal compatriots in other communities as a type of mass protest in opposition against the forces of authority and institutionalism.' The Commission paid attention to the factors suggested in the Adelaide *Taking Control* study, particularly instability in parenting, unemployment and welfare dependence, ill-health and drug abuse, police involvement, physical and/or sexual abuse, anger, self-perception and the adverse perception of Aborigines by non-Aboriginal society.[6]

By comparison, the Maori prison inmate study examined such risk factors as psychological/psychiatric disorders, family, attempted suicide, possible biochemical and genetic factors, exposure to suicidal behaviour, stressful life events, and triggers such as depression or shame. There is an interesting tension in New Zealand suicide research: on the one hand, a strong drive to characterise all suicide as a form of mental disorder, or to give precedence to the psychiatric above the politico-social aspects; on the other hand, an insistence that cultural factors are the key. Thus, of importance is the suicide's relationship to his *whanau* (extended family), his *wairua* (spirituality), his sense of *whakama* (shame), his *whakamomori* (state of mind that can result in suicide), his *iwi* (tribe) and his *hapu* (sub-tribe).

It is self-evident to say that suicide research is quintessentially guesswork — the best available technology and science notwithstanding. The dead cannot explain. Even when they do leave notes — and I have now read all too many in coroners' files — there is little in the way of communicating what really warranted the act. The behaviour exemplified by a 75-year-old Australian who carefully puts his affairs, his house and even the garbage in order, leaves a precise note as to why he now, with terminal cancer, cannot live without his recently deceased wife, is rare in any society. Aboriginal suicides rarely leave notes.

In New South Wales, perhaps unlike the cases in the RCIADIC studies, there is much less in the way of evident 'pretended' shooting in the fleshy arms. Nor is there any *systematic* study in New South Wales or the Australian Capital Territory (ACT), as there has been in New Zealand, of parasuicides when they are admitted to, or discharged from, hospital casualty departments. Even if there were such 'interviews', it is doubtful whether a nurse, hospital orderly or even a trained health professional could elicit anything much better than the 'I-feel-guilty-I'll-confess-to-any-motivation-you-might-suggest-to-me' response from the embarrassed person in a bed in the emergency ward.

The RCIADIC, like so many other studies, tended to confuse underlying factors, or the personal or familial factors involved in a particular suicide, as reasons, explanations or motives for the action. There are many people in this world whose lives are beset by these, or even more stressful, factors who do *not* commit or attempt suicide; conversely, many of those who appear to have endured none of these factors or stressors *do so*.

The need for a broader focus

I am trained in several disciplines, but not in psychology. Doubtless, individuals in trouble need help from people trained in psychiatry, psychology, social work and the related disciplines. But the patient–therapist relationship is, of necessity, confined to just that. It cannot venture much beyond the individual and the immediate family, and it almost never ventures beyond the consulting or therapy room. Aborigines rarely venture into 'by-appointment-only' consulting rooms in medical suites. The space — geographical, architectural, cultural, societal — between potential patient and therapist in this context is, basically, unbridgeable and augurs poorly for any successful resolution of the individual's underlying problems.

To understand why dozens of youth in a particular social or racial grouping take their own lives, and then to suggest ways of mitigating that behaviour, seems a reasonably sensible task: yet this 'group' task can only be approached by a discipline or disciplines which embrace something wider than the individual. This does not mean simply modifying the individual approach to make it suitable for group use. It means using whatever lenses are available to examine this behaviour in particular societal contexts, including the social, sporting, historic, geographic and political. (It is significant that the Australian Psychological Society has called for a 'broadening of their focus' and a widening of their 'analytic and explanatory frameworks' (1999, 17).) Since a good deal of Aboriginal suicide occurs in clusters, we must examine the social context of the cluster — what often looks like a contagion — and not merely that of the individual. But such pluralising of suicide risks the stigmatisation of the group and the dismissing of the individual's behaviour as being merely that of a 'groupie'.

Who or what comprises a cluster? Since the suicides do not occur in the social isolation identified by Emile Durkheim as the key factor in suicide (see Chapter 6), or always in states of classical *anomie* or fatalism, we need to focus on the sort of society in which the suicides originate. Henry Morselli, Durkheim's predecessor, explained, as long ago as 1879, that suicide was no longer 'the expression of individual and independent faculties, but certainly [is] a social phenomenon' (Alvarez 1974, 92). Whatever amelioration psychiatric and other therapeutic treatment might have wrought, it has not been able to stem the rapid and still-increasing rise in Aboriginal suicide rates. It is worth noting the admonition of that notable polemicist and psychiatrist, Dr Thomas Szasz: 'Doctors try to save lives; suicides try to throw them away. It is hardly surprising that the two get along so poorly. Like misers and spendthrifts, all they have in common is their differences' (1974, 76).

Suicide in history

In 1621, Richard Burton's treatise on *The Anatomy of Melancholy* described suicide as tragic but nonetheless a fatal end common to those who suffered from melancholia. This medical model, or vision, was ignored. By the 1600s, suicide was considered one of the lowest possible criminal acts in Britain: the suicide 'is drawn by a horse to the place of the punishment and shame, where he is hanged on a gibbet, and none may take the body down but by the authority of the magistrate' (Szasz 1974, 64). Burial was usually at the crossroads so that carriages would trample the dead, by now seen as a vampire; and if that were not enough, a stake was driven through the heart and a stone placed over the deceased's face — to prevent any rising. A suicide was declared a *felo de se* and his properties forfeited to the Crown rather than passing to his inheritors. This practice was abolished as late as 1882.

Only in 1870 was the law about inheritance and property changed: lawyers invented, in effect, a protection against a silly law which not only deprived a suicide of the right to bequeath but also denied him a religious burial. It would be sensible to remember that the lawyers, not the doctors, devised the notion, and the fiction, that suicide occurred because 'the balance of his mind was disturbed'. Alvarez reminds us of Professor C.E.M. Joad's pertinent aphorism, relevant to so many countries until the middle of the twentieth century, 'that in England you must not commit suicide, on pain of being regarded as a criminal if you fail and a lunatic if you succeed' (1974, 66).

What was once a mortal sin and a criminal offence is now a private vice, something shameful, kept in the closet, something, if at all possible, not mentioned; as Alvarez puts it, 'less self-slaughter than self-abuse'. Stigma always attaches. Szasz makes a good point when he argues that the holy grail of scientists, 'objective' research and 'objective' language, betrays strong emotions: abortion is called murder or feticide by those who disapprove of it; it is called birth control by those who approve. Why not 'death control', he asks, by those who seek it rather than the negative term 'suicide' (1974, 76)?

Suicide ceased being criminal in Britain in 1961 and in Australian states between five and 40 years ago.[7] Suicide, as disturbed balance of the mind, was to become, and remain, the domain of the psychiatrists, the clinical psychologists, a few sociologists and social workers, and a great many statisticians. With 'depression' and 'stress' now bywords in our Western society, suicide is seen as the extreme of both, and hence even more the domain of those who deal in these matters and who are in a position to prescribe antidepressants or even more drastic 'therapies'.

There are several logical slippages in these perspectives of psychiatric and pharmaceutical treatment of 'depression'. For example, it is commonly claimed that at least a third of the population suffers from stress and depression; that depression is a primary cause of suicide; and, therefore, that at least a third of the population commits suicide. This is patently untrue. Or, again, it is claimed that depression is a, if not the, major mental health risk factor in suicide; that antidepressants alleviate or control depression; and that the suicide rate therefore falls markedly across Australia when depression is treated. This again is a nonsensical claim. Medication may prevent a suicide, but this does not mean that the 'depression' is, of itself, the cause of the suicidal impulse. There remains, however, a strong lay (and, regrettably, a medical) perception that the right pill will always solve the problem.

The nineteenth-century label of 'unsound mind' left the burden of suicide, in all its manifestations and consequences, with the health professions. No one else wanted it and, surprisingly, the church was relieved to be absolved of an insoluble 'moral' and 'mortal' problem. Apart from the usual shibboleths about 'misfits', 'wasted lives', 'tragedy', or even 'cost to the state', one outstanding feature of young suicide is that it utterly rejects all of us — everything we can offer by way of love, family, a sense of belonging or of identity, learning, progress, creativity, leisure, pleasure, societal feelings, civility and civilisation and, not least, a belief in a future. The psychoanalyst James Hillman suggests that suicide is 'the paradigm of [their] independence from everyone else' (1997, 91). Society at large cannot accept this rejection, resulting in a counter-rejection or resentment, on our part, of those who commit, or attempt, suicide.

Towards an anthropological approach

From the inception of my study, a number of researchers and policy makers expressed interest in how I gathered my data. Trained in political science, public administration and the law, I have also 'practised' as a sociologist. However, for this exercise, I found it necessary to move towards an anthropological approach: intensive fieldwork, heavy reliance on informants, visits to locales (double-checking with documents where possible), a degree of participant observation and, importantly, the use of what is called in German, *Verstehen*, one's intuitive understanding of situations, especially when one has long experience. To use the old 'onion' metaphor, one must always be aware of what is clearly the outer layer of 'truth', of what comprises the second, third and fourth layers, and, finally, an intuition when one is getting reasonably close to the centre. The finality of self-inflicted death blocks all knowledge of the individual's deeper intentions. There is, therefore, no ultimate 'truth' to be found.

To all this must be added that, in matters of such personal intensity and sensitivity, trust is the key to people talking to the researcher. The RCIADIC inquiry has left a deep psychological scar on many people involved with youth suicide. There was general relief when it was confirmed that we were examining suicide *outside* of custody. Police were wholly cooperative because they were either concerned about youth behaviour in general but were a little fearful lest this was another 'custody' probe, or were relieved of insecurity by virtue of strong letters of commendation about me from their senior commissioners. Coroners were anxious to contribute, again out of concern at escalating youth suicides, and in response to a letter from the Office of the State Coroner approving the research project. Doctors, nurses, mental health workers and juvenile justice staff were willing to discuss anything, with anyone, in the face of the problems confronting them.

Aboriginal trust is another matter. My wife, Sandra, and I were not threatening: we presented as middle-aged grandparents, with some 38 years of working in Aboriginal societies. (Single people, especially younger men, can be seen as a threat.) We had no clipboards, questionnaires or tape recorders, and no vehicles with 'government' decals. My books on Aborigines in sport were reasonably well known, especially the picture-gallery book, *Black Diamonds*. Where communities had not seen the book, I gave them copies for their school or community hall, as a little something in return for what I was to ask for and take away. We would phone and/or fax ahead to a land council or medical service, inform an administrator that we wanted to talk about the problem of 'too many young people taking, or trying to take, their lives', and obtain permission to visit.

Almost without exception, responses were eager, asking, in return, whether we would agree to a meeting, meaning a group session. These became more common: gatherings of anything from three to 20 people, where solidarity gave people the confidence to talk about their own children or relatives and, somewhat surprisingly, to volunteer their own experiences of mutilation and failed attempts at suicide. These meetings could last for two to three hours. I always explained that this research task was a 'mission impossible', but gave my assurance that I would do what I could, without being able to deliver any magical elixir. Everyone was enormously generous with information, their feelings, and the names of people we should contact. Sandra always asked if there was any objection to her taking notes. On the two occasions when there were objections, the notebooks were put away.

We were given abundant witness reports of suicidal behaviour, and first-person descriptions of attempted suicide. We did not ask those who had attempted suicide why they had acted as they did. People discussed family circumstances, their frustration, alienation, anger, resentment and sometimes hatred; they talked openly about the hitherto unmentionable topics of drug abuse, child abuse, child molestation, incest, and the 'abdication' of parenting. They always talked of the need for local people to be trained in appropriate counselling.

(The research project had been approved by Macquarie University's Ethics Committee. However, the ethical protocols do not allow, in advance, for such spontaneous meetings, for unexpected networking and unforeseeable expressions about suicide attempts. Nor, I would add, should they try to cover every such contingency.)

The 'isolation wards of science' usually require that all information be reduced to numbers, otherwise the findings are regarded as merely 'anecdotal'. That word no longer means a narrative of or about an event, but rather a story, or a 'story', bordering on hearsay, clearly unreliable because it is statistically 'unverifiable'. Rather than put as much objective distance between myself and the subject matter, I chose to make the relationship as close and as subjective as possible. Trust reveals the core truth more reliably and more accurately than any other methodology, and in this most intimate of studies is the most important relationship. This trust, the very essence of the counsellor–client relationship, must, by its nature, produce more of value and potential preventive relevance than counting cases in coroners' courts or processing shaky figures from the Bureau of Census and Statistics.

Trust is also a matter of patience. In this field of work, one has to stay around a while, be seen in cafes and supermarkets, in pubs, poolrooms, craft and cultural centres, at local socials, at football practice or at the matches, in hospitals, talking to people, getting the feel of a town and its tensions, however superficially. 'Where are you from?' and 'what are your connections?' are Aboriginal questions as pertinent to me as to any newly arrived Aborigine.

I intend placing copies of our typed, edited fieldwork notes, under restricted conditions of access, in the AIATSIS library in Canberra. Whereas suicide files in coroners' courts are matters of public record, our notes contain names which are not for public knowledge. In this book, I have chosen not to reveal any names. No one insisted on this confidentiality: it is my choice. I have, where necessary, used invented initials to disguise identity. I have also avoided, except where it is used in documents, the term 'indigenous suicide', for the reasons given in Chapter 1.

The sample in this study

Between July 1997 and October 1998, 55 communities were visited in New South Wales and the ACT (Walgett and Forbes had one suicide each, and those are included in Table 2). Two locations (Wollongong and Newcastle) were 'visited' only in the sense of examining deaths in the files of the Office of the State Coroner in Glebe. The two cities are too large, and the Aboriginal populations too scattered, to achieve the same kind of trusting rapport as in rural and remote centres.

The centres visited were carefully selected because there were reliable census figures for the Aboriginal and non-Aboriginal populations; because we knew something of the histories of these communities and something of their repute as 'good' towns or 'bad' towns (that is, good for Aborigines or places of tension and overt discrimination); and because some were on the coast, some inland, some in the central west and some in the far west. In retrospect, there were a few weaknesses in this selection: Dungog, believed to have a small Aboriginal population, has none; the omission of the cluster of towns in southern central New South Wales, namely Griffith, Leeton, Narrandera, Wagga and Junee; and the omission of visits to the Sydney greater metropolitan regions of Blacktown, Bankstown, Redfern, Parramatta and Penrith. Again, the kind of field-work possible in small country towns simply does not work as readily in large urban centres, unless there is a discrete area of community living and infrastructure, as in La Perouse in southeastern Sydney.

We spent five weeks in New Zealand, not to replicate the Australian study, but to gather information from local researchers about suicide research among Maori and Pacific Islanders. In Dunedin, Christchurch, Wellington, Carterton, Auckland, Manakau and Hamilton, we met academic researchers, suicide prevention personnel, police, coroners, Maori psychiatrists, *iwi* counsellors, and Maori residents who had lost children. We learned much from a country which now 'boasts' the second highest male and female youth suicide rates in the world. The comparative and learning-from-another-experience approach offers a sense of perspective (rather than 'solution' or 'explanation'), something easily lost in studies such as this. There are many instances where suicide patterns among young Aboriginal and Maori illuminate each other. The New Zealand material presented here is not intended as a fully-fledged comparison with the Aboriginal portrait. While in South Africa in 1997, I made contact with the leading researcher working on African suicide, hitherto not a problem of any dimension. References to Alan Flisher's work appear in Chapter 9.

We interviewed, in depth, 396 people:
- 208 Aborigines, most of whom were working in Aboriginal agencies;
- 12 Maori in agencies;
- 41 non-Aboriginal people working with or for Aboriginal organisations in New South Wales, the ACT and Queensland;
- 10 New Zealand agency personnel;
- 7 psychiatrists in New South Wales, 4 in New Zealand and 2 in South Africa;
- 5 Australian Federal Police and 5 New Zealand Police;

- 31 New South Wales and ACT coroners, 4 in New Zealand and 1 in the United States; and
- 66 NSW Police personnel.

Although this is a massive sample, the cost — some $40,000 over close on three years (excluding my university salary)—was not expensive, but the fieldwork was time-consuming, difficult, and physically and emotionally draining, requiring fairly regular debriefing and counselling for the two of us.

This study is not simply about Aboriginal youth suicide, about the high rate of Aboriginal self-destruction. Rather, it takes Aboriginal youth suicide as the starting-point for a contextual analysis and critique of contemporary Aboriginal and non-Aboriginal life in rural towns and urban centres. Youth suicide — whether Aboriginal, Maori, Pacific Islander, black South African — cannot be comprehended, let alone alleviated, by the statistics of suicidology. It is imperative that all scholars and agency personnel understand and appreciate the social and political context of this violent behaviour. Until the contexts within which these suicides occur are appreciated and are absorbed into intervention strategies, the present medical and 'mental health' approach, which so often seeks to 'pathologise' Aboriginal youth suicide, will not succeed — beyond, perhaps, alleviating the pain, the 'psychache', of a few individuals with suicidal intent. Significantly, the National Mental Health Strategy now insists that 'mental health interventions must recognise the past for its role in the current health problems of Aboriginal and Torres Strait Islander communities' (2000, 84). A major problem remains: how to educate mental health practitioners about the past — and how to secure their intelligent use of that knowledge?

Notes

1. Alvarez, *The Savage God*, 92–3.
2. Kreitman, 'Definition of Suicide', 343.
3. Goldney, 'Exploring Aboriginal Youth Suicide', 443.
4. RCIADIC, *National Report*, vol. 2, 117–30.
5. Ibid., 117.
6. Ibid., 127–9; see also Reser, 'Aboriginal Mental Health', 274.
7. Tasmania in 1957, Victoria in 1967, Western Australia in 1972, Queensland in 1979, South Australia in 1983, Australian Capital Territory in 1990, New South Wales in 1993, and the Northern Territory in 1996.

4

The Prevalence of Aboriginal Suicide — Definitional Problems

Statistical data on suicide as they are compiled today deserve little if any credence; it has been repeatedly pointed out by scientific students of the problem that suicide cannot be subject to statistical evaluation, since all too many suicides are not reported as such. Those who kill themselves through automobile accidents are almost never recorded as suicides; those who sustain serious injuries during an attempt to commit suicide and die weeks or even months later of these injuries or of intercurrent infections are never registered as suicides; a great many genuine suicides are concealed by families; and suicidal attempts, no matter how serious, never find their way into the tables of vital statistics ... one is justified, therefore, in discarding them as nearly useless in a scientific evaluation of the problem.

— Gregory Zilboorg[1]

Aborigines in vital statistics

Until the mid-1960s, most Aboriginal affairs administrations and other service agencies kept separate statistics on Aborigines because they were a separate legal class of persons in most states and the Northern Territory. They were, in effect, minors, subject to special statutes which prescribed their separate, segregated and incarcerated lives in reserves, missions and settlements. Every aspect of life was separate, and inferior — housing, wages, employment, training, health services, voting rights, social service benefits, and status in the courts. Section 128 of the Australian constitution had precluded the counting of 'full-blood' Aborigines in the national census. Thus, no vital statistics were available, apart from those kept 'unofficially' by special Aboriginal affairs administrations, and health and police services.

The 1967 referendum removed the census preclusion, and Aborigines became, in theory, part of the national count after 1971. Because the initial framing of the 'indigenous' question was awkward, it is fair to say that the 1991 census was the first one to approximate the realities of Aboriginal and Islander demography. However, the disparities between the 1991 and 1996 figures are so great that the former must be disregarded — with the concurrence of the Australian Bureau of Statistics (ABS)—as inaccurate. Between the 1960s and the mid-1970s, most states took refuge in the contention that keeping separate statistics was a form of apartheid and therefore unconscionable. Aboriginal vital statistics were merged into the mainstream data. In the name of assimilation or equality, or both, the dimensions of a range of serious problems were lost in mainstream figures. The administration of Aboriginal affairs operated in a statistical vacuum. Administrations sought parliamentary budgets for unspecified numbers of people in diverse programs. Problems could not be adequately addressed because they could not be quantified or even roughly estimated.

The ABS has published material showing the changes in population between 1991 and 1996. The greatest 'increase' was that of Aboriginal and Islander populations. The New South Wales Aboriginal population 'increased' from 70,019 in census 1991 to 101,485 actually counted in census 1996. Despite the leap from 1991 figures, there is much evidence to suggest significant under-enumeration, even in 1996, of people of 'indigenous origin'. Many minority groups under-enumerate. (For example, demographers believe the under-enumeration of Jews to be as high as 25 per cent. Historic reasons explain why they do not wish to be part of any national 'list'.) It is probable that the growth in Aboriginal numbers between 1991 and 1996 was due to a greater willingness in 1996 to self-identify rather than due to reproductive growth and/or falling mortality. To this factor, the ABS adds 'the higher fertility of Indigenous women' and the fact that 'many children of Indigenous origin have one rather than two parents of Indigenous origin' (1997, 9).

We found many examples of under-enumeration. The 1996 census records Kempsey town and surrounds as having 2273 Aborigines, yet every agency there asserts an 'area of Kempsey' population of 5000; there is no reason to doubt the higher figure. The census records 1134 Aborigines in the region known as Eurobodalla — including Batemans Bay, Mogo, Moruya, Wallaga Lake, Narooma, Bodalla, and surrounds. Police and Aboriginal organisation sources say that the truer figure is at least 3300. For Orange and Bathurst, the claim locally is between two and three times the census figures. It is also improbable that Narooma has only 79 Aborigines. By contrast, in the small town of Dungog, the census shows 393 persons of 'indigenous origin', yet the police sergeant and local publicans claim, at most, two or three. We are convinced of the accuracy of their local knowledge. Cobar is listed as having 372 Aborigines, but the local Aboriginal Land Council considers half that number to be more realistic. On the basis of our 'coverage' of just over a third of the state's Aboriginal population, it is likely that a more accurate total for the state is 130,000, perhaps even 150,000 people.

In sum, Aboriginal demography remains a confused and confusing area. Attempts to define rates of various phenomena — from causes of death to the prevalence of delinquency or renal disease, let alone suicide — must remain speculations, even high-order speculations. There are no 'hard' data. Given that both Aboriginality and the actual population are areas in which it is difficult to collect accurate data, one has to comment that all of the 'quantified' studies of Aboriginal suicide are speculative. One must be critical of suicide studies which blithely assume that official statistics are sacrosanct because they appear in official bulletins. One must also question the claims of studies based on such bulletins as constituting 'original research'.

In the ABS publication *Causes of Death: Australia 1997*, the following statement appears in a very short, but important, paragraph headed 'Indigenous Deaths':

> This publication includes Indigenous deaths data for South Australia, Western Australia and the Northern Territory ... It is estimated that more than 90% of Indigenous deaths in these States and Territories are identified. While other States have provision for the identification of Indigenous deaths on their death registration forms, deaths for these States are considered to be under identified. (1999, 74)

It concerns me to read a claim for better than 90 per cent accuracy in recording 'Indigenous' death in the three states mentioned. The first problem, discussed more fully below, lies in how to determine death by suicide and in its recording as such by coroners. The second lies in establishing the Aboriginality of the deceased. In 1997, in South Australia, 6 Aboriginal suicides were officially recorded as such; in Western Australia, 9; and in the Northern Territory, 11. In New South Wales for that year, there were, at the very least, 28 officially recorded Aboriginal suicides in the 55 locations we examined *in situ* and in the State Coroner's Office in Glebe. I believe that the figure was higher, but Aboriginality, as will be explained, is difficult to determine.

In sum, either New South Wales is grossly aberrant or the figures for the other three jurisdictions are under-reported. The more likely possibility is that in none of the jurisdictions is there any mechanism, such as a set of protocols, for the proper identification of Aboriginal deceased. This leads to one major conclusion from this study: that Aboriginal suicide is under-reported and therefore under-recorded. From information made available to us, it would seem to be perhaps three or four times higher — especially for young males — than stated in official documents and research papers. However, even if there is under-reporting and under-recording, this does not mean that the qualitative factors underlying Aboriginal suicide are beyond reach, or beyond discussion.

The Aboriginal population in this study

In 1997, the ABS published a document on population based on the 'indigenous geography' maps developed from the 1996 census. The ABS gives populations based on actual counts on census night as well as estimates of population. In this way, it attempts to add in people who belong in an area but who were absent from that area on census night. The sample in this study comprises 59 communities: the Aboriginal population in each of the areas covered by this study, based on the ABS publication, is given below. The figures for the Australian Capital Territory (Canberra, Wreck Bay and Jervis Bay) are listed separately. (See the Appendix for full list of sites visited.)

Table 1. Aboriginal (census-counted) populations of sites/communities visited

(a) New South Wales

Armidale	1026	Condobolin	524
Batemans Bay/Bingi Point	324	Coonabarabran	492
Bathurst	828	Cowra	477
Bathurst surrounds	662	Dareton/Wentworth	422
(excl. jail pop.)		Dubbo	2714
Bega surrounds	207	Dungog	393
Bega	148	Eden/Twofold Farm	162
Boggabilla	276	Eurobodalla (excl. Narooma,	650
Bomaderry & North Nowra	492	Wallaga Lake)	
Bourke	868	Forbes*	+417
Brewarrina	607	Forster	399
Broken Hill	772	Grafton surrounds	564
Casino	631	Grafton (excl. 82 in jail)	646
Cobar	372	Gunnedah	700
Coffs Harbour/Corindi Beach	712	Inverell	413
Coffs Harbour surrounds	345	Kempsey/Greenhills, surrounds	2273

Nowra	885	Tweed Heads	1064
Orange	1040	Walgett*	+832
Parkes	478	Wallaga Lake	81
Port Macquarie	517	Wee Waa	254
Purfleet	206	Wellington surrounds	269
Queanbeyan	704	Wellington	743
Tamworth	1626	Wilcannia	406
Taree	667	Wollongong*	+2138
Tingha	166	Woodenbong/Urbenville	403
Toomelah	222		

Total   **40,487**

Notes: Total NSW estimated resident Aboriginal population 1996: 106,294. Counted population in the study as a percentage of the total estimated population: 38 per cent.
*Not visited but suicides in each of these towns are included in the study.

(b) Australian Capital Territory

Canberra and district	2899
Jervis Bay/Wreck Bay	178

Total   **3077**

Total NSW + ACT estimated resident Aboriginal populations: 106,294 + 3153 = 109,447. Counted population in the study as a percentage of the two total estimated populations: 43,564 in a total of 109,447 = 39.8 per cent

---

The recording of Aboriginality in suicide records

Neither police reporting of non-natural causes of death, nor the coronial determination of the causes of such death, indicate the deceased's Aboriginality. Until early 1999, the police protocol form, known as 'P79A — Report of Death to Coroner', did not make provision for Aboriginal or Islander identity. It sought only citizenship, as in 'Australian' or 'foreigner'. The new form, not yet widely in use (even in 2001) includes the words: 'Deceased a native of Torres Strait Islander/ Aborigine'. (Victoria's equivalent Form 83 does not provide for Aboriginal identification, although identification does appear every time a prisoner is placed in custody. The ACT police form does not stipulate Aboriginal identification.)

A typical 79A form, completed by the investigating or reporting police officer, describes the deceased, his or her personal details, the manner of finding the body, the apparent circumstances of the death, and any interviews concerning anyone who might have been the last to see the person alive, and when. Rarely does a reporting officer specify Aboriginality. In some instances, where cause of death is uncertain, or where suicide seems the likely cause, a coroner's file will include witness or relatives depositions taken by police. These can be voluminous. Where the 79A does not mention Aboriginality, which is most usual, where there are no witness statements, and where no inquest is required by the coroner, *there is no way of knowing whether or not a deceased Australian was an Aborigine.*

The Registrar of Births, Deaths and Marriages has a compulsory form known as 'PR13 Registering a Death in New South Wales'. The cover sheet states: 'Ensure that the question about Aboriginal and Torres Strait Islander origin in part A is accurate in all cases'. The Part A questionnaire asks whether the deceased was of either group, or of 'mixed origin'. However, the PR13 requires the funeral director to answer whether there was a medical certificate or Cause of Death issued, or whether there was a coroner's order with or *without* cause of death. Unless the coroner issues an order *stating suicide as the cause of death*, which, for reasons given below, is not something coroners do willingly, we cannot rely on a PR13 as the basis for documenting Aboriginal suicide. The 'PR11 Order of Disposal of Body' form has no Aboriginal question. Put another way, unless someone in a statistics bureau compares a 79A form and its attachments with a PR13 form registering the death, we can never know who was an Aboriginal suicide. The one form almost never mentions Aboriginality; the other, which is required to, does not require the manner and cause of death to be specified.

Inquests are rare, and coroners usually prefer to dispense with them. Occasionally, the parents of a deceased will ask for, or demand, an inquest if they believe there to have been foul play in custody. Such inquests are intense and serious matters, especially since the RCIADIC inquiry. Inquest reports are not a ready avenue of identity. Where a coroner does send a body for autopsy, the forensic pathologist fills in a variety of protocol forms, including one with headings such as external and internal examinations, toxicology and alcohol readings. In no more than 15–20 per cent of cases will the pathologist describe the deceased, for example, as 'an undernourished young Aboriginal male', or 'female of Aboriginal appearance' or 'obese Caucasian male'. Even such bare descriptions are not a reliable index, based as they are on the criterion of skin-visibility, or any other superficial marker of 'race' which appears in the eyes of the beholder. There is no requirement for origin or identity. Nor is there any attempt in New South Wales to establish 'psychiatric' or 'mental' — let alone social

— profiles of the deceased. If we are serious about establishing causes of suicide and strategies for intervention, there is a strong case for a 'psychiatric autopsy', including both personal and social profiles of the deceased.

Michael Dudley and others (1998a) have reported on non-rural youth suicide in New South Wales. They used coroners' records but constructed a 'best guess' psychiatric diagnosis, using demographic data; potential risk factors, including psychiatric symptomatology, past attempts, substance abuse, chronic illness or handicap, criminality, and exposure to suicide; circumstances surrounding the deaths, including precipitants, involvement of alcohol and other drugs, notes left, geographic location and method of death. I could suggest several other topics for such autopsy. The National Health and Medical Research Council has asked for tenders from people who are willing to construct models for such 'psychiatric autopsies'.

I am drawn to the approach used in the United States. In Texas, for example, the *Code of Criminal Procedure*, at chapter 49, allows for the medical examiner (coroner) to 'request the aid of a forensic anthropologist in the examination of a body'. Such a person must be professionally trained and an accredited forensic science specialist. The job is to help determine physical characteristics and also 'the cause, manner, and time of death'. These anthropologists are usually brought in from universities, as consultants. The social and physical aspects of an autopsy are as important, if not more so, than the 'psychiatric'.

The Office of the NSW Coroner, located in Glebe, has a copy of every local coroner's findings. The short reports are in Glebe, while the fuller versions remain in each coronial jurisdiction. Since very little can be gleaned from central records, the search for Aboriginality has to be conducted by field visits to each location. Even then, Aboriginality must be checked with the local Aboriginal community.

Two examples of definitional problems occurred in this study. The first was in a north coast town where the coroner stated he had had only two official suicides. We were given the name of a third suicide by the Aboriginal Legal Service (ALS), a name known to the coroner but one with no apparent Aboriginal connections. ALS checking found that he was Aboriginal, and a known client of the legal service. The second example, in 1997, concerned a man who hanged himself in the cells in Tamworth. One Aboriginal informant, a clinical psychologist, knew him well: she claimed he was not Aboriginal but had 'lived' Aboriginal and had associated only with Aborigines. Another informant employs the deceased's mother who, she insists, is Aboriginal. While in the cells, the deceased said he was Aboriginal. If one accepts self-identification as the key indicator of Aboriginality (see Chapter 1), then he must be accepted as having been Aboriginal. But a suicide cannot self-identify after the event.

In sum, then, how does one recognise a suicide as Aboriginal? The *partial* answer lies in consulting a long-serving local coroner, or a long-serving police officer who knows the local townspeople and who recollects, from local intelligence and local networks, that the deceased was Aboriginal. The smaller the town, the more likely it will be that the deceased is recalled. Although each coroner maintains a hand-written index of suicides by name and by year, nowhere did we find an index which lists Aboriginality alongside the name. The other obvious, but often difficult, source is to talk with Aboriginal families.

We deduced many instances of Aboriginal suicide by reading the witness depositions. The family name of the deceased and of their relatives was often well known. The names of the places of interview, the domicile area of the witness, the clues given by a witness, such as references to 'the mission', and, often, the use of what is clearly 'Aboriginal English' added to a portrait of the deceased. In most cases, certainly for the 55 places visited in this study, Aboriginal suicides were traced and documented for us by relatives, then double-checked with the local coroner's files.

Interviews with relatives and family, interviews with coroners and police officers, checking the local coroner's files, and double-checking in the Glebe records office is an excruciatingly tedious and wasteful way of establishing the picture and prevalence of Aboriginal suicide. Unlike the North Queensland study by Hunter and others (1999), there were no discrete communities, like Yarrabah, Mornington Island and Palm Island, which keep their own records of such events.

There are similar problems in New Zealand. All informants expressed the view that there is under-reporting of Maori suicide, and that even where there is a record of attempted and actual suicide, 'classification' of the person is (too often) dubious. Tension arises, for example, where a research project examines suicidal deaths within a particular geographic area but where the young Maori has taken his life outside of that area. There are two domains of belonging: a Western, geographic boundary for research purposes, and a strong Maori sense that the youth belonged to their *iwi* and will be buried in their *marae*. Thus, the Canterbury suicide project has used geography as a basis for data and for suicide rates, while Dr Erihana Ryan, a Maori psychiatrist in Christchurch, has included Maori victims who belong to that domain but who have suicided outside of it. Coroners and police have sometimes overlooked the Maori-ness of those suicides who take their lives distant from family and who are blonde, blue-eyed and 'non-Maori-looking'.

What is suicide?

There is a strongly adhered-to convention, rather than a law, which regulates coronial dealing with suicide. Kevin Waller's *Coronial Law and Practice in New South Wales* states that 'suicide is not to be presumed. It must be affirmatively proved to justify the finding.' The custom derives from the British precedent, made plain in 1912 and reinforced in 1975 in *R v HM Coroner for City of London*.[2] The Chief Justice held that a coronial presumption of suicide, however strongly suggested, by a man who had climbed over 'effective rails' on the roof garden of his apartment building and fallen, was invalid:

> If a person dies a violent death, the possibility of suicide may be there for all to see, but it must not be presumed merely because it seems on the face of it to be a likely explanation. Suicide must be proved by evidence, and if it is not proved by evidence, it is the duty of the coroner not to find suicide, but to find an open verdict.

This gives rise to a phenomenon I describe as 'kind hearts and coroners'. It has several ingredients, not all of which, of course, are shared by all coroners at all times and in all places. In general, the factors underlying coronial bias against recording a verdict of suicide are:

- the concealment of suicide for humane reasons;
- avoiding the stigma which families see as inherent in 'a suicide';
- avoidance mechanisms through kinder labelling, such as 'accidental death', 'death by misadventure', 'cause unknown', 'open finding';
- Catholic or other religious adherence which generates a reluctance to make a finding of suicide, especially if the victim is a fellow co-religionist; and
- perceived difficulties, real or imagined, about legal, inheritance or insurance consequences.

A considerable number of people in New South Wales die from over-doses of legal drugs and prescription pharmaceuticals, especially where they mix the contra-indicated tricyclic antidepressants (the monoamine oxidase inhibitors or MAOIs) with the selective serotonin re-uptake inhibitor (SSRI) family of drugs or combine their drugs with alcohol. Often the toxic cocktail is inadvertent, with the victim moving constantly from one medical practitioner to another without informing each of their regimen. There are also cases of antidepressant prescriptions which are contra-indicated for people with suicidal tendencies. And there are one or two major '*wunder*-drugs' over which a little cloud seems to hover, in the sense that suicidal (and perhaps homicidal) tendency may be a side effect.[3] There appear to be cases where the victim knows precisely what he or she is doing. Many such deaths result from an overdose, intentional or otherwise, of an illicit substance or combinations of these, especially with alcohol. Yet, in every case, the coronial finding is *not* suicide. Coroners often simply do not know. In the absence of trained 'profilers', the more uncertain suicides — the single-vehicle road accident and the overdose cases — will remain uncertain. However, some people die because they do not care whether they live or not.

The Australian Institute for Suicide Research and Prevention has suggested a three-option model: those cases which are *beyond reasonable doubt* (BRD, greater than 90 per cent certainty), those which are *probable* (PROB, 50–90 per cent certainty) and those which are *possible* (POSS, 20–25 per cent certainty). I suggest that coroners be explicitly allowed what are sometimes called 'error bars', 'margins of error' or 'tolerance levels'. In this way, we might well arrive at a better picture of the phenomenon of suicide in our society.

Most coroners' courts are in buildings either close to, adjacent to, or even under the same roof as, the local police station. There is a strong sense of social mix, of tea and lunch breaks, of camaraderie between police and court officers. There is no inference of collusion, but there is a background which could lead to a well-intended 'corruption of truth' to spare individuals in small towns from avoidable ignominy, stigma or shame. The Australian systems, at least in Victoria and New South Wales, do not require the coroners or coroner-clerks to bring in verdicts of suicide, or even to use the word.

All but two of the coroners interviewed admitted to a predilection for avoiding, if possible, a finding of suicide. Thus, all single-vehicle car smashes, some occurring on good roads, in good weather, without alcohol or drug impairment, and lacking skid or braking marks, are listed as accidental death. Some prefer the term 'misadventure'. Several such cases include reports of the deceased having crosses or rosary beads in their clenched hands. (A preliminary Victorian study of fatal single-vehicle crashes in 1995–96 suggests that in 'less than 5 per cent [of 127 crashes] was there any positive evidence of suicide (note, deceased had told friends)'.[4] Even if only up to 5 per cent of such deaths were suicide, given the relatively small raw number of suicides, the rates of suicide would be considerably altered.)

Most coroners insist on the Waller dictum, the legalistic approach, which they define in this way: in the absence of a note and a presentation overwhelmingly suggesting suicide, suicide will not be the verdict. Even if someone is found alone in a gas-filled room with an open oven door, the suicide has to be proved — otherwise an open verdict must be brought in. Some have gone to greater extremes regarding what constitutes evidence. One example: Coroner XY, at town U, wrote in 1998: 'Z died as a result of Alcohol and Amitriptyline intoxication, however, I am not satisfied on the evidence that the deceased intended to take her own life'. Yet a senior constable had signed the P79A, which included this extract: 'It would appear the deceased [wife of a policeman] had become depressed over an incident on Friday night and during this Saturday night has [*sic*] drunk two bourbon and taken a quantity of tablets with the intent to take her life. A torn up note was located in the rubbish bin which indicates this intention.'

Following the ACT's recent appointment of a senior magistrate as chief coroner, there may well be greater uniformity of suicide verdicts, probably of a more legalistic nature. Until now, the system has meant that five or six stipendiary magistrates have exercised divergent coronial approaches towards making a finding of suicide.

None of the above implies, for one moment, that coroners lack integrity or are anything but dedicated. What is suggested is that the reporting and recording of suicide is deficient, often with good intention. Bias, which should have no place in such matters, is also inevitable, considering the state's system of law and its geography. Two coroners in my research sites have lost sons to suicide. Several have stated that, even though their Catholicism has lapsed, they still regard suicide as sinful. Our observations, from a reading of all the files in all the locations listed in the Appendix, is that the actual raw figures for youth suicide in this state are *at least* two to three times greater than those officially reported.

It may well be that the actual numbers and the establishment of higher rates is really of little consequence, because what we need to recognise is that suicide by the young, both Aboriginal and non-Aboriginal, is rampant and needs serious attention.

Professor Peter Herdson, Director of ACT Pathology, has provided me with the results of a ten-year retrospective study of suicide in the ACT by his colleague, Dr Sene Colomboge. Of 2600 autopsies, only 335 (12.8 per cent) were established as suicide. Only one was Aboriginal, a male, aged 19, recently found in a toilet block with a ligature round his neck. The authorities believe that it was suicide; the parents claim that it was murder; the matter has been referred to the ombudsman.

Of interest is that there were 99 carbon monoxide deaths, 88 deaths by hanging, 50 by gunshot, 47 by prescription drug overdose, 15 by jumping, 7 by stabbing, 5 by drowning, 8 by chemical ingestion, 8 by fire or electrocution, and 2 by plastic bag. Predisposing factors were: marital/domestic disputes, 18 per cent of cases; psychiatric illness, 28 per cent; unemployment, 17 per cent; financial difficulties, 9 per cent; facing trial, 3 per cent; physical illness, 7 per cent; drug addiction, 4 per cent; alcoholism, 3 per cent; loss of a loved one, 1 per cent, and perhaps 1 per cent while in custody. I mention this study for two reasons. First, it may well serve as a portrait of non-Aboriginal suicide. Second, it suggests that autopsy, including 'predisposing autopsy', is more likely to reveal suicide than might the traditional medical inquest. Professor Herdson contends that New Zealand has the best medical statistics in the Western world. However, their system is based on possibly one autopsy in every 20 deaths necessitating the attention of the coroner: he wonders about the nature of the remaining 19. So do I.

There is much less of the imponderable in Dallas, for example. The Chief Medical Examiner has a staff of 10, himself included, and between them they do some 4000 autopsies annually. Importantly, *75 per cent of non-natural deaths go to autopsy*. The only omissions are, for example, where a severely injured car-crash patient lingers and eventually succumbs to injuries.

The British-derived model of not presuming suicide should be reconsidered. United States coroners may so presume. The injunction not to presume is a legacy from the earlier centuries of both stigma and criminality attending the act of self-destruction. Is there any 'positive' way of defining or declaring suicide? Wekstein (1979) describes suicide as 'the human act of self-inflicted, self-intentioned cessation'. There is room for a model which is not predicated on the avoidance of presumption or of circumstantial evidence, but one which

- excludes the presence or participation of second parties;
- excludes, by autopsy, possible or probable homicide;
- examines the deceased by physical autopsy for cause of death;
- excludes 'almost certain' accident;
- investigates, through trained assessors or forensic anthropologists, the personal, social and, where relevant, the community profile of the deceased;
- gives a weighting to the manner of death as a factor in the final assessment; and
- renders a conclusion framed as being 'suicide beyond reasonable doubt', 'probable suicide' or 'possible suicide'.

Using this model, and provided we are willing, as a society, to 'stretch' suicidal behaviour beyond that which is manifestly suicide, as determined by our present forensic or coronial evidence culture, the assessors could achieve most of what coronial inquiries are intended to achieve. A 'full-scale' inquest can always be invoked as the final arbiter. In this way, we should be able to do better than we are doing. We should be able to diagnose or confirm suicide in many of the categories discussed in the following chapter. Some instances — the suicides by omission — simply cannot be substantiated: those, for example, who 'fail' to take their medications or their insulin injections, or those whose indulgence in high-risk activities, such as running red traffic lights, might be hard to differentiate from anti-social behaviour.

Attempted suicide, or parasuicide (I use both terms), has to be viewed in conjunction with suicide. Stengel defines it as 'the non-fatal act of self-injury undertaken with conscious self-destructive intent, however vague and ambiguous'. Attempted suicide has only recently received attention: 'It used to be treated as merely bungled suicide, undeserving of special interest except as a symptom of mental disorder, but in fact requires special study because it presents many important problems of its own which do not arise from suicide' (1964, 11–13). Firestone has coined a new word: microsuicide — 'behaviours, communications, attitudes, or lifestyles that are self-induced and threatening to an individual's physical health, emotional well-being, or personal goals' (1997, 123–4). In short, he is talking about self-destructive behaviours which include what have been called parasuicide, partial suicide, chronic suicide, masked suicide, and so on.

In the mid-1990s, there was a move to have a uniform coronial system in Australia. For reasons unknown to me, it was taken off the agenda. Given the problems experienced in this study, in the work of Hunter and others, and in suicide research in Victoria and elsewhere, I suggest that the uniformity issue be reconsidered.

Who is a coroner?

In Victoria, all magistrates are qualified as coroners but not all of them do coronial work. They usually undergo a two-week coronial training course. Perhaps 10 per cent of their workloads involve coronial matters. Some 90 per cent of these cases do not go to inquest and, in non-inquest matters in the non-metropolitan regions, clerks of petty sessions write up the findings. As in New South Wales, there is a full-time State Coroner and two (rather than three) full-time senior coroners.

In the United Kingdom, some jurisdictions require the coroner to be medically or legally qualified, or to have both qualifications. In some United States jurisdictions, the office of coroner is considered a prize, earned through a hard-fought electoral contest. Few untrained people occupy these positions. For the larger cities, coroners are appointed as medical examiners, that is, they are salaried, qualified and accredited forensic pathologists. In smaller towns, justices of the peace act as coroners and inevitably refer 'uncertain' cases to a forensic pathologist, either locally or in the nearest larger city. In cities like Dallas, the medical examiner has several 'death investigators', men and women with university degrees as well as on-the-job training. They work to, and for, the medical examiner and have co-equal access to death and crime scenes with police.

New Zealand appoints coroners from among the ranks of practising solicitors or barristers, professional people who remain distant and aloof from police procedures. All but three of New Zealand's coroners are legally qualified. Each coroner has at least one full-time inquests officer, a policeman, whose loyalties — at least as judged by interviews with them — reside with the coroners, not with the police. There appears to be no local clerk-coroner system, as in New South Wales. Nonetheless, almost all of our informants confirmed under-reporting of suicide.

In New South Wales, most small town and rural coroners have a mixed set of duties: they act as clerks of petty sessions courts, chamber magistrates, court registrars, licensing officers, and coroners. Very few (of those encountered in this study) have tertiary education. Only one, to my knowledge, has a university degree. Some attended a short training course in Sydney (two days to a week long) in coronial practice; others have not had even that small benefit. Several refer cases to the State Coroner in Glebe, which is staffed by professionals, when they feel a case is too difficult and beyond their ken.[5] All report immediate and positive response from head office. However, self-confidence and self-sufficiency operate in most cases.

Catholic countries tend to show lower rates of suicide than Protestant societies. David Lester — among many other scholars — reports on the perennial problem of the reliability of suicide figures but suggests that, in the United States, there has been some consistency in reporting, even over a period of a century. My task was and is not an investigation of coronial practice, but I do suggest that a study be undertaken of several aspects of this state's coronial system. Several matters, pertinent to reporting, consistency and reliability in suicide matters, warrant attention and improvement.

Who is a youth?

The convention in suicidology, that youth lies between the ages of 15 and 24, has its origins in a consensus World Health Organisation model which was adopted for statistical convenience. I can find no valid social or sociological reason for the confinement of 'youth' within these margins. Moreover, to confine Aboriginal youth suicide to the same 15–24 cohort as would apply to non-Aborigines is to describe the period of youthfulness as constituting differing proportions of quite different life-spans. An Aboriginal man's life has neither the structure nor the seasons of a white American or a white Australian male's life. Compared with non-

Aboriginal life expectation at birth, now close to 80, the Aboriginal figure is, on average, 20–30 years less. In general, Aboriginal life is at least two, even three, decades shorter. There is, undoubtedly, an accelerated ageing in Aboriginal men, with lifestyle diseases occurring much earlier. In many respects, Aboriginal youth becomes older significantly sooner than non-Aboriginal youth: there is earlier sexual development and experience, and earlier exposure to danger, disease and death. Their age of innocence ends much sooner.

Since — rather than if — most Aboriginal males are dead by 50, or even by 40, there is an insurmountable problem in adhering to the WHO definition if we continue to classify Aboriginal youth as 15–24 years. There may be value in devising a new framework for Aboriginal youth, one which attempts to establish a template incorporating both biological age and something akin to 'social maturity'. The 'youth' cohort might more appropriately be considered as 12–18 years. The objective must be better definition and the alleviation of Aboriginal-specific suicide problems, rather than the publication of neat tables of cohorts for statistical comparison with societies which are inherently different and, therefore, not at all comparable.

A growing proportion of Aboriginal suicides, especially in Queensland, are younger than 15. Our study includes a 12-year-old and a 14-year-old, neither of whom should, for WHO-definitional reasons, be omitted. Strict adherence to the WHO model would preclude them. There is, unfortunately, a strong case for establishing a new category of 'child suicide'. This study includes an 8-year-old parasuicide, another 8-year-old possible suicide, and evidence of many self-harm cases among those under 15. It should be noted that, of the 280 Guarani Indians in Brazil who suicided in the past decade, 26 were children under 14: officially, they, too, are not youth suicides.

Notes

1. Zilboorg, 'Suicide among Civilized and Primitive Races'.
2. Waller (1994, 68–71; 1973, 56–8); *All England Law Reports* [1975] 3 All ER, 538–40.
3. It is instructive to read John Cornwell's *The Power To Harm*. He analyses the case which saw the company Eli Lilly on trial, in effect, for 'massaging the data' in clinical tests of Prozac.
4. Personal communication from Annette Graham, research officer, State Coroner's Office, Victoria. The study referred to is 'Characteristics of Fatal Single Vehicle Crashes', Narelle Haworth et al, Monash University Accident Research Centre, September 1997, Report No. 120. Ms Haworth is the author who is quoted as talking with Ms Graham.

5. The Coroner's Support Unit has an inspector, a sergeant and a senior constable in Glebe, a sergeant and senior constable in Westmead, five case officers and four investigators at Glebe, and two prosecutors and two investigators at Westmead. The office contends that it is understaffed.

5

The Prevalence of Aboriginal Suicide — the Data

Scientific studies of suicide have multiplied like flies since the 1920s: clinical investigations, statistical analyses, aspects of this and that, theories of every colour by psycho-analysts, psychiatrists and clinical psychologists, sociologists and social workers, statisticians and medical men; even the insurance companies are in on the act. The contributions to learned journals are unceasing, each year there are new specialised books, most years see another fat volume of essays. As a research subject, suicide, has, as they say, come big; it even has its own name, 'suicidology' ... How much the potential suicide has been helped by all this activity is often not obvious.

— A. Alvarez[1]

The suicide data

Data help delineate the dimension of a problem: they do not necessarily explain the problem, or resolve it. Alvarez, in the quotation above, is not so much berating 'suicidology' as lamenting its seeming impotence in the face of great increases in suicide rates in Western societies.

My primary focus is on explanation and alleviation, and, hopefully, on some understanding of suicide. It is, nevertheless, important to establish what may be a crude portrait of raw numbers and rates. These data illustrate the dimension of suicide among Aborigines, and among youth in particular, but it also presents us with something extraordinary: *that youth suicide, unknown among Aborigines three decades ago, is now certainly double, perhaps treble or even quadruple the rate of non-Aboriginal suicide.* What follows is a portrait of Aboriginal suicide in general over the 30-month period. There is also some narrative commentary on suicides in the sample prior to the study period. The method of death is significant, and is discussed below.

Table 2. Aboriginal suicides in New South Wales, January 1996–June 1998
(Aboriginality documented)

Year	Sex/age (M=male/F=female)	Method	Town
1996	M 16	Train	Wellington
	M 18	Hanging	Menindee
	F 22	Hanging	Tamworth
	M 23	Overdose	Walgett
	M 23	Gunshot	Bourke
	M 25	Hanging	Bega
	M 29	Gunshot	Dubbo
	M 31	Hanging	Grafton
1997	M 12	Hanging	Wilcannia
	M 14	Gunshot	Lake Cargelligo
	F 15	Hanging	Tamworth
	M 18	Gunshot	Forbes
	M 18	Not available	Narooma (suicided in Vic.)
	M 19	Hanging	Bega
	F 19	Hanging	Casino
	M 19	Hanging	Condobolin
	M 20	Hanging	Coffs Harbour
	M 20	Hanging	Dubbo
	M 23	Hanging	Batemans Bay
	M 23	Hanging in cells	Bathurst
	M 27	Hanging	Coffs Harbour
	M 27	Drowning	Macksville
	F 28	Hanging in cells	Brewarrina
	M 29	Gunshot	Dubbo
	M 29	Drowning	Wilcannia
	M 31	Hanging	Broken Hill
	M 31	Carbon monoxide	Nowra
	M 31	Hanging	Wilcannia
	M 32	Hanging in cells	Tamworth
	M 33	Hanging	Coffs Harbour
	M 33	Hanging	Dubbo
	M 34	Hanging	Macksville
	M 36	Hanging	Taree
	M 41	Jumped	Lismore
	M 44	Drowning	Inverell
	M 46	Jumped	Casino

Year	Sex/age (M=male/F=female)	Method	Town
To June 1998			
	M 16	Hanging	Wellington
	M 24	Drowning	Macksville
	F 28	Jumped	La Perouse
	M 29	Gunshot	Bourke
	M 29	Gunshot	Dubbo
	M 34	Hanging	Orange
	M 46	Hanging	Wollongong

Summary of Table 2

Annual figures	Male	Female	Total
1996	7	1	8
1997	25	3	28
To June 1998	6	1	7
Total	**38**	**5**	**43**

Method	Number	% of total
Hanging	22	51.2
Gunshot	7	16.3
Drowning	4	9.3
Hanging in cells	3	7.0
Jumped	3	7.0
Overdose	1	2.3
Carbon monoxide	1	2.3
Train	1	2.3
Not available	1	2.3
Total	**43**	**100.0**

Age	Number	% of total
0–14	2	4.7
15–24	17	39.5
25–34	19	44.2
35–50	5	11.6
Total	**43**	**100.0**

Table 3. Possible Aboriginal suicides in New South Wales, January 1996–June 1998 (Aboriginality undetermined)

Year	Sex/age (M=male/F=female)	Method	Town
1996	M 19	Hanging	Kempsey
	M 19	Overdose	Port Macquarie
	M 21	Hanging	Newcastle
	M 23	Hanging	Lismore
	M 23	Hanging	Newcastle
	M 26	Prescription overdose	Armidale
	M 28	Hanging	Newcastle
	M 36	Gunshot	Tamworth
	M 40	Hanging	Wilcannia
	F 49	Overdose	Port Macquarie
1997	F 8	Drowning	Bourke
	M 18	Train	Kempsey
	M 19	Hanging	Condobolin
	M 20	Hanging	Dubbo
	M 21	Hanging	Forster
	M 21	Hanging	Forster
	M 22	Hanging	Dubbo
	M 23	Overdose	Wee Waa
	M 25	Carbon monoxide	Dubbo
	M 25	Gunshot	Tamworth
	M 27	Hanging	Coffs Harbour
	M 29	Drowning	Kempsey
	M 32	Hanging	Tamworth
	M 33	Hanging	Dubbo
	M 36	Gunshot	Wee Waa
	M 39	Overdose	Tweed Heads
	M 40	Overdose	Wee Waa
To June 1998	M 24	Hanging	Tamworth
	F 28	Hanging	Port Macquarie
	M 33	Overdose	Tamworth
	F 37	Overdose	Newcastle

Summary of Table 3

Annual figures	Male	Female	Total
1996	9	1	10
1997	16	1	17
To June 1998	2	2	4
Total	27	4	31

Method	Number	% of total
Hanging	16	51.6
Overdose	8	25.8
Gunshot	3	9.7
Drowning	2	6.4
Carbon monoxide	1	3.2
Train	1	3.2
Total	31	100.0

Age	Number	% of total
0–14	1	3.2
15–24	13	42
25–34	10	32.2
35–50	7	22.6
Total	31	100.0

There is no doubt that at least 43 Aborigines, between the ages of 12 and 46, committed suicide in the 30-month period between 1 January 1996 and 30 June 1998. In a necessarily superficial analysis of Table 3, I estimate that 16 of the 31 suicides were most probably Aboriginal. For purposes of arriving at the conventional rate of suicide as x per 100,000 of the population, I am disregarding Table 3.

- There were 43 definite suicides in just over one-third of the New South Wales Aboriginal population who comprised the people in our study.

- The combined Aboriginal population for the Australian Capital Territory and the New South Wales sites covered in this study is 43,074. Considering the 43 as the numerator, the rate per 100,000 is 99.76 over the 30-month period. Expressed as the more usual annual rate, this result is a *rate of 40 suicides per 100,000*.

- The Aboriginal population in New South Wales in the 15–24 age group is 20,592. In 1997, ten suicides occurred in that age group, which translates as an overall *youth suicide rate in excess of 48 per 100,000*, double the current Australian rate of 24–26 per 100,000.

- There were ten male youth suicides in 1997, eight in the 15–24 age group and two in the 0–14 cohort. This produces a male rate, based on a sample of 38 per cent of the state's male youth cohort, *of an alarming 128 per 100,000*.

- In the 5–14 age cohort, there were two suicides in 1997. Based on a population of 12,800 in that age group in New South Wales, the 'child suicide' rate is more than 15 per 100,000. By contrast, in 13 selected OECD countries, the highest rate for that younger age group is in Canada, at 1.3 per 100,000, but with Manitoba showing a child rate of 5.25.

In the period of this study (two and a half years), there was only one official coronial finding of Aboriginal suicide in the Australian Capital Territory, a 27-year-old male. However, the former Aboriginal Community Liaison Officer — ACLOs are the men and women employed by the police to assist in their dealings with Aborigines — from Queanbeyan, now working in Canberra, a man with considerable experience in the ACT community, told me of a 21-year-old male who had overdosed in the presence of others and who had left a note. A week earlier, another young male 'took something', fatally, at Ainslie Village. The ACLO's own sister, in her 30s, had overdosed at the same place. Another Aboriginal informant, who works with a great many children in a sporting context, asserts that an 8- or 9-year-old male had died by hanging when visiting his grandmother in Belconnen. Together with the 'ombudsman' case, it appears that there have been six Aboriginal suicides between January 1996 and May 1999. The ACT population sample is small, and could be discounted for statistical purposes. However, I believe that these six suicides since 1996 indicate an overall Aboriginal rate of 76 per 100,000 over the study period.

It has been suggested by some researchers that we should discount figures in rural areas (towns under 100,000) and in remote areas (towns under 10,000) because suicide in those areas tends to be more prevalent in the population as a whole. Since the majority of Aborigines live in such rural and remote towns, it would be quite pointless to do so. As indicated throughout this work, the figures and the decimal points are not all that significant. What must be appreciated is that there is an undeniably high and abnormal rate of young Aboriginal suicide, particularly among males. And the tendency to suicide is becoming more prevalent.

(ACT Police Assistant Commissioner Stoll suggests that research ought to be done into the number of Aboriginal graves at the old Riverside cemetery in Queanbeyan, abutting the ACT. Most are buried 'outside' the main cemetery, posing the question of whether they were buried outside consecrated ground because they were suicides or because they were not considered Christians.)

Suicide was an equally common cause of death for Maori and non-Maori males in 1994, but more common for Maori females than for non-Maori females.[2] Maori male suicides doubled, from 17 in 1984 to 31 in 1994, and female numbers doubled from 5 to 12 in that period. The Maori male rate was 16 per 100,000 in 1994, rapidly approximating the *pakeha* rate of 21.7. The Maori female rate of 6.6 has already overtaken the *pakeha* rate of 4.9. Age-specific rates are not available because of the 'small number of Maori suicide deaths', and because annual variations 'may therefore be misleading or invalid'.

'Hanging'

'Hanging' is a misnomer for this manner of death. It is not hanging in the sense of judicial hanging, where the knot and drop procedure causes the odontoid peg of the axis vertebra to be jerked and to snap through the transverse ligament of the atlas vertebra, crushing the spinal cord and almost immediately causing the cessation of breathing. The popular usage of 'hanging' is really asphyxiation by strangulation, a slower and probably far more painful and unpleasant mode of dying.

The study by Hunter and others found that hanging was the chosen method in 73 per cent of the 137 male and 61 per cent of the 18 female suicides from 1990 to 1997. Both are extraordinarily high rates for one method of self-destruction. The North Queensland study devotes considerable space (almost a third of the report) to hanging, its origins among Aboriginal communities, images, role, effect on the communities and effectiveness as a 'weapon'. (The study was originally commissioned as a study of hanging but was widened to include the historical and cultural aspects of Aboriginal suicide.) They describe it as 'a symbolic statement [which] can be very political as well as poignant' (1999, 26–56). I do not intend discussing or traversing what the Queensland researchers have done so eloquently and powerfully, other than to briefly summarise those aspects of hanging which, I suggest, apply to New South Wales (and elsewhere):

- hanging is dramatic, powerful and confronting;
- it has cultural-specific meanings and associations for Aborigines;
- it has become an institutionalised and pervasive cultural stereotype to which Aborigines are exposed and which they internalise;
- it is often the only method readily available;
- it is a dramatic model for a potential imitator, carrying as it does symbolic meanings such as martyrdom, injustice and pathos;

- it symbolises capital punishment, the legal system, justice and injustice;
- it 'invites' a joining in solidarity with deceased kin;
- it features in many commercial films, and in art, song lyrics, plays, and popular culture generally;
- it is 'paradoxically an expression and statement of no control at the same time that it is a statement of ultimate control';
- it 'is a rebuke and statement of uncaring relations, unmet needs, personal anguish and emotional payback' (Hunter et al 1999, 88); and
- the deaths-in-custody phenomenon has left a strong residual legacy.

Michael Dudley and others report a radical increase in hanging as the chosen method across Australia in the past 10–15 years and 'hanging is now the most common method of youth suicide in most States' (1998b, 78). Annette Graham's unpublished paper in Victoria suggests that suicide by hanging has increased dramatically in the past 18 months: from some 60 to 120 in Victoria.[3] In our study, the hanging figure is 58.2 per cent of the 43 deaths in the 30-month period.

Two additional comments should be made. First, the study by Hunter and others (1999) has reproduced a number of Aboriginal paintings and drawings depicting suicide by hanging. The painting shown in Chapter 10 is significant: the artist, who has attempted suicide on several occasions, perceives successful suicide as death by hanging. Second, Hunter and others state that 'the phenomenon of Indigenous suicide is moving rapidly through tradition-oriented communities in the Northern Territory and, appearing, intermittently, in other regions in Australia'. I disagree about 'intermittent': our study shows much more than that. The point here, however, is that hanging as a method of suicide does not necessarily spread *pari passu* with suicide. The youth at Milikipati, on Melville Island, have taken to climbing power poles and electrocuting themselves on the lines. In 1997–98, at Yirrkala in the Northern Territory, there were three cases of male youths dousing themselves with petrol and then lighting it. Two survived the attempted immolation, a method which is becoming a new form of self-harm.[4]

'Hanging, strangulation and suffocation' is the New Zealand phrasing for this manner of death. It was by far the commonest method of suicide for both males and females aged 15–24 in 1994. The Inquests Officer in Wellington states that he has not seen 'copycat' Maori hanging from a tree, as depicted in the commercial film *Once Were Warriors*. New Zealand law prohibits publication of manner of suicide, lest it suggest methods. Officials generally argue that no teenager needs films or press reports for 'inspiration'.

Comments on individual communities

This study and these tables do not reflect the full picture of Aboriginal suicide in this state. An eight- or ten-year retrospective would have been more illuminating. (I have already stated that there is little value in pursuing 'Aboriginal suicide' in State Coroners' Offices.) However, constraints of time and access precluded a reading of every coronial file in each place visited. Further, staff changes in some towns meant that there were no coroners or police with long service and memory of earlier events. Suicidal behaviour was present well before our time-frame of January 1996 to June 1998. It is important to portray some of this earlier behaviour, and to comment on a few specific cases in Tables 2 and 3.

An Aboriginal informant, who worked as a mental health counsellor in Newcastle from 1989 to 1992, claims that as many as three in ten Aboriginal patients had attempted suicide and that several females were in the 9-, 10- and 11-year-old bracket, pregnant as a result of incest.

Apart from two in Table 3, Kempsey had two other possible Aboriginal male deaths in 1997: males aged 28 and 41, both by hanging. There were three definite suicide attempts by girls in 1997–98. Informants say their motives were: (i) to 'get a buzz'; (ii) 'they didn't want to live'; and (iii) 'they were sexually abused by fathers'. Of the three, one had a mother who was alcoholic, a second girl's mother was a removed child, and the mother of the third was a domestic violence victim. The local coroner describes Kempsey as 'depressing and depressive, with lots of white suicides'. Taree had two attempted suicides by males, aged 21 and 24, in 1997. One attempted hanging, with his football sock, in the A-grade surveillance cells; rather than being rescued through intervention by the staff meant to view him, he changed his mind and desisted.

Macksville is clearly a key area. Three male suicides in a short period is high for an Aboriginal population of 650 (the combined figure for the three neighbouring towns of Macksville, Nambucca Heads and Bowraville). One of the males, who drowned himself, had a 'strong connection' with cannabis, as did a 21-year-old male who suicided in 1988 alongside his own cultivated cannabis plot. Another drowned victim was saturated with pharmaceutical sedatives and antidepressants. There were two attempted youth suicides in Bowraville in 1997.

Informants at Port Macquarie stated that an Aboriginal female hanged herself in the cemetery in 1998 and that a 19-year-old male had overdosed in 1996. We have not recorded either case. There was also one attempted suicide by a male.

In Coffs Harbour, a coroner's case of an Aboriginal man in 1995 was not listed as suicide: the coroner now regards the case of that man walking in front of an oncoming truck as a suicidal act. Therefore, in a population of almost exactly 1000, there have been four young suicides in three years. The pregnant girlfriend of a popular 33-year-old sports-man who suicided, attempted suicide shortly after his death.

Nowra may well have the best infrastructure of all small towns in the study. There is an active, energetic and progressive Aboriginal Legal Service, an excellent Young Offenders Program, accomplished Aboriginal health education officers and mental health counsellors, dedicated ACLOs and a Koori Habitat program that collects potentially wayward children from the town streets at night and ensures their safe return home. Although there was only one suicide in 1997, there had been several, all in one family, between 1993 and 1995. An older man hanged himself at Mumbala Village; later, his son did the same thing and was found with his fingers hooked under the wire hanger in an apparent attempt to stop the act. Another relative from Wreck Bay hanged himself. In the same year, a musician, related to these two men, hanged himself with a tea towel. There is an interesting story about this victim. After the senior member had hanged himself, the family received a message from Central Australia that the family had been 'sung'. Thereafter the son killed himself, the musician, a nephew, took his life, and a grandson was murdered. Another son, who had been out on bail, having possibly been involved in three murders, was found dead, after he had heard about the murder in the family, of no known cause. The Nowra ACLO, who knew him well, told me that this man had been drinking straight tequila for almost three days. This death could well have been a suicide.

A young male suicided in the cells in Grafton in 1983, and there may have been a second young male in 1996. There were two serious attempts in Woodenbong, including a female of 16. Bega had one suicide during our study period, and there is also some evidence that a young woman who overdosed had suicided. Wallaga Lake has had several attempted suicides by men under 20. One Wallaga Lake youth, included in Table 2, took his life in Victoria. A Lithgow male of 21 committed suicide in Mt Victoria in 1990, as did a 27-year-old male in Wellington. In 1991, Dubbo recorded a male, in his 20s, drowning and a 39-year-old female overdosed in 1995. In Coonabarabran, a 20-year-old male deliberately ran in front of a freight truck in the early 1990s. In Broken Hill in 1994, a 24-year-old male hanged himself, as did a 24-year-old in Moree in 1995.

Brewarrina, where a 28-year-old woman hanged herself by her bra in the cells in 1997, had an extraordinary case in the late 1980s. A 16-year-old female consulted the local doctor one morning. He prescribed Digesic, a powerful analgesic. The chemist dispensed a pack of 50 tablets. When the ambulance driver was called that evening, he summoned the doctor for cause of death. He was reported to have said that he 'expected something like this to happen'. She had consulted him about being upset at a broken relationship. (This case raises some issues which are discussed in Chapter 10.)

The Toomelah community, which has experienced much anguish, trauma and publicity over the years, is generally reluctant to talk about suicidal behaviour. However, there is one young man, aged 16, still in a Sydney hospital following an attempted hanging. He had a serious cannabis 'problem'. As in the Hunter and others report (1999), many of these suicides or attempted suicides are associated with alcohol (alcoholism or binge-drinking), or with cannabis, or with a combination of substances. The Wilcannia cases, including the 12-year-old recorded suicide, were associated with petrol-sniffing. Two Aboriginal researchers who have worked in Wilcannia state that '65 per cent of the population has played at suicide'.

The Bourke community has a sad history of death by non-natural causes. In 1991, an Aboriginal man of 37 shot another Aboriginal man, then shot himself. There was another Aboriginal male murder in the same year. In 1993, an Aboriginal male of 20 drowned while intoxicated. In 1996, a male of 23 shot himself, a young chronic alcoholic male died (ostensibly of hypertension), and an Aboriginal male struck another man following an argument over a wine flagon, killing him (but claiming self-defence). In 1997, a 34-year-old female, with toxic levels of alcohol in her blood, died of pneumonia; and an 8-year-old female, a good swimmer, drowned near the wharf, possibly a suicide but she may have been held down in a prank by another child. In 1998, a male of 29 shot himself.

In communities like Murrin Bridge, expressions like 'there is an attempt every second day' are doubtless exaggerations. But there is no doubt that risk-taking, dangerous and self-harmful behaviour is a norm among Aboriginal youth. Stengel contends that, in general, non-fatal suicide attempts are estimated at between six and eight times as numerous as suicides. Some North American studies suggest that there are between 50 and 200 attempts for each completed suicide. It is not possible to quantify Aboriginal attempted suicides in this (or in any other) study, but it is an omnipresent feature of contemporary Aboriginal life.

Notes

1. Alvarez, *The Savage God*, 99–100.
2. Ministry of Health, *Suicide Trends in New Zealand*, 7–13, 24.
3. Personal communication. See also Australian Psychological Society, *Suicide*, 5.
4. Personal communication from Stuart McMillan, Darwin.

6

Towards an Explanation of Aboriginal Suicide

Suicide is only a medico-legal term and a mode of death. Self-destruction is a more comprehensive term for investigation. But the term suicide is too deeply entrenched. It also has a mystique and fascination in its sibilants. Suicide is ... 'the human act of self-inflicted, self-intentioned cessation.'

— Louis Wekstein[1]

... a serious suicide is an act of choice, the terms of which are entirely of this world; a man dies by his own hand because he thinks the life he has [is] not worth living.

— A. Alvarez[2]

Suicide is the end result of a process, not the process itself. In most behaviour disorders we have at least part of the process at hand for examination. In suicide all we usually have is the end result, arrived at by a variety of paths. Unravelling the causes after the fact is well nigh impossible.

— Joseph Zubin[3]

Suicide theories

Emile Durkheim's *Le Suicide*, perhaps the most seminal work in the field, took a long time to be translated into English. Research has moved on since he formulated the categories of *egoistic, altruistic* and *anomic* suicide. Egoistic suicide is due to slight or poor social integration into family, religious or state life. Importantly in the context of this study, Durkheim contended that suicide rates fall during great crises because the society is more strongly integrated, with the individual participating more actively in social life. The rarer altruistic suicide results from excessive identification and integration. The individual makes himself or herself subservient to higher commandments of a religious or political kind. Anomic suicide follows trauma, catastrophe or a loss, with resultant alienation, social isolation and loneliness.

The only category of any use in this study is anomic suicide. Even then it does not quite suit. Despite Aboriginal society's being in crisis, and therefore, following Durkheim's theory, being more 'integrated', suicide is increasing rather than decreasing. This could be seen as Aboriginal society's disintegration (as discussed in Chapter 2) rather than integration, in response to its current crisis. Much suicidology since Durkheim has concerned classification. Hillman disparages this approach, arguing 'for all their research, their clues to suicide from case studies and diagnostic classifications yield trivia' (1997, 42). Amid a plethora of classifications since Durkheim, I have found Louis Wekstein's taxonomy the most useful, even though he also deprecates most attempts at definition, including his own, as 'leaving much to be desired'. His descriptions are more convenient than attempts at definition, motivation or explanation. They also expand on the traditionally narrow 'mental-ill health' approach.

Chronic suicide is the masking of an orientation towards death by the excessive use of alcohol and/or drugs. This overlaps with several of Wekstein's other categories. Serious research is required into whether Aboriginal substance use and misuse has some positive attributes, as Hunter contends,[4] or whether such chronic abuse is nothing more nor less than large numbers of people masking an intended cessation of self. Is chronic suicide perhaps the most lingering form of suicide? More frightening, in many ways, is the question of whether this is tantamount to a form of mass suicide?

Neglect suicide occurs where the victim ignores reality factors, for example the diabetic who indulges in dietary indiscretions and 'forgets' to take his or her medication. Another dimension of *neglect* by Aboriginal youth is the ignoring of risks and of danger, discussed below.

Sub-intentional suicide is allied to *neglect*, where, for example, the person drives through red lights, denying the intent while, in fact, simultaneously promoting self-destruction.

Surcease suicide is what Wekstein describes as 'rational suicide', an auto-euthanasia, where the person's plight is, in fact, irremediable; this is another form of 'rational', or even 'political', suicide.

Psychotic suicide occurs where the victim does not intend dying but attempts to excise, extirpate and, in effect, exorcise his or her psychological inadequacy.

Focal suicide is the idea of partial death, where a limited part of the body is killed. Self-mutilation, maiming, contrived accidents and some types of sexual impairment, such as deliberate genital damage, fall into this category. This may overlap with the previous category. (This may also be part of the present phase, or craze, in the language of identity and selfhood: what Carl Elliott (2000) calls the popular culture of self-discovery, self-realisation, self-expression, self-invention, self-knowledge, self-absorption, exemplified by (non-traditional) body piercing and tattooing, so prevalent in the United States and becoming more so in Australia. But I doubt that many Aboriginal youth are 'into' this preoccupation with self.)

Automatisation suicide is the attempt to relieve pain or to achieve sleep or an altered state of consciousness by the use of medicinal or illicit drugs and, when no prompt result is noticed, to continue taking the drugs, robotically, until death ensues.

Accidental suicide is the result of misinformation or poor timing — a miscalculation or a blunder.

Suicide by murder is not a fiction of television movies. It occurs when one attacks a person of superior strength or weaponry in order to promote or effect one's own death.

Existential suicide, of significance in this study, is the notion of Albert Camus, the (French) winner of the Nobel literature prize in 1957. He postulated the idea of suicide as ending the burden of hypocrisy, of the meaninglessness of life, of the ennui and lack of motivation to continue to exist. This category seems me to have the greatest relevance to Aboriginal youth suicide. In similar vein, Viktor Frankl's philosophy and therapy, originating in a Nazi concentration camp, was that only those who are imbued with a *purpose in life* survive (such conditions). I believe that much of Aboriginal suicide is, broadly speaking, a Camus-type ending of the meaninglessness, or a Frankl-type lack of purposefulness, and that it has nothing to do with mental illness. Such theorisation may not be the kind of 'science' Norman Kreitman would like it to be, but it illuminates a great deal more than quantitative science has done.

Suicidology is much concerned about attempted suicide and 'suicide ideation'. Several experts argue for a more concerted approach to *intent*, that is, differentiating intent as between (a) the suicide gesture; (b) the ambivalent suicide attempt; (c) the serious suicide attempt; and (d) the completed suicide. Clearly there are gradations between thinking about suicide and achieving that end. But the line between ambivalent act and serious attempt is difficult to draw. This is even harder where someone is interrupted in the attempt, as has frequently happened among Aboriginal youth. Wekstein refers to American conferences which defined 'attempted suicide' as any act which appears to have a life-threatening potential or carries such a potential and intent, but which does not result in death. Regrettably, this must include gestures and ambivalences, in short, everything short of actual suicide. Firestone's term 'microsuicide' covers such labels as indirect suicide, partial suicide, instalment-plan suicide, slow suicide, inimical patterns of behaviour, embryonic suicide, masked suicide, hidden suicide, parasuicide and chronic suicide (1997, 123). An examination of the methods of attempted suicide might help to differentiate the gesture and the ambivalent gesture from the serious act. Certain methods are almost inevitably lethal, as in jumping from a great height, gunshot to the head or heart, or the use of weed-killer.

The time frame of suicide is important. We commonly assume that suicide is an act of immediacy, committed (for whatever reason) as quickly as it takes to pull a trigger, jump off a roof, or, at worst, to linger a little longer while strangling, gassing or poisoning. We ignore, quite without justification, the slow, the chronic, the masked, the hidden, the pill-popping, the neglect, and the sub-intentional forms of self-destruction. The people involved don't leave notes, often don't exhibit 'at risk' behaviour, don't confide in friends, don't phone hotline services and don't make appointments with therapists.

In the previous chapter, mention was made of Stengel's views on attempted suicide: that attempts are about six to eight times as prevalent as completed suicides, that conscious self-destructive acts, 'however vague and ambiguous', are serious and require special study. (Many reports, especially from Alaska, suggest that attempted suicide is not six to eight, but between 50 and 300, times as prevalent as completed suicide.) Two of Stengel's concepts are worth particular examination: first, his somewhat strange notion that 'self-destructive behaviour not associated with the idea of death is not suicide' (1964, 12–13). There may be some similarity between this and Wekstein's category of accidental, or even focal, suicide. His second idea needs careful reflection: that the suicide, 'while it seems to aim solely at destroying the self, is also an act of aggression against others' (1979, 27–30). This approximates Joseph Reser's 'reactance' theory — suicide as a form of protest against the forces of authority and institutionalism. Some of what I have to say below suggests that much Aboriginal youth suicide falls into this category.

The classic profile of youth suicides

Traditional or classic youth suicide is characterised by, *inter alia*, severe depression, feelings of hopelessness, social isolation, anger, impulsiveness, poor or disturbed interpersonal relationships, unemployment, dramatic changes in the nature of family life, and a disjunction between 'theoretical freedom' (to be independent, free of constraints) and experiential autonomy (Hassan 1995, 53–61). Seligman would add learned helplessness and pessimism as key factors.[5] Some of these factors and values are relevant in all cultures, but many relate only to modern Western, 'Anglo' and middle-class lifestyles. Herein lies one of the key problems in Australian suicidology: it is universally 'Westernist' in its value system and its concerns tend to be with the 'Anglo' bourgeoisie — where suicide is seen to be aberrant or, perhaps nowadays, 'normal', given the stresses and depressions of modern competitive life.

Barry Maley's 1994 study showed a statistical correlation between male suicide and unemployment. The 20–24 age group, with a longer period of unemployment, was most at risk: they had no prospect of making a living, no prospects of enduring relations with women and no social status. Isolation, especially in rural areas, was both physical and social. The lack of social and interpersonal relations appeared to be the most significant risk factor, followed by unemployment and its meaning for self-esteem, and then by family circumstances.

Aboriginal youth suicide(s) do not fit the conventional profiles:
- There is little evidence of clinical depression in the accepted sense.
- There appears to be little or no correlation between suicide and diagnosable mental illness.
- There has been little change in Aboriginal family life over the past 30–40 years. The formalities of Christian marriage and the sociology of the Western nuclear family are not part of the subculture. Most Aboriginal communities today are matriarchal, held together by the women. There has been no sudden change due to the rise of feminism, the liberation and changing roles of women, or the reversion to single-parenthood now being manifested more frequently in non-Aboriginal family life.
- Aboriginal youth have never had the 'theoretical freedom' which Hassan presents as a norm: they have, on the contrary, an early, practical autonomy that is quite singular, one castigated by white society as lax, and lacking in care or supervision. While some Aboriginal suicides appear to centre on broken love relationships, the majority do not. Most Aboriginal youth have an altogether different perspective on sexual and love relationships, which are not dependent on suitors having social status, a decent job or the solidity of a 'good living'. With a few exceptions, the 'classical' notion of suicide appears irrelevant to an understanding, let alone the alleviation, of Aboriginal suicide.
- While there is certainly alienation from white society, there is no internal social isolation in the sense that Durkheim understood or

intended the term. There is much Aboriginal 'togetherness' or integration, especially among the youth. In the chapter following, I discuss the Aboriginal propensity to commit minor offences in order to be sent to Minda, a juvenile facility, and then to re-offend immediately on release in order to return to that facility. There is togetherness and a strong sense of integration — in Minda even — away from family.

We are left with anger, hopelessness, lack of purpose, ennui, and pessimism. Norman Farberow, the American scholar, is the only researcher I have read who inverts the usual order of risk factors and suggested causes of suicide (Peck et al 1985, 196). The great majority begin with 'current conditions', such as abusive and suicidal parents, broken homes, excessive mobility and transiency. From these, they move to 'causal constructs', such as delinquency, substance abuse, antisocial behaviour, school failure, and negative personal relationships. Then follow 'precipitating factors', such as poor school performance, joblessness, loss or threatened loss by divorce or rejection by lover, and rejection by 'a significant other'. These, in turn, lead to the 'reactive states' of depression, anxiety, guilt, shame, inadequacy, confusion, and ambivalence. What follows are 'dependent constructs' — feelings of worthlessness, helplessness and hopelessness. Farberow argues, as I do, that *we need to understand the overwhelming importance to the individual of these dependent constructs*. They matter more to the individual and are the more immediate causes of suicide than the 'current conditions', 'causal constructs' or 'precipitating factors'.

These 'constructs' do not necessarily explain the propensity for self-cessation of life, but they go a great deal further towards understanding the motivation of the suicides. There is a need to look further, and to this end we need to examine some facets of suicide-threatening and parasuicidal behaviour before arriving at a proper portrait of the youthful Aborigine who commits suicide.

The movement towards suicide

'The incompletes are bad and scary, the kids who are not trying to live.' That remarkable analysis is from an Aboriginal worker in the Homeless Youth Unit in Taree. She is talking about boys who threaten suicide every time they are taken to cells, and about girls who 'slash up'. Importantly, she is not talking about a few individuals, but about a plurality, a collective and group phenomenon. The significance of this must be stressed: *the suicidal behaviours in these communities have become patterned, ritualised and even institutionalised, perhaps even contagious*. David Lester, among many other suicide researchers, has come to recognise that attempted suicide and completed suicide fall 'on a continuum of varying suicidal intent' and are not separate, less serious actions (1989, 109–10). The threat, and the actuality, of self-harm in the cells is universal, and serious. 'I'll neck myself', or 'I'll neck myself and you'll be in trouble', is common across the state. There is an urgent need to examine the female propensity for 'slashing up' when in custody or in trouble with the police. Throughout this study, youth was conveyed as being male, with minimal attention to, or concern about, girls.

Female suicide is relatively neglected. The numbers and the rates are much lower, but there is evidence that attempted suicide is much more frequent in females than males among Aborigines, Maori and most North American Indian groups. The difference is probably due to the method of choice rather than difference in intent. Aboriginal men use rope, cord or gunshot, and invariably succeed. Women, and girls in particular, swallow whatever tablets are to hand. Often — and here illiteracy may be some kind of mixed blessing — they cannot read the labels on their mothers' medication packages, and so take non-fatal substances such as vitamin tablets or hormone prescriptions. Paracetamol in excessive quantities does kill, but in many instances these parasuicides are managed quite simply in casualty, rather than in intensive care units.

'Slashing up' is common. Several informants contended that it is most common among those who have been sexually abused, and that the slashing begins at an early age. A suggestion worth serious consideration is that slashing and other similar forms of mutilation are not suicide attempts, but rather the reverse: a letting of blood in order to feel the warmth and the vitality of life, an *affirmation* that one is alive.

The responses to attempted suicide differ widely. Some police view it as a 'neo-suicidal' action based on despair and hopelessness. Others see it, not as an egotistical cry *for attention* but, if they were to use Mark Williams' words, as 'a cry *of pain* first, and only then a cry for help' (1997, xiii). Some police describe, in their own words, what Shneidman calls a certain kind of psychological pain, or 'psychache' (1996, 4). Some police insist that it is a threat that only occurs under drug or alcohol influence and that it is either bluff or bravado — or both. One ACLO contends that the threat is a macho thing, producing hero-worship for he who dares. An experienced ACLO from Queanbeyan tells me that 'young people of today have got no fear of dying. That's the least of their worries; rather it's a fear of living.' Another ACLO says it is a matter of 'talking silly'. Others again see the threats as a political statement, a weapon, an evocation of the simplest reprisal weapon available to 'disempowered' people, namely, an action which could lead to royal commission-type investigations. Another Aboriginal perspective is that there is often a need for alcohol to disinhibit the normally present but suppressed and masked suicidal feelings.

There is an abundance of suicidal behaviour in communities, yet most service personnel and almost all Aboriginal family members insist that there are no warnings, no signs, and few preceding actions which warrant serious attention. The Aboriginal health education officer in Narooma insists that 'when young people threaten, they try it'. He also describes what he calls 'indirect suicide', people living on the edge, who engage police in car chases, or who drink and then climb cliffs, the 'kids who have no care about tomorrow'. Many others have endorsed this perception of '*kids who don't necessarily want to be dead but don't want to be in life either*'. In both Kempsey and Taree, there is evidence of young people, especially girls, running in front of trucks at night. One can speculate that such knife-edge and dangerous behaviour is born out of a realisation that life is short indeed, especially for males. These young-sters do not read articles about their poor life expectation, but they do attend, from a very early age, an astonishing number of funerals of young relatives. In most towns in this study, one funeral a week would be the norm, the deceased often being a young victim of disease, accident or violence.

A few examples illustrate my contention about the movement towards suicide:

- A police officer in Narooma related the following story about a 13-year-old girl 'who is out to self-destruct'. She had not only been sniffing petrol but also drinking it. Her father reported her to the police as a runaway. The police officer found her but could not find anyone to consult professionally in Narooma. The stepmother took her back home but found her too aggressive, and so she was taken to Sydney. Two days before this interview (with me), the girl jumped from the third floor of her Sydney accommodation and broke both legs. The officer believes she has even injected herself with petrol.

- At Taree, many young people are seen as 'risk-runners'. One case of 'sub-intentional' suicide is worth reporting as a speculation. A man of 24 was in hospital for chronic golden staphylococcus infection, which was being treated with antibiotics, intravenously administered. Despite being warned repeatedly to complete the treatment, he discharged himself from hospital one Saturday in order to play competition football. He died on the field.

- A professionally qualified Aboriginal mental health worker told me the story of a 25-year-old male, a chronic alcoholic, who had left school early and had spent his whole life in town Z. He has low literacy skills. He threatens that he will get a gun, shoot all the nurses and then hang himself. He tells police he will shoot them all and hang himself. My informant is convinced that he will do all or some of the above. He publicly displays his intentions by, for example, walking down the main street of Z with a coil of rope around his neck. He has attempted suicide in the cells and has been cut down. He provokes police. When he gets no response, he beats up women. My informant says that there is no professional help for this young man in Z.

- An Aboriginal health education officer in Nowra relates the life of a woman, removed from her parents at age 2. She told my informant that, at the age of 25, she wanted to die because she was 'old'. She was first raped when she was seven months pregnant with her first child. When the child was little, she was raped again. She has three children, all in care. She began painting as personal therapy, catharsis and self-salvation.

- The Aboriginal mental health counsellor at Nowra is treating a man of 50, a stolen child from the age of 2, placed in Bomaderry until the age of 7. At Mt Penang juvenile institution, from the age of 7 to 18, he was repeatedly raped. Hired out to do farm work, he was again repeatedly raped. Two years out of institutional life, he found his natural father, who raped him while drunk. He has attempted every conceivable form of mutilation and damage to himself.

- At Menindee in the far west, an 18-year-old hanged himself in the local park. He had mugged a kindly old lady and believed that she had died. She had not. Since his death, three Aboriginal men meet at the cemetery to visit the grave. One, aged 15, has attempted suicide; one, aged 25, is heavily sedated on Prozac and other antidepressants (he persistently burns himself with cigarettes); and the other is a 28-year-old who has tried hanging six times. With a carton of beer, they commune with their dead friend: each drinks one beer, and they pour one onto the grave mound for the deceased, until a sense of communion is achieved. I talked individually and at length with each man, and believe, as do their parents, that they will probably suicide before long.

- At Wilcannia in 1998, a girl of 8 placed a rope around her neck and tried to jump from a branch. Her 12-year-old female companion rescued her. The latter was interviewed by a female ACLO, a respected town elder, who asked her whether the 8-year-old was involved in an accident or a 'game gone wrong'. The answer was 'no', that this was a serious attempt. The girl is small and immature for her age. She is related to a 12-year-old who hanged himself in the town. In New South Wales in 1999, the senior children's magistrate ruled that a (non-Aboriginal) 10-year-old boy, who deliberately pushed a 6-year-old into a dam, could not be tried for manslaughter because he was *doli incapax*, that is, because he was between 10 and 14 he lacked the mental capacity to commit a crime. This case raises the question of how an 8-year-old can, and does, form the intention to take her own life. My conclusion is that death is more readily familiar to Aboriginal children in their socialisation processes than it is to non-Aboriginal children. But I am not certain of the answer to a question about their knowledge of *self*-death?

Documenting and quantifying the attempted suicides is an impossible task. An important New Zealand study interviewed 129 attempted suicides in 'semi-structured interviews ... to retrospectively construct a life history'.[6] Interviews used a variety of standard psychological tests, including: the Parental Bonding Instrument, a 25-item questionnaire containing a 12-item subscale; and the Structured Clinical Interview for *DSM–III–R* to diagnose selected mental disorders. The study found that 90.1 per cent of those who made a serious attempt had a mental disorder.

In Lismore, a public health nurse at the Public Health Unit has produced a protocol for use by admitting doctors or nurses at the local hospital.[7] Each protocol questionnaire has multiple-choice questions under the headings: Thoughts, Plans, Psychiatric Disorder, Mood, Means, Medical Problem, Suicidal History, and Support. Apart from the inappropriate language, and the inappropriateness of the actual questions for Aborigines, the realities are: first, that Aboriginal parasuicides tend to hide, treat themselves, or seek out ambulance officers for non-hospital attention; second, they are most unlikely to respond to the phrasings of these protocol questionnaires; third, I suggest that it is unlikely that anything like 90 per cent (as is claimed in New Zealand), or even 50 per cent, were suffering from a mental disorder.

Many Aborigines have a strong antipathy to hospitals. They see Health, Mental Health, the hospital, and related agencies as the equivalent of 'the Welfare', and it was 'the Welfare' who used to dislocate families and remove children.

Professor Mason Durie, a Maori psychiatrist and educator, has given us an explanation that may well capture the attitude of Aboriginal youth to hospitals, 'welfare' agencies and questions about attempted suicide. He says that the reason behind Maori objection to *pakeha* intervention is that 'it's not just the whiteness, it's the style'. 'How do you feel?', he argues, is a classic, white middle-class question. For 'kids on the edge', he says, 'this question drives them either to explosion or no answer'. However, I suspect that, in the case of Aborigines, whiteness is as strong an emotion as style. Noteworthy is Durie's conviction 'that mental ill-health is not the biggest cause of suicide; that the mental health strategies are too narrow and that mental health services for Maori are often hopeless'.

Two Aboriginal health workers in Coffs Harbour talk of suicide by negation of help, that is, people reject what the hospital has to offer for reasons of distrust mentioned above, or for spiritual reasons. The grandfather of one of these informants had been the last tribal man to be fully initiated in the Coffs Harbour area. He developed gangrene in one foot. He refused to go to hospital, stating that amputation would destroy his spiritual wholeness. He died, untreated. Finally, there was hardly an interview conducted in which the Aboriginal interviewee did not mention either a personal attempt or attempts by one or more immediate family members. They consider themselves, in their words, 'survivors'.

The extent of the idea of suicide among Aborigines is best demonstrated by the responses in a large number of in-depth interviews conducted by the professional staff at Bennelong's Haven — site of the original Kinchela Boys Home — a major drug and alcohol rehabilitation unit. Interviews with 129 women residents from 1 July 1992 to 15 July 1997 revealed that 53, or 41 per cent, had attempted suicide. Of 435 males interviewed between those dates, 223, or 51 per cent, had attempted suicide, making a total of 276 parasuicides in a sample of 564, that is, 49 per cent of the residents in the program! It would be unwise to dismiss this finding on the ground that it was confined to addicts in one program. There are, literally, legions of professional people in this state who offer the same information about their experiences with attempted suicide.

The Ministry of Maori Development gave us some preliminary, and unpublished, figures for attempted suicides.[8] Two advisers on Maori policy talked at length about the under-reporting of Maori suicide and of attempted suicide. In the latter category, and based solely on hospital sources, the Maori female numbers were exactly five times the *pakeha* figures, and the Maori male numbers three times the non-Maori. This is consistent with the findings of the Maori Suicide Review Group (1996, 25), which recorded that, in 1992, Maori had the highest hospitalisation rates for self-injury at 85.7 per 100,000 persons, compared with a *pakeha* rate of 78.

Aspects and categories of Aboriginal suicide

The novelist and suicide, Cesare Pavese, once said that 'no one ever lacks a good reason for suicide'.[9] While there are some factors, or 'reasons', in Aboriginal suicide which are seemingly universal, there are important aspects which make it different. These differences need to be stressed, recognised, absorbed, appreciated and acted upon, if any prevention or alleviation strategies are to be attempted. There are also regional differences

— not only between states and territories, but within states — requiring specific attention. Continuing a philosophy and policy of locating Aboriginal suicide in 'mainstream' suicide, or of footnoting or sidelining 'indigenous origin' suicide as an interesting but marginally different genre, is unacceptable and unproductive.

There is a separate Aboriginal suicidology — perhaps even separate Aboriginal suicidologies. What follows are some factors specific to, or extreme in, Aboriginal suicide.

'Yaandi'

There is much evidence from witnesses that youth suicide is commonly associated with cannabis, or *yaandi*, an Aboriginal term for the substance. The association can be categorised not so much as an addiction but as an *obsession* with the substance. In at least six instances in our study, young men, aged between 16 and 20, insisted on being physically near a constant supply. A few left solid family circles to live out bush, where they could be close to their own small cultivation. Several were found hanged at those sites. Many autopsy reports reveal the presence of cannabis.

Police across the state were adamant that the worst-case scenarios for them are dealing with youth in pubs at closing time, where the drinkers are also cannabis users. They rate, in degrees of difficulty, a plain drinker as a 3 out of 10 problem, a cannabis user as a 6, and a mix of the two as an 8 or 9. They assert that, despite an apparent calm and laid-back quality to the marijuana men, they are prone to unexpected outbursts of violence. There can be no doubt that, in the past 20 years, Aboriginal youth has taken strongly to this substance: it is omnipresent, is used regularly, and is cultivated and sold in several communities. There is evidence that hydroponically grown cannabis magnifies behavioural change. It is also said to be more addictive. It is chemically more potent and produces more explosive behaviour in situations of violence, arrest, and detention in cells. It is also probable that a form of psychosis results from cannabis obsession and overuse.

Suicide notes

Notes are extremely rare in Aboriginal suicide. We have seen notes in no more than four or five cases for the periods 1995 to 1998. Coroners vary in their estimates of note-leaving in non-Aboriginal suicide, but commonly suggest — or, rather, guess — 50 per cent. (The inquests officer in Dunedin informed us that possibly 60 per cent of Maori youth suicides in the South Island leave notes.) I refer here to the incidence of notes among confirmed suicide verdicts only, not those whose overdose is registered as being accidental, or those who crash into the only tree on either side of the road.

There are many evidentiary signs of suicide apart from a note. I believe that the note is an exaggerated facet of suicide, deriving from nineteenth-century fiction and twentieth-century films. At best, it is indicative of literacy skills, which few young Aborigines have, and of a premeditative, reflective and contemplative disposition or action (as shown in the not uncommon case of German Jews, discussed below).

Illiteracy as a contributing factor

Illiteracy is a key to much of suicidal behaviour. The majority of Aboriginal youth showing suicidal behaviour cannot read or write, or cannot read sufficiently well to absorb other than the most elementary popular materials, like picture magazines. In a group, the one or two who can read cover for the others, as interpreter or spokesperson. Disguise of illiteracy is commonplace. The illiterate can become surprisingly well informed through omnipresent television and radio, even without tuning into the 'serious' wavelengths of electronic communications.

Illiteracy creates its own frustrations and anger. Incomprehension alienates, as does being inarticulate. Violence is often the only means of expressing feelings: physicality, of whatever kind, is a substitute for a lack of verbal skills. Most Aborigines speak Aboriginal English. It is a *lingua franca*, a language of its own, with a different grammar, syntax, vocabulary, terminology, idiom, sign language and body language. This should not come as a startling discovery: several educators and linguists have for long advocated Aboriginal English as a medium of school instruction. Those providing services ought to be informed of, and educated about, this language. Resorting to pidgin and child-talk is not appropriate. In short, there is no intellectual intercourse between youth and the people they deal with in their external lives. The ensuing frustration is relevant to the violence, slashing up, self-mutilation and self-destruction.

There may even be an important correlation between illiteracy and deafness, and between both and suicide. The Maori Health Research Unit at the Dunedin medical school funds a program to install grommets in children's ears to help with chronic 'glue ear' infection, a common cause of deafness. At least 20 per cent of Maori prison inmates who are considered to be at risk for suicide are seriously deaf.[10] We know that there is widespread hearing deficiency in Aboriginal youth, and the relationship between 'glue ear', illiteracy and suicidal behaviour is worth pursuing.

A different typology of suicide

It may be possible to construct a profile or paradigm of Aboriginal suicide, partly from existing theories, classifications and categories, and partly from some innovative classification arising from this study. The following might prove worthy of consideration, as a way towards achieving an understanding of that which Hillman calls the 'soul' of the suicide.

The 'political' suicides

'Political' may seem a bizarre word to use in this context. It is also difficult to define when used in the phrase 'making a political statement'. Konrad Kwiet has given us an insight into 'political' suicides by German Jews as early as 1933. In a farewell letter, Fritz Rosenfelder said he was 'unable to go on living with the knowledge that the movement to which national Germany is looking for salvation considers him a traitor to the fatherland ... I leave without hate or anger ... and so I have chosen a voluntary death in order to shock my Christian friends into awareness' (Kwiet 1984, 147).

At best, this type of suicide is a public declaration of anger or grievance designed to gain a hearing, possibly even a response. It is an attempt at power, in Robert Dahl's classic sense that power is involved where A has power over B to the extent that he can get B to do something that B would not otherwise do. In my context, it is an effort to move someone, or something, to a response. Some of Aboriginal suicide is of this kind: an 'I'll show you', 'I'll get even with you', a 'you'll be sorry', 'you'll lose your job', 'you'll pay for this ...' statement. A 14-year-old in central New South Wales shot himself in front of his assembled family in 1997. There had been a row about his staying out late at night, and then brandishing (what turned out to be) an unusable rifle, which was taken from him. He found another, usable weapon and announced his 'equation': his life in exchange for their loss and sorrow. Several weeks earlier, his 18-year-old cousin, at another central New South Wales town, had shot himself in front of the family, again after a row about his late night hours. These cases appear to be the beginning of a new pattern, namely shooting in front of an audience, with assertions, or 'political statements', about independence, status or lack of care.

The 'respect' suicides

An even more disturbing variant is the demand for a respect which was seen as not accorded, or *was* not accorded, in life. Interviews with immediate relatives have confirmed that X and Y, from aged 12 upward, had been 'nobodies', seemingly unwanted, often neglected (even though not socially or physically isolated), disrespected or 'dissed'. That Black American expression has not yet reached our shores, but the idea has. These young men are often 'disempowered' by the stronger wills or personalities of younger siblings and see themselves as displaced family members. They will take on their older siblings, or older boys in general, although they are thumped in basketball games, lose the fist fights, the snooker or pool games, the video games. They are given no respect by anyone. Their response has been articulated and overheard in more than a handful of cases: 'You'll all have to come to my funeral'. And, of course, everybody does.

The 14-year-old mentioned above was a 'nobody' all his life. Constantly moved by his young mother between and within states, he lived with a succession of his mother's de facto partners. His funeral was something to behold. Four hundred people, including two busloads of Aboriginal prisoners from Broken Hill and another cohort of prisoners from Long Bay in Sydney, came to a town of a thousand residents. (The RCIADIC recommended that funds be available for prisoners to attend funerals of kith and kin.) At least 30 additional police came to the town to supervise the well-attended wake. The church was overflowing. The lad had his 'respect'.

Although his case was more 'political' in my sense, it illustrates a dictum posited by Sigmund Freud: that 'our unconscious does not believe in its own death; it behaves as if it were immortal'. Alvarez comments: 'thus suicide enhances a personality which magically survives'. In other words, young suicide is an act of physical destruction, but the psyche, or soul, or the unconscious, is conceived as continuing to live. Listening to many of the threats, it appears to me that many of these young people believe that they will be there to witness the sorrow, regret, remorse, revenge or respect that their acts will, or did, create. It is suggested in the verb they always use: 'I'll *see* you in trouble'. The Christchurch suicide researcher, Annette Beautrais, tells me that suicide notes from 14- to 18-year-old New Zealanders contain messages to the effect that 'we will be around watching out for you as we know what you're doing'.

There is no doubt that much of this kind of suicide occurs in clusters, in families, or in small communities. Five in one Nowra family is an extreme case, perhaps, but the two gunshot suicides discussed above occurred in reasonably proximate towns by boys who were first cousins. I believe that this form of 'respect' will increase and so will the clusters. The universally used term by informants throughout this study is that youth lack 'self-esteem'. It is a [misused] mantra that hopes and seeks to explain and to solve: self-esteem, once achieved, will bring an end to assaults, drug- and alcohol-taking, even suicide. However, what constitutes self-esteem is the gamut of factors and forces described thus far in this book. In the final chapter, I describe one or two potentially positive programs which may help illiterate, angry, frustrated, helpless youth to articulate their goals and I discuss the obstacles which have to be overcome to achieve them.

The grieving suicides

Much of Aboriginal life in New South Wales, as elsewhere, is consumed by grieving for relatives who die in infancy, or die young, or from premature disease, or from accidents or various kinds of violence. 'Old' death, as in a granny or aunty of 80, is much less common. Much time is spent at funerals and mourning rituals of a more Western kind. The wakes that follow cost large amounts of money, especially for quantities of alcohol and food (that the children look forward to consuming). There is almost none of the expiation, purgation and catharsis which stem from the organised ritual mourning ceremonies still practised in Aboriginal northern Australia. One North American study, discussed in Chapter 9, mentions 'prolonged unresolved grief' among Indian youth suicides.

There is, then, a perpetual cycle of grief. The suicide of a popular 33-year-old sportsman in Coffs Harbour, a role model for all, resulted in grief all the way from Sydney to Tweed Heads, and then west, lasting almost a year and a half. He was mourned even by those who were not blood kin. A commonly used term in the suicide literature is 'copy-cat'. It has a pejorative ring. But what it is, when seen in context, is communing, emulating, joining, and not merely imitation. The Menindee grievers are the starkest example we encountered, but there is much evidence from relatives of young male suicides that their lives centred on grief of this kind. There are no mechanisms in place, certainly no appropriate mechanisms or avenues, in any of the communities we visited, for grief counselling.

The 'ambivalently rational' suicides

My sense of 'rational' is quite different from Wekstein's notion of the irremediably ill person who plans an auto-euthanasia. A psychiatrist colleague, Michael Diamond, suggests to me that there is sometimes an ambivalent suicide, in the following sense. A youth feels socially integrated, alive, comradely in his gang or group membership. He feels a 'high' in a venture, such as a break-and-enter, especially if there is no detection. He may still feel on a 'high' when the group faces arrest, then remand, then court with lawyers representing him. He may retain that 'high' when placed in custody. However, when, for example, he falls foul of a warder and is placed on various penalties, or in isolation, he suddenly runs into a brick wall: there is no camaraderie available, no social integration to assist him. He sees, in a rational moment, an answer to his seemingly insoluble dilemma: suicide.

The 'appealing' suicides

Emanuel Marx's study of the social context of violent behaviour (in Israel) contends that appealing violence occurs when a person 'has reached the end of his tether, and feels unable to achieve a social aim unaided by others. It is a "cry for help"' (1976, 2–3). It is partly a cry addressed to the public, 'and partly an attempt to shift some of their obligations towards their dependants onto others'. The person who cannot make that public appeal for help, nor persuade his or her family to share (personal and social) responsibilities, engages in violence towards others and finally towards self, as a desperate means to regain the support of family or kin.

An Aboriginal elder and leader in Fingal, south Tweed Heads, believes that suicides occur 'because life at home is too awful! There are very few normal family relationships.' In an earlier fieldwork study, I reported the case at Raukkun in South Australia, where an Aboriginal man attacked his brother with an axe early in 1989. Admonished later by the local policeman's wife, he replied: 'Sorry, I'll never do that again: I'll only hurt myself'.[11] The director of Booroongen Djugun, near Kempsey, tells me that 'sometimes kids hang themselves, and in the process you can see that they're not sure, you can see it on their dead faces'. He is not the only informant to talk of finding youngsters hanging, but with fingers desperately trying to reverse or stop the process.

'Empowerment' suicides

Aboriginal youth rarely experience autonomy, self-fulfilment or personal sovereignty over their physical, material or internal lives. The vague modern term, 'disempowerment', does, however, convey this condition. There is an overlap between this phenomenon and the lack of respect discussed above.

Elsewhere I have discussed the motives of a number of Aboriginal sportsmen and women: they see sport as the only arena in which, even without education, income and opportunity, they can compete on equal terms. It is their only chance to pit their bodies, minds, energies and skills against an opposition.[12] Henry Collins' view of boxing expressed this outlook: 'I felt good when I knocked white blokes out. I knew I was boss in the boxing ring. I showed my superiority ... they showed it outside.' This embodies what the German sociologist Max Weber meant by power: 'the chance of a man or of a number of men to realise their own will in a communal action even against the resistance of others who are participating in the action' (1970, 180).

Several parasuicides have indicated that they perceive suicide as their only avenue to 'realise their own will'. It is their moment of autonomy and empowerment, suggesting that the only 'thing' they own is their physical life. For once, fleetingly, they can manage it, dispose of it, even against the opposition of those close to them or of those they see as antagonistic. Hillman has a poignant phrase for this: that, within this 'negative selfishness', there is *a small seed of selfhood* —the suicide's 'ultimate empowerment' (1997, 92, 196–7).

The 'lost' suicides

Many Aboriginal youth feel the direct effects of racism and alienation. Some articulate a sense of emptiness, a loss of culture, especially ritual and spirituality. Others know there is a 'hole' in their lives but don't know what it is. They suffer the label 'Aborigine', yet cannot comprehend what it is in 'Aborigine' that causes such antagonism or contempt.

Dr Erahana Ryan, New Zealand's only female Maori psychiatrist, talks of Maori youth who suffer 'stress of loss of who they are'.[13] She talks about 'the emptiness of blighted, warped, eviscerated urban Maori life'. There is a likely parallel in contemporary Aboriginal life.

Whom to turn to?

Hopelessness is a universal among youth in such contexts. Phrases like 'no light at the end of the tunnel', 'hopelessness', 'no horizons', 'no skills', come off most people's lips. An important difference, or variation, in the Aboriginal world is that there is no one in their universe to act as guide, mentor, sign-poster in a transition to betterment. They really do have to make decisions *unaided*. The home is filled with family in like circumstances. There is no classical ministering priest. The school counsellor, even if seen as a guide, is overworked and never available immediately. The usual welfare agencies, even if considered, are there only by appointment, inevitably on their own premises, 9 to 5 on week-days. The only constantly available resources are police officers and ACLOs. The police are neither trained for this nor, clearly, are they trusted by youth. The ACLOs do yeoman service, but their overload is staggering.

As discussed earlier, there are no 'guru' figures, respect figures, trust figures in their young lives. More importantly, they do not have an 'enlightened witness' in their lives, the kind of person who, psychoanalyst Alice Miller says, is not cruel to them and who enables them to become aware of the cruelty done to them by parents or family members. Miller sees the role of a witness as 'supporting' and 'corrective' (1990, 167–75). Such witnesses have knowledge of the truth of what is being done to the young person, thus allowing them to believe in something while retaining a sense of belonging to humanity. Once they lose that thread of connection to parent, immediate family or enlightened witness, all is lost.

Asked what they would like to do in life, several Aboriginal youngsters have told me that they would like to change their present circumstances. But none has any comprehension of how to commence the move from point A to point B. A great many cannot even read about techniques to alter their situation. By contrast, in much of middle-class Australia there is a plethora of help: teachers, counsellors, careers advisers, tutors, ambitious parents, computer programs, website information, good doctor–patient relationships, access to all manner of advice bureaux — places of help to which they can be directed.

Conclusion

There is much written, and generally believed, about suicide being a 'mental health' problem. Peter Neame, for example, quotes from the *Guidelines on the Management of Suicidal Patients* prepared by the New Zealand Ministry of Health in 1993: 'Although the causes of suicide are complex and a number of factors may combine to lead any individual to take their own life, it is generally accepted that at least 94% of people who die by suicide were suffering from a mental illness at the time of their death' (1997, 9). The Australian Psychological Society repeats this belief: 'There is a clear majority view that mental illness is an almost certain precursor and comorbid risk factor in youth suicide'; and again, 'many researchers agree that at least 90% of suicides in all age groups are associated with psychiatric or addictive disorders' (1999, 27, 9).

I do not accept that generalisation. Without a detailed profile by competent assessors, it is impossible, unreasonable and immoral to maintain 'mental illness' as the key causation in Aboriginal suicide. On the contrary, my information — derived from interview with kin, and with those who provided services to the deceased and to the parasuicides in this study — is that mental illness, in the strict pathological sense, was rarely a factor. The 'bible' of mental illness is known as *DSM–IV* (*Diagnostic and Statistical Manual for Mental Disorders, 4th edn*). It defines 'substance abuse' and 'antisocial conduct' as mental disorder. If heavy resort to cigarettes, alcohol, drugs and other 'uplifters' is a symptom of mental illness, our whole society is in deep trouble.

As discussed further in the final chapter, to be perturbed, disturbed, stressed, uneasy, *dis*-eased, anxious, confused, aggressive, delinquent, obnoxious, aggressive, *is to be normal.* These conditions are *not* diseases, the *DSM* notwithstanding. There is an all too common mischief abroad that only good or appealing feelings and behaviours are normal and that objectionable ones are abnormal and, therefore, indicate illness. (Viktor Frankl expresses all this most elegantly in the headnote to the next chapter.) Put another way, compliant behaviours are deemed normal, and all other behaviours are 'pathologised'. A current fashion in psychiatry and related disciplines is to be aggressive about biological or genetic factors as explanations of 'abnormal' behaviour. Some even call it 'biological triumphalism'.

Ordinary language, plain language, has suffered — perhaps irreparably — from psychiatry. Misuse of language has produced what Thomas Szasz calls 'professional mystification' (1974, 24–7). Whoever first defines the situation, he argues, is the victor; his adversary or patient, the victim. If the *DSM* defines something as antisocial or abusive or addictive as 'mental illness', it is not surprising that researchers find that 90 per cent of suicides are 'ill'. But there is no evidence by the *DSM* compilers, or by all those who comprise 'the clear majority view', that there is observable, demonstrable pathological mental illness in youth suicide. Empirical, physical or even social examinations are not involved; even if the researchers do examine individual cases, they are diagnosing, in most cases, after death.

Szasz argues that those who behave in a way that is unacceptable are labelled as troublesome, mentally sick, deviant. Why is it that we so often give quick medical diagnoses to people whose behaviour annoys or offends us? Here sociology is as much at fault: the sociology of social problems and of deviance defines a social problem, or deviant behaviour, as that which the majority views in that way. Aborigines are labelled, daily. The word 'Aborigine' is a label of both hidden and overt metaphor: ignorant, poor, uncivilised, alcoholic, unemployed, unemployable, hopeless, helpless, unworthy, reckless, promiscuous, welfare-dependent and, in the context of suicide, mentally ill. It ought to be a sobering thought for those who constantly urge that the remedy for suicide is to improve or acquire 'self-esteem'. How does a victim who is constantly portrayed as having no self-esteem begin to fight for it?

The issue of 'mental illness' is a major one, especially in matters of criminal responsibility. Joel Feinberg has done a great service in examining 'What Is So Special about Mental Illness?' in relation to responsibility (or excusability) in criminal cases. His contention is that many types of 'mental illness' have no more bearing on a criminal's behaviour than a physical illness would have (1970, 272–92). If Ned Kelly had, incidentally, had high blood pressure or cancer during his bank robberies, no excuse or explanation would have lain therein.

Why then, in our discussion of suicide, do we persist in seeing every disorder that can be included under the broad heading of 'mental illness' as either a cause or an explanation for suicide or as bestowing *non-*responsibility for suicide? Certainly, some people who suffer from such illnesses do commit suicide. But is their illness always the *direct cause* of this very active action or is it, in many cases, an incidental factor? Suicidal behaviour differs from illness behaviour in at least one significant respect: most patients, physical or mental, tend to be passive about their illnesses, delegating its management to doctors and hospitals. But most suicide is, above all else, an active event, managed by the individual, usually alone. The all-consuming passion for seeking out and identifying 'mental illness' as the unique explanation of Aboriginal youth suicide is, I believe, the greatest single obstacle to the beginnings of alleviation.

One of the 43 in this study drowned himself on the eve of serious charges of child molestation and sexual abuse. The evidence we have points to 'rational' suicide as a way out of a bleak future. From our reading of the files, and from interviews concerning about half of the 43 suicides, it would appear that only two of them were being attended to and being treated for a 'mental illness', such as severe depression, bipolar disorder, and the like.

An attempted broad, albeit speculative, model of Aboriginal suicide could be expressed as

- a broad-based community norm of Wekstein's chronic suicide, that is, a use of alcohol or drugs or both to mask an orientation which suggests 'a preference for obliteration rather than life'; in conjunction with

- a general lack of purpose in life, a hopelessness about the present and future, an ennui that is all-pervasive, that manifests as existential suicide, whether in symbolic form or as actual self-destruction.

Within that broad compass, there appear to be clear, or seemingly clear, cases of

- accidental or indirect suicide or sub-intentional suicide — the risk-runners, those who dice with danger;

- focal suicide — the slashers, the self-mutilators, those who 'kill' an offending part of the body;

- political suicide — those making an overt statement about their lack of care, or about their desire for revenge or retaliation;

- respect suicide — those who perceive themselves as being so utterly forlorn and forsaken that suicide is the only way to command a focus on self;
- grieving suicide — the surcease (in Wekstein's terms) not of irremediable illness but of irremediable grief;
- rational suicide — those who find an inspirational answer to that which appears unanswerable;
- appealing suicide — violence to others and then to self, as an appeal for support and assistance;
- empowerment suicide — much akin to respect suicide, where the person feels so unempowered or disempowered that suicide is the only way to exercise autonomy or personal sovereignty, to exert his or her will in a successful action; and, possibly,
- 'stress of loss' suicide — where no meaning is to be found in an Aboriginality which is meant to produce an inner sense of belonging from within and which is, simultaneously, the basis of so much antagonism from without.

The chairman of the Fingal Bay council has a much more succinct perspective on young Aboriginal suicide:

- they are tired, worn out, worn down, even the young ones;
- they have no physical or mental stamina left;
- they are tired of the same depressed lifestyle;
- it is a quick way out of dilemmas.

There is much talk in suicidology about the proximal and the distal causes of suicide. The medical–psychiatric approach is to examine proximal risk factors, those considered close to the point of origin of the problem: depression, a family history of suicide, past attempts at suicide, substance abuse and personal conduct problems. Certainly this is one way to obtain clinical data about those who seek or are sent for treatment, for any of the above reasons. The health professionals tend to see the distal or socio-environmental approaches, those more distant from the essence of the problem, as important but of little use in clinical practice.

My conclusion is the antithesis, namely, that unless health care practitioners — psychiatrists, psychologists, general practitioners, nurses, social workers, mental health workers, health educators — become holistically knowledgeable about the wide variety of Aboriginal societies who encompass 106,000 or possibly 150,000 people in New South Wales, their clinical, proximal (and increasingly biological) approach will touch but a few of the many who are involved in suicide behaviour. They need to comprehend more than a history of oppression and the legacies of colonialism. What is occurring is a new violence, of which suicide is but one facet. And, within that facet, there are behaviours motivated or occasioned by many things other than the personal family histories of suicide, aggressive behaviour, substance abuse, 'depression' and other mental illness.

Notes

1. Wekstein, *Handbook of Suicidology*, 27–30.
2. Alvarez, *The Savage God*, 74.
3. Ibid.
4. Hunter, *Aboriginal Health and History*, ch. 5, 90–132.
5. Seligman, *The Optimistic Child*, chs 1, 2 and 3.
6. Beautrais et al, 'Prevalence, Comorbidity of Mental Disorders', 1009–14.
7. Dietrich and Kempton, *Prevention of Deliberate Self-Harm*, 87–93.
8. Tane Cassidy and Helen Leaky, Wellington.
9. Alvarez, *The Savage God*, 99.
10. Dr John Broughton, personal communication.
11. Tatz, *Obstacle Race*, 320–2.
12. Ibid., 111.
13. Personal communication.

7

Contributing Factors — Aboriginal Community Values

Existential frustration is in itself neither pathological nor pathogenic. A man's concern, even his despair, over the worthwhileness of life is an existential distress but by no means a mental disease. It may well be that interpreting the first in terms of the latter motivates a doctor to bury his patient's existential despair under a heap of tranquilizing drugs. It is his task, rather, to pilot the patient through his existential crisis of growth and development.

— Viktor Frankl[1]

Suicide prevention agencies reach only a small minority in need of help. They are unlikely to reduce drastically the suicide rates. This can be expected only from suicide prophylaxis which begins at birth and even earlier ... The preservation of the family, active membership of a religious community or some other social group, the fight against alcoholism, good mental and physical health, good medical services, full employment, are all powerful factors against suicide.

–Erwin Stengel[2]

Social factors in suicide

Two Australians prominent in the suicide field have advocated the consideration of those social factors likely to initiate a decision to attempt suicide. Riaz Hassan (1996, 4–5) suggests the following:

- marital status — suicide is lower among the married, that is, among people enjoying 'domestic integration';
- economic cycles — suicide is higher among the unemployed and during an economic depression or stock market crash;
- occupation — lower status and income, poor promotion opportunities and less job satisfaction are more commonly associated with suicide;

- migration — non-English-speaking migrants, who adjust less easily to the everyday stresses of life in Australia, have higher rates than native English speakers;
- ethnicity, as occurs with Aboriginality — where suicide is more common due to 'devaluation of their culture and self-identity', together with 'a sense of anomie, hopelessness, despair and depression', all aggravated by 'poverty, economic insecurity, alcoholism and subjection to racism';
- extent of public welfare — good or adequate social welfare systems have kept suicide rates among non-Aboriginal people in the 'middle range';
- locality — rural suicide is higher than urban, possibly due to downturns in the economy, difficult access to health and welfare facilities, and a 'macho' sense of 'rugged' self-sufficiency.

Pierre Baume suggests two sets of factors: the global and the personal.[3] High suicide rates are found in countries suffering global problems, such as a high divorce rate, high youth unemployment, extremely high alcohol intake, a high number of unwanted pregnancies, and low church or other religious participation. Personal factors include the death of a family member or close friend, divorce and domestic upheaval, break-up of a relationship, physical or social isolation, the excessive use of alcohol and drugs, confusion over sexuality or rejection because of sexuality, and contagion, that is, through an awareness of friends committing suicide, of media reports of suicide and of musical or sporting heroes taking their own lives.

Not many of the Hassan and Baume factors pertain directly to Aborigines. Formal marriage and divorce do not assume great importance in Aboriginal life. Nor do unemployment, poor job status or lack of promotional opportunity. These are such common Aboriginal experiences that they are taken to be the norm rather than being perceived as major stressors. Access to mental health and welfare agencies is not their problem; the services are, by and large, provided. Rather, it is the Aborigines' own rejection of such help which constitutes the problem. Ruralness or remoteness do not cause problems for Aborigines; they are the norm, as they are the locales in which they have chosen to live, or which they or their immediate ancestors were coerced into 'choosing'. Unwanted pregnancies are not perceived as being an issue, since many Aboriginal girls, as young as 13, seek pregnancy as a pathway to an independent income (from the supporting or single-parent benefit). Aborigines may, indeed, be physically and socially isolated from mainstream life, but *not* from each other. There is much movement between communities which are empathic towards each other's social disadvantage or which have sympathetic kinship or geographic ties.

By contrast, other adverse factors — many of them politically caused — prevail in Aboriginal communities: generalised poverty, overcrowding or lack of adequate homes for large and often much extended families, low income from social service benefits or the equivalent CDEP payments, chronic and sometimes severe alcohol and drug consumption, the constant experience of racism in their contacts with non-Aboriginal society, and the omnipresence of deaths and funerals of kin and friends.

Specific Aboriginal factors

At least eight factors operate within the politics and sociology of Aboriginal communities, adding to actual or attempted suicidal or high-risk behaviour. These factors need to be recognised and then accommodated in prevention strategies. These are specific, smaller in scope and more tangible than the overarching and broader issues presented in Chapter 1 as part of the social context. Some can be addressed and are remediable; others will ineluctably remain integral to Aboriginal life. Some are within the province of Aborigines themselves to address; others can only be ameliorated with the assistance of organised non-Aboriginal society.

No sense of purpose in life

Although this is no place for a discussion of existential philosophy, Nietzsche's dictum is relevant: 'He who has a *why* to live can bear with almost any *how*'. Viktor Frankl contends that all people need a *will to meaning* (rather than a Freudian *will to pleasure*). He opposes those who contend that meanings and values are nothing 'but defence mechanisms, reaction formations and sublimations' (1984, 121). Frankl contends that he survived the experience of having been in a Nazi concentration camp because he had a conviction that life could be meaningful even amidst the hellish world dominated by grossly indecent people. (The late Primo Levi also talked about those who had purpose as being the 'saved' and those who perished as being the *sommersi*, the 'drowned'.)

I have spoken with a number of Aboriginal youth during this and previous studies. Most will talk about sublimations — of achieving a time, space and place different from their present existence. Most state, with simple realism, that neither these goals, nor the will to achieve them, can be achieved unless they move, in mind and in body, to another 'place'. They appear to have no concept of how such goals can be attained and/or how to alter their own circumstances, whether at home or some place 'away'.

Sporting success is an attainable goal. There are increasing numbers of models, hero figures who have achieved a new place, status and, above all, social acceptance and respect within both Aboriginal and non-Aboriginal society. For example, Evonne Goolagong-Cawley, Cathy Freeman, Anthony Mundine, David Peachey, Darrell Trindall, Ricky Walford, the Ella family, Michael O'Loughlin, and a host of others, are identifiable successes and, moreover, are often kin. A path to the big arenas extends from local clubs, junior and reserve ranks, through the omnipresence of club talent scouts. There is a rough map of how to proceed from point A to point B.

Apart from sport, there are few activities which present such maps or routes: rock music and country and western, and the artistic worlds of painting and dancing. Again, there are role models for those with enough talent to compete in these fields. For the majority, life happens, as dictated by wills other than their own. There is a collective sense of ennui, of hopelessness, of an inability to exert their wills in any competitive arena. Petty crime is a group action, an exercise in 'will to meaning' — for the moment. Suicide is sometimes both an individual and a group 'will to action'—to physically make that change in time and place, to move both body and spirit from one place to another, *unaided*.

Suicide is rare in societies engaged in struggles for racial, religious or ethnic survival. Africans in South African rarely committed suicide while the struggle against apartheid was fierce, incessant and unequal. Since the election of an African government, the spur of alienation has gone, leaving other struggles — for job, house, food, dignity. Suicide is now a factor. In Aboriginal life, there is no equivalent 'enemy'. The anti-apartheid movement was based on a belief that life could be made better if apartheid were destroyed. Aboriginal communities — despite now being free of the 'protectors', the managers of reserves, and the matrons of hostels — have had no such liberation movement and, tragically, therefore, no belief that life could be better. The struggle for apology or for some form of treaty has none of the universal and all-embracing vitality demonstrated in the anti-apartheid struggle.

Some Aboriginal groups in this study, notably in Boggabilla and Orange, have opted for Pentecostal religious movements. The adherents do indeed articulate purpose, just as Black Islam has brought cohesion to many African-Americans in the United States. Purpose, and the often ugly coercion that appears to go with it, is overwhelming in such communities; it is cohering and meaningful to a people now confident of their present and future.

A few communities have embarked on enterprises with both economic and purpose goals. Forster has developed a powerful CDEP workforce, sought after for its expertise in lawn-mowing, weed control and land-scaping. It also has a stable of some 20 artists, working on canvas and on kitchen and bathroom tiles as commercial ventures. There is full employment in the community, with varied choices of work, and there is a strong sense of communal enterprise. The Aboriginal community also owns large tracts of land.

The Minjungbal Museum in south Tweed Heads, offering camping trips to re-acculturate Aboriginal children, is another example of such enterprise. The Yarrawarra training scheme at Corindi Beach, near Coffs Harbour, is a successful project: here young Aborigines are given skills in mapping culture trails and in providing traditional Aboriginal foods for tourists. An even larger, and equally successful, venture of this kind is the Umbarra cultural centre, operated by the Aboriginal community at Wallaga Lake.

CDEP has given an uplift and a dignity to communities. From a trade union point of view, it is defective: working for what is normally a legal entitlement, at hourly rates not consonant with union rates, often for work which would command higher rates, with little or no supervision, no opportunities for promotion, little if anything in the way of training in a trade or skill, no holiday or superannuation benefits. Commonly, it is as it is described—'shit work'. But to see people eager to go to work, arriving on time, having titles attached to their jobs, receiving pay rather than dole packets, is to witness something close to a miracle of morale-boosting. Until the May 1999 federal budget, CDEP places were pegged at 32,000 nationally. The scheme needs to be universal and without ceilings. It is, after all, the money to which the recipients are already legally entitled.

Few role models and mentors

Aboriginal innocence ends at a young age. All children of early primary school age desire to become pilots, astronauts or rock stars. By 8 or 10, some of the starker realities prevail. When Aboriginal children articulate their goals, it is to be like father or uncle — perhaps a shearer, railway ganger, forest or CDEP worker (now seen increasingly as of higher status, as in contract fencing or landscaping). The Australian Psychological Society quotes an author who suggests that young people 'are engaged in a tussle between hope and cynicism' (1999, 21); that may be true, but in the Aboriginal case the tussle is more likely between hope and realism.

There are too few publicly recognised role models who show that education, study, training or an apprenticeship is 'the way to go'. In the 1960s, I wrote that the football field and the boxing ring were *the* models for Aboriginal parents looking for a future for their children. At that time, there were only two Aboriginal graduates as models for emulation: Margaret Valadian and Charles Perkins. Almost 40 years later, there are now some 8000 Aborigines in tertiary study of some kind. Despite this improvement in academic endeavour, the rugby league and Australian football fields are still perceived as much more accessible and acceptable avenues to status, income and acceptance. Significant Aboriginal achievements in intellectual endeavours, in the arts and literature, and even in professions such as medicine, remain relatively obscure when compared with sporting possibilities. In part, this is due to an Aboriginal propensity to consume the 'popular culture' found in commercial radio and television, in the tabloid newspapers and in their magazine counterparts.

In every community there is always need of a mentor, a 'guru' figure, a person of respect to whom to go for guidance, information, advice, succour, even confession. (I use 'mentor' here as someone different from the 'enlightened witness' discussed in the previous chapter.) In all of the communities we visited, there was a constant lament that there were no longer any resource people available as 'trust' figures for children and youth. When we suggested a return to the 'elders', the common response was that many of the 'elders' no longer commanded respect, and that some have become abusers or molesters. The kinds of person they saw fulfilling these roles were, most often, sportsmen — like Tony Mundine (former professional boxing title-holder in four weight divisions), a solid and sober man who has avoided the general fate of most professional fighters.

Because of the tendency to hero-worship sporting figures, the suicide of the young sportsman in Coffs Harbour was devastating for all. He was a model indeed: a surfing champion, a man who had travelled to competitions in Hawaii, had married, was working with the police service, was a church-goer, a non-smoker and non-drinker. His choice of suicide has initiated a very different kind of role model.

For the girls, the traditional granny or aunty is often suggested as the mentor figure. However, most grannies and aunties are burned-out, exhausted by life, by keeping communities in one piece, by loss of their own children, by ill-health, and, most significantly, by forever acting as surrogate mothers because their children's generation have 'abdicated' their own parenting.

There is no ready answer. There are no training schools for 'respect figures', and it is fortuitous if a community produces a man or woman of stature, personality, wisdom and, most importantly, possessing a neutrality that does not locate the person as being from an alien or 'enemy' family or clan. Several ACLOs are fulfilling this role, but they have a burden of work best described as gross. Some mental health workers are seen in these roles, and so, too, are female heads of councils or agencies.

Ineffective parenting

Riaz and Baume, among others, regard domestic disintegration as a social factor in suicide. The sociology of the Aboriginal family is possibly unique. Generally, motherhood commences at a very young age, with single parenting, a propensity for de facto rather than contractual marriage relationships, many half-sibling relationships because of several partners, large numbers of children per mother, a greater loss of children through illness, and extended family networks and domicile arrangements.

Several staff in support agencies complain that they cannot locate who is responsible for a particular child because the 'care' people are so numerous. The problem is not that there are too many carers, but that there is a 'dilution of responsibility' in parenting and parental responsibilities. Girls bear children at 15 and 16, even at 14 and 13. This is driven primarily by two economic imperatives: first, an encouragement to fecund girls to produce children and enhance social service benefit income to families who subsist, in the main, on such income; second, a personal desire to acquire that benefit as a way to independence and to 'escape' from dysfunctional households. Parenthood for such young mothers is not, however, a reliable recipe for independence. The novelty soon wears thin and there is no willing grandmother to take over the baby to enable the child-mother to complete her schooling.

Many of these young mothers still want a social life. It is common to see toddlers and slightly older children playing outside pubs and clubs while their mothers socialise, play bingo, poker machines or darts, or drink, usually on social service benefit paydays and the few days following. Children 'grow each other up', producing an independence of spirit and of physicality from a very young age. Parents complain that they have no 'say' over children — as young as 8 and 10 — who roam the streets late at night. In one large northern coastal town, youth of 10 to 14 have been congregating outside all-night pubs at two and three in the morning, engaging in fights with broken bottles. Many fathers, if they do remain part of the family, simply allow their children to develop along whatever lines they may choose.

The 12-year-old who hanged himself at Wilcannia in 1997 was not found for at least two days. Police and others made much of this 'abdication' of care. The mother assumed that he was with a granny or an aunt, something common to this lad's daily pattern. Each relative believed he was with another. The mother is an alcoholic and often 'fostered him out'. She was still drinking when his body was found. The mother's anguished response to all this was that she really loved the boy, a statement made to us by many who have lost children in this way. There is no doubt that parents love their children, but the issue under discussion is not 'love' but physical and emotional *care*.

In Kempsey, for example, at least 70 per cent of local crime is committed by Aborigines aged between 10 and 24. Between 1 January and 15 April 1997, there were 39 Kempsey, 33 Taree, 3 Forster, 2 Port Macquarie, and 1 Macksville Aboriginal juvenile appearances before the children's court. Even allowing for a greater propensity by police to arrest Aboriginal youth, for whatever reasons, the fact is that many Aboriginal youth commit crimes. Significantly, the majority break and enter and, in the majority of those cases, the theft is to obtain food.

Perhaps the most telling consequence of the dilution of parental responsibility is the predilection for young children to be incarcerated in Minda, the juvenile justice facility. As we did not visit the institution, we are unable to confirm what we have been told of the youngsters' direct accounts of life there. Ex-inmates and many others involved in juvenile justice are of the strong opinion that youngsters like to go there and that they re-offend soon after release in order to return. There is much talk of 'warm bed and three square meals a day'. More cogent is wanting to be away from households where alcohol, drugs, constant domestic violence and overcrowding are often the norm, and where meals are available only when there is money to spare.

There are two forms of parental dilution of responsibility: first, abandoning responsibilities in the belief, or hope, that others will do what has to be done; second, not having the skills to parent in the first place. Parenting skills *can* be taught. The parenting issue belongs squarely in the Aboriginal domain, and they are the only people who can decide to address this monumental problem. However, direction and leadership may have to come from outside the distressed communities. Removal of children from their parents has produced several generations who have no role models and no traditions to guide them in this special under-taking. Furthermore, improvement in Aboriginal child-rearing practices requires a great deal of assistance.

Sexual assaults

Molestation and abuse of children occur too frequently. Every community in this study expressed distress at the levels of abuse, which is not only unreported to police or other agencies but also goes unpunished within the groups.

In a so-called 'riot' in a town adjacent to one of our sample towns, 8- and 9-year-old girls had climbed onto the roofs of houses under construction and were throwing tiles at people down below. When we asked why the elders or the men on the local council did not intervene, we were told, by more than one witness, that the anger and tiles were aimed at those very elders who had been sexually misusing them. Like most people, Aborigines have a penchant for exaggeration and for vilification of those seen as 'enemies'; however, there cannot be calumny behind every report of sexual abuse. Not only is there evidence from counselling agencies, but also from Aboriginal parents and the young people themselves.

We do not have direct evidence of the correlation between sexual assault and suicide in each of the 43 suicides in this study, or in the many more who have attempted suicide. One professional, who operates a first-offenders post-release program, says that those who slash have been sexually abused; he adds that it is usually the same relative who is the abuser in each family where it occurs. There is also strong anecdotal evidence from parasuicides that sexual abuse is a major factor in their lives.

In Chapter 2, I used the phrase 'disordered societies'. Child molestation and sexual abuse have always been absolute taboos in all Aboriginal societies. Penalties ranged from physical beating, through ritual spearing and exile from the community, to death. Traditional Aboriginal systems of incest prohibition remain the world's foremost model. Yet, in practice, most of the structure and discipline have fallen away, to the point where the abuse is committed with impunity.

Alcohol and drugs

The stereotype is that all Aborigines drink to excess. However, many do not drink at all, and there are 'dry' communities in several areas. Hunter has shown that heavy drinking is the norm in some communities and that such drinking has origins, motives, patterns and rituals quite distinct from those pertaining to non-Aboriginal drinking. When august bodies define alcohol or substance abuse, they do so from an ethno- or class-centric stance: what they observe is what happens in their mainstream societies. Among the many theories and explanations, my view is that Aboriginal drinking is for 'surcease'—for obliteration of their present existence, and probably to mask a suppressed wish for permanent obliteration — in effect, Wekstein's 'chronic suicide'.

Drug use, almost unknown in Aboriginal communities until some 30 years ago, is rampant. Cannabis is the substance of choice and availability. Some Aboriginal communities, particularly in the coastal regions, are heavily engaged in cultivation and selling. 'Green money' dominates a handful of communities which have become (relatively) wealthy from its cultivation.

Several of the autopsy reports on the people in our study mention the presence of cannabis. As indicated in the previous chapter, many young males are obsessed with, rather than addicted to, the drug. There is a strong correlation between drug use and the consumption of alcohol, with both parents and police alike deploring the explosive and violent behaviour ensuing from the combination. Children as young as 6 have been observed smoking pot, and group behaviours clearly lead to younger group emulation.

The historian Richard Kimber has informed me of the views of a traditional Warlpiri man of 40 in Alice Springs, a keen footballer, sophisticated in both traditional and non-Aboriginal lifestyles. This man insists that *all* the young men who had suicided in that region had been heavy cannabis users. Kimber asserts that cannabis usage began in the Yuendumu and Papunya areas in the 1970s, possibly through the influence of (Jamaican) reggae singer Bob Marley, a popular figure with Aboriginal youth.

Binge-drinking is often reported among the younger boys. I am unsure of what 'binge' means but suspect that it involves heavy episodic drinking, as when either money or the substance becomes available. We did not record all autopsies which showed a heavy alcohol presence, but we know that a number of suicides had high alcohol readings, especially those who had drowned themselves. It is clear that alcohol is often associated with the suicide at the time of the attempt.

Animosity and jealousy

Factionalism pervades many Aboriginal communities. Even small communities, of perhaps 300 or 400 people, can be split into two or more factions, vying for whatever resources may be available, such as land allocations, jobs in agencies, CDEP, housing, and so on. Factionalism is often corrosive, not negotiable or remediable. One informant told of 'deadly animosities in the mission'. In one town I know well, a sports centre has not been built for some 25 years, despite allocation of land and funds. Three separate clans vied for control of the complex. Each would rather see it not built than see it entrusted to the 'wrong' people.

Suicide is not directly correlated with factionalism, but clearly there are Montague and Capulet type relationships. Clan strife sometimes intrudes on interpersonal love or friendship. Suicide, we discover, is perhaps the one unifying event: funerals of the young are places of mutuality and of common grief.

Ernest Hunter used an interesting word in his work in the Kimberley region of Western Australia: 'jealousing', as in 'he jealoused me'. We found a similar phenomenon. It does not mean envy, in the usual sense of someone coveting another's prized possession; rather, it is a feeling that since he or she does not enjoy success or a possession, the person who has the status or object has shamed the person who does not have it. The premise appears to be that neither should have it, rather than both. A young girl in the far west was recently taken by her father from the local government school to a private school. At the former, she was 'jealousing' the other girls by her good marks, resulting in her mental and physical abuse for letting down the non-achieving group. For these reasons, the private boarding school option is now being exercised in quite considerable numbers by Aboriginal parents, especially in the coastal towns in northern New South Wales.

Again, it is not possible to correlate jealousing and the 'tall-poppy' syndrome directly with suicide, but it is a cause of much unhappiness, especially among girls who want an education but whose families cannot afford private schooling.

Grief cycles

The cycle of grief was discussed initially in Chapter 6, in the section on 'grieving suicides'. In Australia, there is no other group of people who experience the numbers of deaths, especially early deaths and deaths from non-natural causes, as does Aboriginal society. All social indicators and vital statistics which illustrate age structures, or causes of death, or morbidity and mortality rates, support that statement. The frequency of funerals in small towns is the real yardstick of death, and of the grief that follows.

Aborigines in New South Wales observe the traditional Celtic ritual of the wake, which means more alcohol than usual. Wakes are all too common. In at least eight of the communities we visited, appointments were either deferred or changed, or even cancelled, because of funerals and their associated wakes. There is a constant cycle, or procession, of grief. There is no time to complete the grieving before another death ensues, and there is almost no grief counselling available.

A house in Bourke, formerly occupied by an Aboriginal suicide, has become something of a shrine. Youth visit there, attend the wall the deceased had painted and decorated, and vent their grief. The grave of the young man at Menindee, discussed earlier, is also a shrine and 'communion place' of a similar nature. Dr Archie Kalokerinos once told me to visit the Aboriginal cemetery at Collarenebri to see how many children under 5 were buried there, in order to appreciate the unacceptable brevity of many Aboriginal lives which so determine the poor life expectancy statistics. I did, and have since visited many other cemeteries. They are exquisite, in the sense of care, attention, grooming and decoration. They are, indeed, loving shrines. But graves and their adornment are not counselling mechanisms, and the cycles of grief need urgent attention.

In earlier visits to New Zealand, I was a guest at Maori funerals. These events were more ceremonial, certainly more ritualistic than among Aboriginal communities in this study. Protocols appear to be fully observed and there seemed, to me at least, to be a coherent orchestration of grief.

Illiteracy

There is a sense in which Frankl's purpose in life, and one's existential distress, cannot be overcome by any person, or by his or her 'pilot', without the aid of reading and writing skills. In a generally illiterate society, illiteracy may not be a hindrance. But in a society which increasingly resorts to the printed word — on paper, poster, warning sign, brochure or on screen — the audience must be capable of receiving the messages.

Any Aboriginal agency office or support service facility, such as a health counselling unit or doctor's waiting room, has more brochures than could be read (by me) in perhaps a two-hour stretch: AIDS, contraception, diabetes, renal disease, pregnancies, homophobia, childhood illnesses, inoculations, tobacco and alcohol material, drugs, antidepressants, depression, sterilisation, domestic violence, and so on. The material simply isn't read, because most of those attending cannot read. Diagrams abound but, however simply they are presented as explanations of syndromes or causal connections, they are not always understood.

Our entire service and health industry is predicated on literacy. A person consults a doctor and is given a prescription, which is then dispensed by a pharmacist. He or she labels the package with the required dosage administration at appropriate times, together with warning labels about contra-indications and avoidances, such as alcohol or driving a car, or taking medication without food. All professionals involved in the cycle assume both comprehension and compliance.

As a heart-bypass patient myself, I am inclined to discuss medication and regimens with men with a similar condition. Only one Aboriginal man was aware of dosages, frequency of intake, times of efficacy, and things or medicines to be avoided. Asked, for example, how many coated aspirin he takes, a man would typically call out to his wife to tell him, since he couldn't read the label. Often, his wife or partner would say she didn't know but would ask the doctor on the next visit, usually weeks or months ahead.

The bypass men are not likely to suicide. But youth (who do) believe they can get by with television, video pictures and picture magazines. They often mask their illiteracy or they fake literacy. School is *not* the answer. There they are regarded by teachers as hopeless, deficient, lazy, undisciplined and not worth any effort. Many drop out, and many 'muck up' in order to be expelled. In Taree, there are 32 children who did not register for high school on the first day of term: accordingly, they are in limbo because, having never signed on, they do not 'exist'. There are possibly double that number in the Coffs Harbour region. Aboriginal mothers now run special after-hours classes for these non-school-attending children, who are very much of school age.

The new federal government initiatives on illiteracy will not reach most Aboriginal youth. In Chapter 10, I expand on the literacy techniques of Ann Morrice, funded (until recently) by Bryce Courtenay's literacy foundation. She is able to achieve literacy among Aboriginal (and non-Aboriginal) people in the space of months, even weeks.

Senior decision makers have to be persuaded that, while Education Department culture and technology works for most of the population, it is inappropriate for people who, by and large, are not attending school. They also need to heed the evidence that literacy is not necessarily achieved only at or by the mid-levels of high school. In South Africa, mining companies find it imperative that all underground workers speak and read a lingua franca, called *fanagalo*, to prevent death or injury. It has a working vocabulary of 350–500 words. It is taught, and learned, in three weeks. Full literacy in English or Afrikaans often follows, in 9–12 weeks. Where there is an economic imperative, there is a way.

What is also important in this context is that Aboriginal youth have neither confidence nor trust in helping agencies. Confidence is absent for many reasons, not the least being a self-knowing inability to communicate a point of view, other than in angry four-letter invective. (Chronic obscenity is often a barometer of self-loathing.) Help to overcome self-destructive inclinations, help in achieving goals, and help in conquering distress and frustration require communication. With reading skills will come writing skills, and with both there may well be a way forward to verbal skills. These skills may not stop suicide, but they can be eliminated as a factor in the chain of causation of suicide.

Addressing and redressing the social factors

In no sense do I discuss these factors as a way of blaming the victim, or of explaining the problems as biologically, culturally or socially inherent in their Aboriginality. The danger, as mentioned at the outset, is that the material presented here will be misused by those of ill-will. There is, however, a sense in which only Aboriginal people themselves can remedy many of these contributing factors.

For much of this century, Aborigines have been *administered*. They have been moved, cajoled, coerced, disciplined, and their behaviour proscribed or prescribed. The eras of treating them solely as a 'welfare problem' have ended, with some exceptions. There is now an era of (relative) freedom and free will. Aboriginal leader Noel Pearson talks of the poison of welfare and its 'parasitic' legacy. However, a serious problem remains: that many of the legacies of what was done to Aborigines by others can now only be addressed by the victims of those actions. Many Aborigines still tend to project both blame, and redress, on to others. Importantly in this suicide context, it must be said that only Aborigines can address and redress some of these suggested causal factors. Only they can handle the alcohol issue, the parenting problems and, above all, the endemic sexual assault issue. Only they can ameliorate their internal enmities. Only they can find mentors for the young, and the older, within their own society.

Some matters require outside assistance:
- initially, the Ann Morrice literacy skills program (discussed in the final chapter), which Aboriginal teachers could adopt after a short training;
- conflict resolution skills, to confront aggressive and destructive behaviour;
- grief counselling, to be used internally after appropriate training;
- parenting skills, to be taught by Aborigines and non-Aborigines;
- life-goal aspirations, based on American and New Zealand pilot projects (discussed in the last chapter), using Aboriginal and non-Aboriginal 'mentors'.

Perhaps *will to meaning* can flow from reductions in existential distress. Aboriginal youth need the help of people of goodwill — Frankl's 'pilots'. I agree with his profound view that *none* of this is 'mental disease'. I disagree only in his choice of the medical practitioner as the quintessential pilot.

Notes

1. Frankl, *Man's Search for Meaning*, 125.
2. Stengel, *Suicide and Attempted Suicide*, 11–13.
3. House of Representatives Standing Committee on Family and Community Affairs, *Aspects of Youth Suicide*, 8–9.

8

Contributing Factors — Societal Values

The true believer in Medicine is convinced that, with modern science guarding their well-being, people have opportunities for a happy and healthy life such as they never had before: anyone who would want to leave such a life prematurely must be mad — or bad. In either case, he must be prevented from doing so.

— Thomas Szasz[1]

In a real sense, Aborigines have been invisible. In the areas of civil and human rights, society saw fit, often still sees fit, not to see them. In the domains of land settlement and squatting, of modern mining and development, for purposes of dubious law and alleged order, the exclusion from pubs, clubs and teams, society has seen fit to make them all too visible. Aborigines are simultaneously invisible and ultra-visible.

— Colin Tatz[2]

I wish to focus on some of the values in mainstream society which impinge on, or relate to, the suicides involved in this study. First, the general attitude to suicide — which is so often seen as something catastrophic, a blot or blight on society, offensive to our notions of the sanctity of life, and therefore as something to be addressed urgently through improved medical diagnosis and treatment, and new or better strategies for prevention. Second, the pervasiveness of racism in much of Aboriginal life, a burden that few other sectors or groups in society endure in their day-to-day contact with fellow Australians. Third, the perpetuation of an attitude of 'welfare colonialism', one in which Aborigines — always seen as plural or as a collective — are always dependent on the ministering services of a 'superior' society. Fourth, and allied to the third, the seeming contradiction of the 'disempowerment' of individual Aborigines even as government policies aim to 'empower' the Aboriginal 'people'.

Attitudes to suicide

Suicide is seen as an indicator of crisis in a society, a serious phenomenon most worthy of our attention. Therefore, broader questions should be asked, such as:

- Is suicide indeed at the very summit of all manners of death, requiring the considerable energy and expenditure now involved in prevention strategies?
- Why do we all respond to suicide as emotively as we do?
- Do we see it as a rejection of 'us', an affront to a civilisation we prefer to see as capable of offering hope, faith, spirituality, learned optimism, knowledge, technology?
- Is suicidal intent always a problem of ill-health, a 'mental disorder' which health care personnel can treat or prevent?
- Is suicide an act of free will which society does not want the individual to exercise?
- Does a person's life 'belong' to society at large rather than to that individual?

It is noteworthy that in the four major professions or areas dealing with suicide — sociology, law, theology and medicine — there is prejudice against suicide. In James Hillman's important book, *Suicide and the Soul*, he examines suicide, not as an exit from life but as an entrance to death. He is searching for a metaphor, befitting an analyst, which goes to the core of our ideas on death. His concept of 'soul' embraces any of the following: mind, spirit, heart, life, warmth, humanness, personality, individuality, essence, purpose, morality, sin, virtue, wisdom, death, and perhaps God. In his struggle for an understanding of the soul, he has rejected the ideas about suicide prevention inherent in sociology, law, theology and medicine. I summarise his admonitions about the attitudes of these disciplines to suicide (1997, 24–55):

- For sociology, suicide is always negative. It presents a loosening of the social structure, a weakening of group bonds, and disintegration. 'As an open enemy of society, suicide must be opposed and prevented … suicide prevention for sociology means group reinforcement, which of course reinforces the root metaphor of sociology itself.'
- Roman law, church law and English law declared suicide criminal. Again, Hillman argues, prevention is the main end in view. In law, death is 'an act of God' and a *'force majeure'*. Durkheim noted that, in most instances, 'the causes of death are outside rather than within us'. Thus, the law recognises death as something emanating from without. To take one's own life, to originate death from within, is neither *'force majeure'* nor an 'act of God', 'but a one-sided abrogation of

contract', and thus a breach of the law. Western law has judged suicide from the viewpoint that man belongs first to God, then to King, then last to himself. There are many instances of justifiable homicide, at the behest of God, King or in self-defence; however, until very recently, the law prohibited being 'mine own executioner'. Insanity thus became the only loophole.

- The three monotheistic (Abrahamic) religions have their root metaphor in Creation: 'Almighty God created life. It is His. We are, therefore, not our own makers, and so we cannot take our lives because they are not ours.'

- As to medicine, the root metaphor above and beyond all others is to 'promote physical well-being, that is, life'. He contends that, in the present era, it has come to mean not just promotion of life but *the prolonging of life*. Suicide, or the threat of self-death, cries for 'the immediate action of locks and drugs and constant surveillance — treatment usually reserved for criminals'. Good life equals more life. The physician, he says, 'is obliged to postpone death with every weapon he can command'. Suicide is death, the arch-enemy. Accordingly, there can be no objectivity about suicide in the medical approach.

Thomas Szasz, a radical and often disparaged psychiatrist, has long supported Hillman in asking that we re-examine our attitudes to suicide. Al Alvarez, David Lester and, more recently, Mark Williams have put forward cogent arguments which confront the restricted views of suicide as madness or badness, as being near-criminal, as a condition warranting coercive treatment or special strategies such as prevention agencies. Szasz condemns R.E. Schulman, an American lawyer and psychologist, who argues that even if a person does not value his life, society does and is entitled to preserve it. Schulman insists that suicide 'surely falls within the province of the law': he calls suicide 'self-murder'.[3] Szasz disapproves of Phillip Solomon for treating the would-be suicide as an unruly child. Solomon wrote that physicians 'must protect the patient from his own [suicidal] wishes'. Szasz is even harsher on Shneidman, who says that 'suicide prevention is like fire prevention', which Szasz contends reduces the would-be suicide 'to the level of a tree' in a forest fire! Szasz quotes a telling passage from Stefan Zweig, the renowned Austrian writer and biographer, who committed suicide in 1942. In Zweig's novella, *Amok*, his protagonist says:

Ah, yes, 'It's one's duty to help.' That's your favourite maxim, isn't it?
... Thank you for your good intentions, but I'd rather be left to myself
... Sir, I won't trouble you to call, if you don't mind. Among the 'rights of man' there is a right which no one can take away, the right to croak when and where and how one pleases, without a 'helping hand'.[4]

In citing these authors, I am being neither anti-medicine nor anti-prevention. Rather, I suggest a reconsideration of our approach towards suicide, customarily seen as something so horrific that, even though it occurs far less frequently than other deaths, we have to marshal enormous resources to cope with, and prevent, it. In too many instances, we label suicide as resulting from 'depression'. Suicidal behaviour is not always within the domain of mental ill-health. We need serious reflection on why we react to suicide the way we do, why we perceive youth suicide as more calamitous than, for example, young deaths on motorbikes or in fast cars, or from drug-taking. We need to ask why we continue to be so affronted, or confronted, by those who would rather not remain, with us, in life.

Endemic racism

Aboriginal children — unlike disenchanted, dislocated and disaffected non-Aboriginal youth — are socialised from birth to an endemic and all-pervasive racism. This racism originates in a perception that Aborigines are different because of their physical attributes, such as colour and facial features. These differences are then equated with social characteristics, such as stereotyped notions of culture or lifestyle. These physical–social characteristics are then considered socially significant and inferior. And then, most importantly, the perceiver believes he is therefore *justified* either in having negative attitudes towards people with those physically based social attributes, or in taking some action against them.

Racism is more than prejudice. The latter is a mind-set, a mere predisposition. In the thirteenth century, St Thomas Aquinas phrased it as 'thinking ill of others without sufficient warrant'. Racism is prejudice which is then acted upon.

In a hostile world, every racial or ethnic minority, every marginalised group in society, learns to cope with an all-pervasive discrimination if they are to survive and flourish. Many racially discriminatory attitudes and practices are passively accepted, absorbed and, in effect, tolerated by the defined group. Other attitudes and practices, which are more direct and hurtful, cannot readily be handled or shrugged off as 'a fact of life'. The dilemma for the oppressed is to find an acceptable way of coping.

Employment

In several of the towns in this study, a number of men in their 40s and 50s talked to us, often with pride and pleasure, about their years of employment as stockmen, sheep-shearers, fencing contractors, vegetable-pickers and cotton-chippers. They tended to see themselves as a dying breed, with few similar options now available to them or to their children. Jobs are now perceived almost exclusively as CDEP occupations, limited by budgets, profit opportunities which may come from good contracts, or by CDEP programs which are often not really work but simply the occupation of time.

Jobs are now seen in terms of what is available within exclusively Aboriginal communities, not within the mainstream. While CDEP commends itself as occupation which restores pride and dignity, it nevertheless has a negative value in that it denies people any incentive, and further closes off the already limited outside world.

Jobs in towns for young Aboriginal males and females are rare. In 1997, only two Aboriginal girls in Moree had supermarket checkout jobs, and no boys were employed by town enterprises. (Initiatives by Aborigines in 2000 saw a marked change in this employment profile.) In Narrabri, an Aboriginal girl could not obtain work experience in a retail shop, the owner confessing (with chagrin) to the girl's mother, an old school friend, that he would lose customers if the daughter was seen 'up front' in the store. In 1997, a bright young man in Gunnedah, with a Higher School Certificate, made 53 unsuccessful job applications. In one coastal town, the meatworks, with a staff of over a thousand, employs only three Aboriginal men. However, the town boasts an Aboriginal watchmaker.

This pattern pervades New South Wales. The employment of Aborigines exposes them to, among other things, rejection by the non-Aboriginal society with whom they must deal in their day-to-day work. So they become reliant on extremely limited opportunities and resources. The only world, outside of the CDEP world, into which they can move is the sphere of support services — for Aborigines. In our study, there were perhaps 60 men (and two women) employed by the police service as ACLOs. The list of people who were interviewed shows the available agency employment: land councils, legal aid services, medical services, Aboriginal corporations, mental health units, Aboriginal rehabilitation centres, and so on. While no Aborigines or non-Aborigines could complain about Aboriginal staff servicing their own organisations, it has to be recognised that that is the only service employment available to them. Exclusions and restrictions, once enforced by law, have been maintained through continuing social attitudes and values.

Earlier in this book, I wrote that unemployment and unemployment benefits are now a norm in Aboriginal life. These financial benefits do not remove from Aboriginal youth the feelings of alienation and exclusion. They see themselves as unwanted in mainstream Australian society. And even though there is group 'togetherness' in this sense of rejection, and a degree of social integration in being a band of unemployed or unemployable youth, there is still the overwhelming Durkheimian sense of social isolation.

Housing

Without exception, every town in this study had a shortage of Aboriginal housing. Every informant insisted that real estate agents discriminated against prospective Aboriginal tenants. A few agents denied this, and when I published a newspaper feature in December 1997 which referred to this, I received several long letters of 'correction' and denunciation from aggrieved townspeople. (There are ways in which housing discrimination can be empirically tested, but this must be left to others.) Because the Aboriginal evidence was often highly specific as to names, places and date, my disposition is to accept it.

Housing has always been an acute problem. Aboriginal housing authorities and funding bodies really do not know how many people to cater for. Available houses are constructed as standard Western homes, predicated on nuclear families of one set of parents and perhaps three children. Rarely have projects encompassed the structure of extended Aboriginal family life. Overcrowding, lack of privacy (such as a desk at which to study), and lack of personal space produce an element of 'claustrophobia'. Certainly, as the young people insist, it produces a need for space — which means the streets.

Sport

Elsewhere I have discussed the importance of sport in Aboriginal life, arguing that sport is more essential in sustaining Aboriginal life than it is in non-Aboriginal society.[5] Sport has also been a major factor in reducing Aboriginal juvenile delinquency: where there is active competition, and access to it, delinquency declines. In the absence of competition, delinquency escalates quite markedly (Tatz 1994b).

Sport is relevant to the suicide pattern, in the sense that it is purposive and purposeful. It has simple, clear goals; it has well-worn and well-known methods of achieving them; it has inbuilt mechanisms for belonging, for loyalty and for treating disloyalty; it has uniforms which signify true membership and equality; it has elaborate ritual and its own special idiom; it has support groups, fans, audiences; it has, always, the promise of rewards at best, of improvement at least. In 1995, I wrote that the Wilcannia Boomerangs and their victories provided some kind of *raison d'être* in a town where purposelessness and meaninglessness pervade.

My 1994 sport–delinquency study discussed the absence of sporting facilities and lack of access to organised competition in many communities. I drew attention to the relative absence of delinquency and suicidal behaviours in towns with active sport: in particular, Nguiu (Bathurst Island) and Barunga (Bamyili) in the Northern Territory; Port Lincoln and Gerard in South Australia; Cherbourg in Queensland; and Condobolin in New South Wales. However, despite increased attention to Aboriginal sport by the Australian Sports Commission — which has effectively taken over sports funding from ATSIC — there has been a marked regression since my 1989–91 fieldwork.

Facilities in towns vary. The Gingie Reserve near Walgett has an 'oval' covered in scrub, with no goalposts; Moree has the use, for a large leasing fee, of an oval with lights. Grounds, equipment and travel money are hard to come by, and expensive, but the most serious problem of all is lack of opponents. The exclusion of the Australian football team, Coomealla, from the Millewa League in 1993 meant that Aborigines in the Dareton–Wentworth area no longer had competition sport. 'Unduly rough play' and 'language' were cited as reasons for the expulsion. In Bourke, non-Aboriginal youths recently switched from Australian football to rugby union in order to avoid Aborigines. In 1998, the Aboriginal team, which had been expelled from the football league, was readmitted on appeal, whereupon the other teams withdrew from the competition. The (then) local police commander in Bourke guaranteed to meet half the travel costs of these teams, to prevent spectator violence and to ban alcohol from the matches — to no avail. The Moree league team has found itself in a situation of being banned 'for life'.[6] Sometimes the problem is not this kind of racism, but a shortage of resources. In 1997–98, Menindee could not muster a team, which meant that the Group 12 competition, to which they belonged, ceased, leaving Wilcannia also without sport.

Funding for junior sport is a serious problem. Without exception, parents claimed that the costs of junior sport — for shoes, equipment, travel and registration fees — are beyond their means. Some service personnel claim that, since there is money for alcohol, there should be money for sport. There is little point in debating choices: the people spending the money are exercising their preferences, and the money in question is social service benefit money, the bulk of which is unemployment relief, which in turn is deliberately predicated below a level which would be self-sustaining.

The role of Police and Community Youth Clubs

The newer name for the once-popular Police Boys Clubs system is Police and Community Youth Clubs, or PCYCs. Most major towns and urban centres have such clubs, until 1999 run by police staff in a separate administrative unit. Most clubs have a staff of two and operate in buildings ranging from the palatial, as in the ex-Returned Servicemen's Club building in Port Macquarie, to the cramped and under-equipped. Each club has a board, comprising interested citizens. Sponsorships and donations must be sought, and operational funds raised. The police staff are paid by the police service.

I have long been an admirer of the work done by, in my view, underpaid and ill-recognised youth workers. They come to the job with little training and no avenues of promotion. The officer who seeks PCYC work is seen by colleagues to be stepping outside the lines of promotion. During my fieldwork, the police service commissioned an inquiry into the future of PCYCs. Most staff were jittery about the outcome, fearing the truth of a rumour that they were either to be closed down, or the service operated and staffed solely by civilians. In the end, the decision was that PCYCs would continue with police staff but that the officers in each club would come under part of the area or local commander's staff, to be directed as to the time spent in PCYC work or in general police duties.

PCYCs are often 'the only game in town'. Clubs — with staff, gyms, playing areas, equipment, sometimes fields — are open seven days a week, with very low membership fees. The staff are often the closest that Aboriginal youth come to having 'enlightened witnesses' in their lives: people who see them regularly, who observe patterns of dysfunctional or reactive behaviour, and who are aware of their lack of food and their poor health. These clubs are the greatest opportunity for an intimate, non-confrontational interaction between Aboriginal youth and the police. It is a relationship *capable* of producing care and trust, of 'witness' and assistance.

There are, however, negative aspects. Several PCYCs are inappropriately staffed. Some staff are uninterested and bored. Some even dislike Aborigines. Some try hard, but their clubs are in areas remote from Aboriginal living, or in areas where Aborigines feel ill at ease. Some officers have taken their services to a community hall in areas where Aborigines live, as in Tamworth, since the youngsters will not come to them. One former senior PCYC officer, now on general duties in Kempsey, organised a mobile PCYC, a large truck fitted out with movable equipment, and computers on board for driving-licence instruction. The truck moves to where the youth are, and where they are more likely to respond, especially to the 'sausage sizzler' that travels with the unit. Some officers, as in Bathurst, collect the youngsters, provide an early morning meal, deliver them to their schools, and run afternoon homework classes. The

Port Macquarie club provides a bag of chips and a sandwich for a dollar and, if payment is not possible, accepts help in the kitchen in exchange.

Some PCYC officers have sought permission to give lectures on suicide to schools. They have been refused, allegedly on the ground that the school has a counsellor on staff and that to talk openly about suicide 'might put ideas into kids' heads'. The PCYC concept could be the most important agency for monitoring behaviour, mitigating it, and at the same time providing an alternative to the boredom that besets so many youth in country towns. The reality is that most Aboriginal youngsters avoid these clubs, claiming that fees are too high, the premises too far away, and the regimens too formal.

The attitudes of police service personnel

The people who have most dealings with Aborigines are the police. There is an important historical dimension. The *Aborigines Protection Act 1909* created a Board for the Protection of Aborigines, with the Inspector-General of Police (later, the Commissioner) as chairman *ex officio*. The Board's task was to distribute blankets and food, to maintain 'the custody, maintenance and education of children of Aborigines', and to 'exercise a general supervision and care over all matters affecting the interests and welfare of Aborigines'. In 1936, 'any Aborigine (or person apparently having an admixture of Aboriginal blood) living, in the Board's opinion, in unsanitary or undesirable conditions, can be ordered by a stipendiary magistrate to a reserve'. The Act was not repealed until 1969. Most of the statutory power to 'supervise', protect and remove to reserves lay with the police.

When 'freedom' came after the repeal of special legislation, and especially after the 1972 federal election, police resented the loss of their role in Aboriginal matters. For nearly two decades, police in general railed against Aboriginal legal aid: here was 'intrusion' into the police domain and 'defiance' of the authoritative and authoritarian police regulation of Aboriginal conduct.

In an ironic sense, little has changed. Police no longer have a formal or statutory role in Aboriginal affairs. Many police officers now cooperate with, and even applaud, the work of legal aid and similar agencies. A remarkable change in police culture has taken place since my first ventures into Aboriginal centres, and even since my 1989–91 fieldwork. The 'new breed' say the right things, for the most part, and often do the right things. Officers with inappropriate attitudes remain in some sensitive locations, but there is a much greater sense of police being 'on side'. The irony, as I see it, is that the only people who are available to communities exhibiting distress signals are the police, whom most Aborigines still purport to despise and distrust.

Most police stations operate 24 hours a day, seven days a week. Much of the violence, especially of the domestic kind, occurs over weekends. The only resource people available are police, who need to act as social workers, mediators, confessors, and 'dampeners' where possible. Most police object to these roles, contending that they lack the necessary formal training or skills. Be that as it may, it is the ACLOs who take the burden of this work. It is this body of men and women who suffer gross overload and who are under-rewarded, in salary and status, for the work they do.

The allegation by Aborigines and by police is that the normal 'welfare' agencies — the departments of community services, juvenile justice, health, the mental health units—'switch on their answering machines at 4 p.m. on a Friday and switch them off again at 9 a.m. on a Monday'. The proffered justifications are budget restrictions and cuts in overtime, but it leaves the police, especially ACLOs, as the only personnel — apart from ambulance and hospital casualty staff — able to respond to calls for help.

Service providers tend to see Aborigines in the generic plural rather than as singular or individual. 'They', 'them', 'these people'—common phrasings — are treated, not only as being 'different' but as a collective, exhibiting group symptoms and problems and, clearly, requiring 'group solutions'. There are instances of one-on-one relationships, such as in treatment or therapy contexts. A number of such relationships are caring ones, often commented on as such by Aboriginal patients or clients. But there remains a deep-seated and pervasive sense that Aboriginal communities have one set of values, needs, wants, behaviours and responses. The *communitas* model, discussed in Chapter 2, is misconceived, inaccurate and inappropriate as a way of proceeding towards strategies in any field, let alone the complex area of suicide.

'Disempowerment'

Empowerment means giving someone the authority to act. To 'disempower' is to remove that authorisation. However, it has come to mean that a person has no sense of confidence in his or her ability to make decisions unaided. If power is intended in its political, or Weberian, sense of a person being able to exert his or her will in competition with others, then 'disempowerment' can, at a stretch, be taken to mean 'powerless', or the condition of powerlessness.

In Chapter 6, I discussed various categories of suicide which may arise from this sense of powerlessness. The desire or the need to express autonomy, or 'selfhood', for perhaps the only time in their lives — even, or only, by the act of suicide — is a possible explanation for some forms of self-destruction. I also discussed existential suicide, embracing as it does the notion of hopelessness and futility.

In the broader sense, there is communal 'disempowerment'. In the 1960s and early 1970s, the late Professor Charles Rowley and I declared that what Aborigines needed was 'more lawyers and fewer welfare officers'. We meant that legal recourse, to discover and recover rights, was a better avenue than the 'welfare' model, and the best way for Aboriginal people to go forward was to protect themselves by forming associations or corporations with distinct artificial legal personalities. The legal cocoons provided by incorporation would make the 'naked individuals' less susceptible to treatment meted out by government agencies. Western society has always had greater respect for corporate power than for individual rights. Thus, we argued, there could well be greater respect arising from contests initiated by 'organisation' people, rather than from conflicts waged by individual men and women.

From the early 1970s, Aboriginal groups began their systematic incorporation as legal associations. By 1996, the *National Directory of Aboriginal and Torres Strait Islander Organisations* occupied 511 pages, subdividing land rights and councils; community groups; community aid groups; housing and accommodation bodies; women's groups; preschools and day-care centres; employment, education and training organisations; and legal and civil rights associations. The *Directory* is incomplete, but New South Wales has at least 108 land councils, 50 community corporations, 62 housing associations, 22 women's group associations, 34 health corporations, 35 preschool bodies, 43 educational and training associations, and 25 legal aid and/or advice bureaux. A safe figure is 400 corporations, servicing a population of about 109,000 people (producing a somewhat absurd-looking statistic of one corporation per 272 people). These are in addition to the services provided by the regular governmental agencies.

It seems that Rowley and I were wrong in one unexpected sense. The plethora of associations has led, not to 'empowerment' but to 'disempowerment'. The associations, albeit with detailed mission statements and articles of incorporation defining their reasons for being, compete for a share of what they call 'the money bucket'. That bucket is finite. Jurisdictions or agendas often overlap. ATSIC and other authorising bodies are reluctant to refuse requests for association status, and all too often one clan decides it wants to form an association because of factionalism. Either for unintended and unforeseen reasons, or, as some Aborigines would have it, for 'divide-and-conquer' reasons, these associations can be divisive rather than cohesive, antagonistic rather than cooperative, 'jealousing' rather than moving forward.

The structure of Aboriginal corporate bodies causes additional problems. They are based on a Western legal template for corporate organisation, with agendas, meetings, quorums, minutes, presidents, vice-presidents, treasurers, auditors. It is an alien template that has been imposed, as such structures are rarely consonant with (what were) traditional methods of decision making. Those in positions of power claim they have neither the time nor the patience to construct more culturally appropriate mechanisms. However, this essentially assimilationist philosophy — which insists that the 'colonised' accommodate to metropolitan models and values — has long bedevilled Aboriginal administration.

Deloria argues that American Indian corporations are the new tribe, one that should aim at ensuring as beneficial a life as possible for its members. He sees it as a 'technical weapon by which Indian revivalism can be accomplished'. Importantly, 'at the same time it is that element of white culture closest to the tribe and can thereby enable it to understand both white and Indian ways of doing business'. Aborigines, like Amerindians, can absorb the corporation 'as a handy tool for its own purposes' (1988, 230–42). I agree. But the sadness is that most corporations are still too heavily engaged in 'siege and fortress' activity, of meeting deadlines set by white agencies and of beating off financial investigations.

The other sadness is that Aboriginal children are rejecting the corporation life. These are the children whose parents occupy senior, paid positions. These youth are children of *literate* parents: yet many demonstrate their preference for illiteracy, and for *not* following parental footsteps and progress up the mobility ladder. Several young informants said they hate the in-fighting, the power play and the internecine strife involved in this corporation world. For these young people, this alien world of power, prestige, income, status and skill is to be avoided.

Notes

1. Szasz, *The Second Sin*, 85. Thomas Szasz is a practising psychiatrist and academic in the State University of New York. There is much disapproval of his style, manner, sharp pen and gadfly interests, and there is a great deal of controversy, especially among the more conservative, about his often logical attacks on what he calls 'the theology of medicine'. Szasz has written

strongly about medicine's attitude to suicide, and I have come to share some of his values.

2. Tatz, *Obstacle Race*, 24; see also Tatz and Tatz, *Black Gold*.

3. This is interesting terminology: a dozen European languages use variations of the German *selbstmord*, and the Dutch *zelfmoord*. In Afrikaans, the word is *selfmoord*; in Danish and Norse, *selvmord*; in Swedish, *självmord*; in Serbian, *samebistvon* and in Hungarian, *öngyilkosság*, which is, literally, 'self-murder'.

4. Schulman, Solomon, Shneidman and Zweig, all quoted in Szasz, *The Theology of Medicine*, 68–85.

5. Tatz, *Obstacle Race*, ch. 13, 'Sport and Survival'.

6. The ban, as of 1998, was from the Group 4 rugby league competition. Group 4 was the home of the Moree Boomerangs team in the 1980s. In November 2000, Group 4 voted to readmit the Aborigines under certain conditions. In January 2001, the Group executive decided *not* to overturn the 1998 motion on their books. The Boomerangs had, in the meantime, secured a sponsorship, introduced a code of conduct and placed a ten-year ban on alcohol at its matches — to no avail.

9
Lessons from Abroad

Understanding is never a collective phenomenon. It is based on sympathy, on intimate knowledge, on participation. It depends upon a communication of souls and is appropriate to the human encounter, whereas explanation belongs to the viewpoint of the natural sciences. Understanding attempts to stay with the moment as it is, while explanation leads away from the present, backwards into a chain of causality, or sideways into comparisons.

— James Hillman[1]

Unfortunately, Professor Tatz appears to be unaware of data demonstrating a high degree of prevalence of mental disorders in those who have suicided in a number of different countries, including indigenous groups in Taiwan and also, more recently, in a diverse population in India.

— Robert Goldney[2]

Comparative suicide studies

Much of my professional life has been devoted to comparative studies: in race politics and, later, in genocide studies. Comparison may not bring understanding, but an examination of similarities and differences can help us to learn and to distil some general principles, always with the aim of improving or, idealistically, ameliorating or preventing racist and genocidal behaviour.

I am less certain about the value of comparison in suicidology. As Hillman contends, to compare is to move sideways: it deflects from the path towards understanding, and it decorates rather than illuminates the heart of the matter.

First published in 1965, the second edition of Hillman's *Suicide and the Soul* has a 'Postscript of Afterthoughts'. Discussing who owns the soul, he says he tires of the individual versus collective argument:

We need a wider context that embraces both. So, this Postscript proposes the anima mundi [literally, the soul of the world] as that context, and a definition of self as the interiorization of community. Suicide, literally 'self-killing', now would mean both a killing of community and involvement of community in the killing. (1997, 198–200)

Just as Dr Jack Kevorkian's assisted suicide campaign in the United States has very publicly opened the issue, so Hillman pleads that suicide should be judged 'by some community court', comprising legal, medical, aesthetic, religious and philosophical interests, as well as by family and friends. In this way, self-death can 'come out of the closet'. The act of suicide will still remain individualistic, but assessment of the suicide as part of, or interior to, a community may help to liberate Western civilisation's 'persecutory panic' when suicide, or the threat of suicide, arises. We must, he concludes, get away from 'police action, lockups, criminalization of helpers, dosages to dumbness'.

In this context, it is worth seeking some lessons from abroad — from communities which *may* approximate, but which can never parallel, let alone be identical to, diverse Aboriginal communities. If it could be shown that mental disorders figure prominently, or at all, in Aboriginal suicide, then there may be cause for examining the prevalence of mental disorders among suicides in indigenous populations in Taiwan and in 'diverse populations in India'. But since, as I have shown in earlier chapters, there is a large body of evidence in the literature that it is in social and political contexts that we are most likely to find explanation, Taiwan and India hardly come within the comparative social and historical ambits of North American Indians, Brazilian Indians, Maori, Pacific Islanders, or black South Africans.

South Africa

South African literature provides a little insight into Aboriginal suicide. The demography and the politics, and even the nature of the racial discrimination and oppression, are so different that direct comparison is not appropriate. However, some pointers can be obtained from South African research.

Alan Flisher and others (1992, 77–80) report what is possibly the world's highest rate of adolescent mortality from external causes: 56.8 per cent of 16,348 deaths between the years 1984 and 1986. The researchers pointed to the 'far-reaching social and political changes that [even then] were taking place in South Africa, resulting in instability and, hence, health-damaging behaviour (such as substance abuse and interpersonal violence)'. A high urbanisation rate exposes teenagers to road accidents, the commonest form of death among the adolescents. 'Risk-taking behaviour may contribute to these deaths.'

Flisher and his colleagues then studied risk-taking behaviour in a sample of 7340 Cape Peninsula students in all racial groups from 16 high schools (1993, 469–73). They combine an interesting, if not curious, set of risk-taking behaviours: suicide, cigarette-smoking, alcohol use, drug use, road behaviour and sexual behaviour. A comprehensive theoretical framework, incorporating the psychological, social and environmental dimensions of adolescent health behaviour, was used. In search of a syndrome of risk behaviour, they sought instances of attempted suicide within 12 months of the administration of the research instrument. Of the 7340 students,

- 19 per cent had 'seriously thought about harming themselves in a way that might result in their death';
- 12.4 per cent had told someone that they intended to end their lives; and
- 7.8 per cent had actually attempted suicide.[3]

In the period 1984–86, the suicide rate for youth aged 15–24 was 25.75 per 100,000 for white males and 9.5 for white females. For black Africans, it was a low 2.3 and 1.1, respectively.[4]

The lowest incidence of suicidal feeling in the high-school study was among the Xhosa-speaking black youth. The researchers attribute this 'to the adverse social circumstances of these students'. They quote Lester as arguing that suicide is less likely where people have an outside source to blame for their misery. Other factors might be cultural taboos, the prevalence of relatively close family ties, and 'a propensity for expressing emotions in somatic [physical or bodily] terms'.

Mayekiso, at the black University of Transkei, reports on the paucity of research among black youth. In a study of 80 adolescents, aged 15–19, at the Ngangelizwe High School at Umtata, he found 'perceived causes of adolescent suicide'.[5] The results are fascinating:

- 100 per cent did not approve of suicide in principle;
- 64 per cent did not consider suicide an option; and
- 36 per cent said suicide was an acceptable option in certain circumstances.

Students were asked what they perceived to be the causes of suicide:

Causes	Per cent
Impulse	8
Teenage pregnancy	22
Loss of loved one	6
Conflict with parents	38

Peer group conflict	1
School problems	1
Love relationship problems	8
Financial problems	11
Substance abuse	5

More interesting were the reasons advanced which deterred individuals from self-destroying:

Answers	Per cent
Concern about their parents	26
Fear of God's punishment	25
Concern about other family members	13
Fear of death	7
Hope for a solution	14
Social support	5

His conclusion is *'suicide is generally unacceptable to Blacks'*.

The South African material is refreshing in that it seeks an understanding of suicide from within the living adolescent cohort. However, several aspects of this research are, regrettably, simply not possible in Australia. First, there is a Christian aspect to black African lives which is uncommon among Aboriginal Australians. The virtues of virginity until Christian marriage, the sanctity of indissoluble marriage and the fear of God's punishment are not part of Aboriginal mores. Second, the Flisher and Mayekiso studies are based on questionnaires, self-administered by youth, in their mother tongues. Africans prize education. In the pre- and post-apartheid eras, learning is revered and is seen as the avenue to social mobility and betterment. It is highly unlikely that Aboriginal teenagers would respond to such questionnaires, administered in high schools which most perceive as being 'alien' — places in which most would rather not be.

Finally, Flisher tells me that black suicide may well increase with the advent of black majority rule. The centuries-long 'struggle'— an overarching and overwhelming force in African life — is, in theory, at an end. Misery as struggle against an all-too-visible and powerful enemy is one thing: plain misery is another. If Flisher, Lester and I are correct, then inculpation of 'the system' means extending blame for one's pain onto others, thus providing an explanation for one's misery. It seems contradictory, then, that Aborigines, who almost universally locate blame on factors outside of themselves, commit suicide in such numbers. Although I have always argued that alienation is a spur to achievement, or at least to survival, Aboriginal suicide occurs despite a world replete with alienation of every kind.

Canada and the United States

The literature on suicide among Native American and Canadian Indian, Alaskan Native and Canadian Inuit has grown remarkably in the past decade. In 1989, for example, David Lester's *Suicide from a Sociological Perspective* covered New Mexico Indian suicides in three pages; in 1997, he was moved to publish a full-length book on *Suicide in American Indians*. Indian suicide is increasing each year.

In 1994, the American and Alaska Native Mental Health Research Center published the proceedings of a major conference. *Calling from the Rim* may well be the most important and coherent account of youth suicide among indigenous peoples. Dozens of medical and psychiatric journal papers cite quite diverse rates of Indian suicide within tribal groups, while others point to sharp differences in prevalence between tribes.

As discriminating as these studies appear to be, there remains the problem of the all-embracing title of 'tribe'. *Custer Died for Your Sins* by Vine Deloria Jr, a well-known Indian rights advocate and a former executive director of the National Congress of American Indians, remains the most searing, and unrebutted, indictment of American Indian policy, and of white academic attitudes, especially those of anthropologists. He deplores the Little Big Horn and wigwam stereotyping of his people, and I suspect that, while he has not written specifically about suicide, his admonitions of anthropology would apply as strongly to suicidology. In essence, he condemns academe for creating 'unreal' Indians in their attempts to establish 'real' Indians. Thus, the 'bicultural people', the 'folk people', the 'drink-too-much people', the 'warriors-without-weapons people', the 'between-two-worlds people' are academic constructs imposed on a people who then came to believe, and live out, these external perceptions. Deloria reminds us that when academics talk of the Chippewas, the Sioux or the Potawatomi, they appear not to recognise that 'there are nineteen different Chippewa tribes, fifteen Sioux tribes, four Potawatomi tribes', and so on (1988, 17).

Anthropology may well have committed many 'sins' against Indian peoples. But the anthropological approach at least attempted to get to know 'their' people and 'their' tribes. Other social science and medical disciplines have adopted a distant, statistical approach, even where there are attempts at differentiation between reservation and non-reservation residents, as in a Manitoba study (Malchy et al 1997). There is no detail of lifestyle difference, only difference in geographic domain. In short, there is no context — social, historical, political — provided in these studies, apart from stating the inevitably obvious that these communities are impoverished, with high rates of unemployment, and so on.

Every study is concerned about under-reporting and about inadequate protocols for identification. The 'Manitoba aboriginal' paper states that 'suicide among aboriginal people cannot be studied through the use of such traditional data sources as vital statistics records, since ethnic background is not recorded on the death certificates in any jurisdiction'.

Every study reports more attempts by females, but makes an important point that clustering is commoner among females and that more females succeed in their purpose when among the cluster. Without being explicit, there is a strong message that attempted suicide by female youth is in need of serious attention.

The following summary gives us an overall picture of annual rates of youth suicide per 100,000 of a Native American and Canadian Indian, Alaskan Native and Canadian Inuit population generally, or for particular periods:

- The rate per 100,000 for Shoshone and Bannocks in Idaho is now 98, but it was as high as 173 in the period 1972–78 (May 1995, 8).
- The Shoshone rate for the United States is 100 (Lester 1997, 14).
- The rates vary enormously: from 4 for the Lumbee in North Carolina to as high as 230 for Shoshone-Arapaho (Lester 1997, 131).
- The rates in New Mexico range from 175 for the Apache, to 46 for the Navajo and 79 for the Pueblo.[6]
- The Indian rates for Yukon, Alberta and Saskatchewan are 62, 52 and 35, respectively.
- The Manitoba rate is 32, but there are interesting differences between those living on the reserve, 84, and those off the reserve, 60. Noteworthy is that the rate is 5 in the 10–14 age cohort, 22 in those aged 15–19, and 56 in those aged 20–24 (Malchy et al 1997, 1135).
- Canada, as a whole, has an Indian suicide rate of 38, compared with the national rate of 14.
- In the Alaskan town of Alakanuk, in a population of 550, there were 8 suicides in a 16-month period, a figure which would equate to a rate some 20 to 24 times the national figure.[7]
- The Alaskan attempted suicide rates are alarming: in 1971–77, between 205 and 302 per 100,000. Between 100 and 251 youth had to be hospitalised. The Indian male rate of attempted suicide is 2.7 times the national figure; the female rate is 7.5 times the national rate (Lester 1997, 23–6).

Lester provides the best statistical summary of youth suicide, albeit with data at least a decade old. Despite regional differences, there is a sameness about many of the figures and ostensible causes. The 'indigenous' rates are at least *ten times higher* than the national rates. The attempted suicides are vastly more prevalent.

Lester admits the unreliability of standard psychology tests when used with Native American and Canadian Indians. His checklist of the 'standard' underlying factors is similar to the one in common use in Australia and in New Zealand: depression, hopelessness, immaturity, aggressiveness, a history of suicidal behaviour, psychiatric problems, substance abuse, parent and family conflict, lack of family support, physical and sexual abuse, and recent stress. He lists the sociological factors as social disintegration, cultural conflict and family breakdown. However, he adds, 'rarely is cultural conflict listed among the precipitating causes'. It is not clear whether he is being critical of that omission or whether he, himself, believes it not to be significant.

David Bechtold is one of the few researchers who talks about 'culturally sensitive risk factors' for males aged 12-plus:

- physical and intellectual developmental precocity (in the 12–14 age group);
- conceptual maturity regarding death;
- conceptual familiarity with suicide through family or peer group or media exposure;
- substance abuse, depression, antisocial behaviour;
- previous suicide gestures and attempts;
- cultural mismatch between the youth and the environment;
- suicidogenic messages from family, especially parents;
- family disruption and dysfunction;
- availability of lethal means.

Bechtold is the only author I have read who may have read Deloria. He is concerned about the negative impact of suicide publicity and asks how one establishes unequivocal moral proscriptions against suicide without calling undue attention to suicide. He also asks whether we can delineate a generalisable, culturally relevant set of risk factors for Native American and Canadian Indian people. 'Or do we have to do it by tribe or clan? Is tribal-specific research methodologically possible?'[8] Deloria's plea is for 'a leave-us-alone-law'; 'what we need is a cultural leave-us-alone agreement, in spirit and in fact' (1988, 27).

What we can learn from this brief excursion into North America is that there may well be room for a philosophy which is neither proactive nor intrusive, one which waits patiently until one is asked to intervene, to explain or, better still, to understand. Of all human behaviours, suicide may, however, just possibly be the one that *always* needs attention, that cannot be ignored and left alone, but which needs attention of a very different kind from the strategies commonly proffered at present.

The Pacific Islands

Geoffrey White has a valuable metaphor in relation to suicide studies: 'The international literature is full of studies which have compared suicide rates of different nations or social groups, as if this was a more or less straightforward way of taking a society's pulse' (Hezel et al 1985, 2–12). In many ways, the 1984 conference on suicide in the Pacific, held at the East-West Center in Honolulu, provided a salutary lesson about the reasons why we should broaden suicide studies by subjecting them to analysis by academics from different disciplines, with different approaches.

This is not the place to summarise all the commentaries and reports on Pacific suicide. I touch only on those aspects which could be useful in Australia and New Zealand.

The 'Pacific' in this set of studies includes the Northern Mariana Islands, the Marshalls, the Federated States of Micronesia, Nauru, Kiribati, Western and American Samoa, Fiji, Tonga, Vanuatu, the Solomons, New Caledonia, Tuvalu, Tokelau, and Papua New Guinea. While there are significant variations in suicide causes and methods, it is clear that many Pacific suicides have little to do with the 'pulse' of Western, industrialised societies. For example, among the Truk (in the Caroline Islands) and the Samoans, young male suicide is closely associated with parent–child relationships and specific cultural routines for communicating about conflict. In other words, 'suicide is a social action which usually involves not just a single individual, but an entire family or community'. This is what Hillman says is true of all suicide, but something which most of us, in the West, refuse to acknowledge.

In each of the Pacific regions, there are 'reasonably coherent explanations' of suicide, based in traditional patterns of culture. Researchers understand the customary manner of dealing with emotion and conflict and the traditional manner of achieving a resolution. 'Cultural concepts shape suicide as a meaningful social action.' White concludes his overview with the strong assertion 'that a concern with cultural meaning is not separate from medical or public health concerns with suicide prevention'. No one who is ignorant of cultural interpretations of suicide can deal effectively with the 'complexities of either suicide counselling or prevention'.

Western Samoa is of particular interest because many of the islanders have migrated to New Zealand, where suicide of a similar kind to that of the homeland is evident. This takes the form of young males and females swallowing paraquat, a weed-killer which causes a painful, lingering, untreatable death. In the 1980s, the Western Samoan male rate for the

25–34 age group reached 167 per 100,000, and for 20- to 24-year-olds it was 76 (Hezel et al 1985, 15–20). There has been a dramatically increasing use of paraquat (which was introduced into the region only in 1972).

The research also shows a marked increase in parasuicide, 'more often female than male', among those who have 'no history of mental illness'. The author, Bowles (1985), describes these parasuicides as occasioned by flight from 'an intense and intolerable situation, with death not always the well-formulated goal'. 'There is an element of ambivalence, risk-taking, a surrender to fatalism and chance in many cases.' They involve a communication directed at significant others, 'with an operant quality which puts pressure on this complementary person to respond in some way'. This, I believe, is an adequate description of what is occurring among young Aboriginal females. It is also a description which does not require medical diagnosis or prescription. However, Western Samoans, like so many Pacific people, and unlike Aboriginal people, have a long cultural tradition of suicide. Words for the act were first recorded in the 1860s. Hezel and others note that 'suicide, embedded as it is in Trukese culture, will no doubt remain as endemic to Truk as cholera' (1985, 123).

A 'national awareness campaign' — 'to reduce the incidence of suicide in Samoa' — began in the 1980s. The program had sophisticated philosophical premises and goals, which were significant in the understanding of suicide. I discuss this at some length in Chapter 10.

Micronesia has had an 'epidemic' of youth suicide since 1960. The rate was 8 per 100,000 in 1960–63, increasing to 48 in 1980–83, and to 111 by 1987 for the 20–24 age cohort.[9] The suicides are 'patterned culturally, in terms of the characteristics of the actors, the method, and the situations'. The predominant relationship involved in suicide is one of tension between adolescent and parent. It is the youth's conflict about parental authority, support and recognition that leads to self-harm. The method most commonly used is hanging, in some 85 per cent of cases.

The suicide rates vary in Papua New Guinea's Highlands — from 34 to 72 per 100,000 for both sexes. Pataki-Schweitzer has given ten 'ranked' causes for this latter group: 'bereavement, no reason, witches, quarrelled, scolded, adultery, accused as witch, frustration, misfortune, and fright'. He believes the causality is much more complex than the list suggests. Of note is the consistency of scolding, as in a parent admonishing a child, as a major factor in many Pacific suicides.

The research consensus is that 'suicide is deeply embedded in the unique cultural context of the local situation, and that suicide is often attributed with more than a single meaning within a locality' (Hezel et al

1985, 210–16). Suicide should not be studied apart from the cultural context which provides its patterns and meanings in each of these societies. Hezel suggests three 'divisions of labour': attempting to elicit the cultural patterning of suicide; inquiring into psycho-social aspects of suicide; and suicide prevention. Under cultural patterning, he suggests the following domains of questioning:

1. Historical — What is the historical, ethno-historical or mythological occurrence of suicide in the culture? Is there a lexical term for suicide? What were the typical methods and traditional interpretations of suicide?

2. Contemporary — Is there a cultural script for suicide today? What are the commonly recognised situations, methods, actors, emotions, and messages communicated by the suicides in a culture?

3. Cultural evaluation — Do members of the society evaluate suicide positively or negatively? Do people make attributions or accusations of responsibility or blame for other people's suicide?

Several of Hezel's questions have validity in my Aboriginal context. Hitherto I have criticised the mono-dimensional 'mental health' approach and suggested the co-relevance of historical, political and social factors. On reflection, some of these cultural evaluations must even be included in groups which appear to have none of the strong traditional relationships which sustain Truk or Palau or Samoan societies.

Hezel's psycho-social questions are also pertinent:

1. Social cohesiveness — Do villages or areas of high suicide rates show evidence of a lack of, or a disruption of, cohesiveness, due to cultural change, political fragmentation or conflict, etc?

2. Social bonds — What is the strength of affiliation between victims and their family, kin group or society? Are victims usually marginal individuals?

3. Psychological profile — What is the psychological profile of the victim? Is there any mental abnormality? Can certain high-risk personality types be identified? Are suicide victims typically described, in local cultural terms, as being 'strong' or 'weak', etc?

4. Impulsivity — To what extent is the suicide an impulsive act? Do spatial or temporal clustering, or other signals, suggest a high degree of impulsivity in the suicide acts?

5. Emotions — What are the emotions generally associated with suicide? Especially, what is the nature of 'anger' and 'shame' and how do these two emotions interplay in cultural interpretations of suicide?

These questions form a useful agenda for those seeking prevention strategies outside those which I later describe as the 'conventional' mould. Several key 'political' questions need to be added, such as the role and effect of racism, and the exclusion of native peoples from many values, systems, rights, decision-making roles, benefits, goods and services available to mainstream societies.

New Zealand

My professorial inaugural lecture at the University of New England in 1972 addressed comparative race politics in Australia, Canada, New Zealand and South Africa (Tatz 1972). While disputing the commonly expressed *pakeha* (European) view that 'New Zealand has the best race relations in the world', I found much that appeared positive, at least compared with Australia, in a period of radical social and political change. Rereading the lecture, I note that I presented separatism in a positive light, not as apartheid but as a way of both reviving and maintaining cultural, social and political values while still participating in mainstream societal institutions. I talked of the need for 'accommodation', a notion totally antithetical to assimilation, one in which administrators and decision makers modify their strategies in view of 'indigenous realities'.

Accommodation requires a radical change of attitude and thought processes, including the abandonment of 'them' and 'us' as superior and inferior; it requires a mind-set willing to view diverse peoples as having equivalent cultural sophistication, with each achieving, in its own way, for its own time and place. While it is clear that the various Maori cultures are not the same, invidious comparisons and distinctions block the path to accommodation, to achieving what Richard Thompson calls the necessary 'community of communities' in New Zealand. He argues that the Maori role is not simply 'separatist': 'it is not a threat'. 'It serves a necessary and positive function in a shared society; it anchors identity and is a source of confidence and self-esteem' (1998, 103–12).

Thompson's new discussion document, *The Challenge of Racism*, provides an excellent summary of all that has changed, or not changed, since my 1960s research in New Zealand. There is no need to traverse his discussion points, except to say that Maori suicide, like Aboriginal suicide, must be seen in the cultural, social and political contexts of the nation. Maori suicide is not simply an incidental subset of New Zealand suicide.

The 1996 census lists 2,879,085 people of *pakeha* descent (72.5 per cent of the population); 523,374 of Maori descent (13.2 per cent); 202,233 of Pacific Island descent (5.1 per cent); and 173,505 of Asian descent (4.4 per cent). Maori have tired of the array of definitions of them. They claim that self-identification is the only acceptable approach:

'Being Maori is a state of mind'. Of interest is that the introduction to the census states: 'People have Maori ancestry if they consider they have Maori ancestors, no matter how distant' (Thompson 1998, 13–15).

As an irregular visitor over a period of 30 years, and bearing in mind my Aboriginal-oriented lenses, there is much that is positive in and about Maori life. I do not forget Moana Jackson's admonition that New Zealand is 'the land of myths, lies and deceit, where things are never what they appear to be'. Whatever the truth *within*, Maori strength appears impressive from *without*: regular inclusion of Maori as stakeholders in public and social policy formulation; virtual bilingualism, at least in government language, in official documents and on public occasions; increasing use of Maori words and concepts as part of the national culture; a powerful Maori presence in national politics; an extraordinary presence, and applause, on sporting fields and in the artistic world; Maori perspectives as part of the national media, no longer relegated to quaint documentaries; Maori Studies as part of university curriculums; and the new 'ball game' as a result of the Waitangi Tribunal and the resultant reparation, as well as restoring ownership and management of dispossessed lands. I have one especially important yardstick: that the medical school at the University of Otago has introduced Maori material into every sub-discipline, and the material is examinable. For me, that is both 'separatism' and accommodation at its best.

New Zealanders dispute whether *Maoritanga* — Maori being, love of Maori-ness — is the exclusive property of Maori or should be available for all to share. 'Our culture is our business' is fairly common. At times, this assertion of sovereignty, exclusivity or even militancy spills over into matters like suicide. At the start of our research, we were 'warned' by a number of people that Maori are seeking to exclude non-Maori from this domain. Not so. Maori researchers, officials and parents of deceased youth were not only polite but sharing.

Maori suicide

The Skegg, Cox and Broughton study (1995) examined Maori suicide from 1957 to 1991. The Maori male rate was one-half, and the female rate one-third, of the non-Maori. For the 15–24 age cohort, the male rate was 35 per 100,000, and the female, 6 per 100,000. What the researchers found disturbing was the doubling of the Maori female rate, and a trebling of the male rate, over the 35-year period.

The 1987–91 figures show an 'equality' of Maori and *pakeha* youth suicide. Equally disquieting, according to John Broughton, is that youth steeped in *Maoritanga* are suiciding, whereas several opinions are that it is only, or mostly, the alienated-from-culture youth who take their lives.

Poison is the chosen female method, and hanging, the male. In the 15–49 age group, 71 per cent of Maori suicides in the period 1980–88 were by hanging while in custody.

The study concludes that the under-reporting of Maori suicide is as high as 28 per cent. This is because 'the recording of Maori ethnicity on a death certificate depends on the undertaker ascertaining that the person had 50% or more of Maori biological origin'. Death certificates use biological definition, whereas self-identification has been the census protocol since 1986. The researchers believe that Maori suicide rates, 'already a cause for concern', might now be even higher than non-Maori.

There is very little suicide beyond the age of 55. The researchers suggest that elders have a greater involvement in cultural life, and that it is the culturally deprived or alienated youth who suicide. They see culture as 'providing a sense of belonging and purpose, and so a sense of meaning and self-worth, and a moral framework to guide [our] conduct'. Despite reports of culturally 'orthodox' youth committing suicide, there is clearly a much greater sense of security for Maori youth in family, in a *hapu* or *iwi*, than for their Aboriginal counterparts in New South Wales rural areas.

The Maori Suicide Review Group was established because of alarm that, between 1971 and 1995, 47 incarcerated Maori committed suicide.[10] Nowhere near the 'awesome' apparatus and agenda of the RCIADIC inquiry in Australia, it nevertheless covered some common ground, especially on 'inmate management'. The 17-page account of 'Suicide by Maori' is comprehensive.

As could be expected, the Group examined risk factors in the 'literature review': psychological/psychiatric disorders, social and cultural factors, family factors, behavioural risk factors, genetic and biochemical factors (which I discuss in Chapter 10), exposure to suicidal behaviour, stressful life events, and triggers. The custody suicides were believed to involve high levels of substance abuse and 'psychiatric disorder', poor 'coping skills' and social disadvantage.

There is a significant difference between the Aboriginal and Maori experience of imprisonment: Maori experience 'strong feelings of shame', whereas Aborigines appear to experience anger and a sense of retaliation rather than shame. The Group also found that Maori inmate suicides were more likely to be those serving longer sentences for violent offences. By contrast, much of Aboriginal suicide in custody occurs within the first 24 hours, a period of high risk. Contrasting with the New Zealand finding on long-serving suicides, the RCIADIC found that many Aboriginal custody suicides were, and are, by people jailed for short periods of time for minor infractions or alcohol-related misbehaviour.

The Group examined 'factors specific to Maori'. Maori, who comprise 13 per cent of the population, formed 47 per cent of the prison population, as at the 1993 prison census. By comparison, Aborigines, some 2 per cent of the New South Wales population, are now 16 per cent of the prison population. Of the Maori inmates, 43 per cent were under 25. Most were unskilled, unemployed, and one in four was 'more likely to be affiliated to a gang'. Most were in jail for aggravated robbery. All Maori had longer criminal histories. In short, 'it appears that Maori inmates are a higher risk group before they arrive in prison'. This is consonant with my view, expressed in Chapter 2, that suicide in custody has less to do with custody than with the factors which are conducive to suicide *before* custody.

The Group postulates that there is 'increasing mental illness among Maori'. They are unsure whether this is something new, or something that has been evolving. They considered 'economic and social disadvantage', quoting Mason Durie as defining this group (of inmates) as 'caught between two cultures, isolated from both Maori and general society'. Two submissions to the Group are noteworthy:

(a) You could almost write the lives of each of these people. They grew up in sheer hell and hell is all they have lived all their lives and the only escape for them is death.

(b) The fact that they are in prison is not the cause. It is an avenue which allowed them to do what they intended to do; and what they have done spiritually for months before that. The rope was just ending the physical side of an already spiritual death.

The Group analyses, at some length, the cultural factors, especially the ingredients which make for a healthy person. In Australia, we have no such equivalent analyses; nor can we say, with any certainty, that there are no Aboriginal, or vestigial Aboriginal equivalent, cultural factors. *Te taha wairua*, the spiritual quality (or Hillman's 'soul'), is the most basic and essential requirement for health. *Te taha wairua* also accounts for something very important in Maori life: *mana*, or status.

Then follows a detailed exposition of *whakama*, where a person perceives he has less *mana* than particular others or has lost *mana* because of his, or someone else's, actions. This is seen as an 'illness with a spiritual dimension, an unease which affects the whole person, body, mind and spirit'. When *whakama* goes untreated, it can lead to breakdown. There may, possibly, be some cultural equivalent in Aboriginal 'jealousing', discussed earlier. Doctors diagnose *whakama* as 'psychiatric disorder'; Maori call it *mate Maori*, Maori sickness. Again, we have the intransigent problem of who is the first, or the loudest, to define the diagnosis and thereby determine the nature of the treatment.

Non-Maori suicide

Suicide studies in New Zealand are, if one may so describe them, efficient, professional, compact and strongly directed towards the medical/ psychiatric model. Coggan and Norton (1994a), who have done important work on youth suicide in Auckland, have also published strategy papers for reducing 'self-directed harm'. Their work illustrates two themes I raised earlier: first, self-harm, of the suicide variety, 'has significant individual and societal costs, compared with other health problems'; second, a strategy is needed 'to improve the identification, referral and treatment of persons at high risk of suicide by various caretakers and "gatekeepers" in the community'. ('Gatekeepers', in this particular context, no doubt means health care personnel.)

This work is reasonably typical of non-Maori suicide research: it is steeped in the medicalised public health model, with an occasional reference to cultural factors or to socioeconomic disadvantage. Rarely is there mention of the historical and political dimensions. New Zealand research generally suggests the unlikely, namely, that there is more death, and more cost to the nation, in suicide than in road accidents, in alcohol consumption and drug abuse, and in criminal behaviour. It recommends an approach which Szasz and Hillman, among others, have shown to be quite unrewarding in terms of the prevention and handling of suicide: 'treatment' by 'caretakers' and 'gatekeepers'.

The Canterbury Suicide Project, and especially the work of Annette Beautrais, is renowned. The researchers have examined many facets of suicide: from risk factors among the 13- to 24-year-olds, to the prevalence and co-morbidity disorders among the parasuicides, to child-hood circumstances and adolescent adjustment among parasuicides, to access to firearms and the risk of suicide. The paradigm in most of this material is that there is probably dysfunctional or disadvantaged family circumstance to begin with. This leads to increased vulnerability to problems of personal adjustment and to psychiatric disorder, both increasing the likelihood of suicide.[11] Further, the 'odds of serious suicide attempt are related systematically to the extent of exposure to disadvantageous childhood experiences and family circumstances, adverse sociodemographic factors, and an individual's current psychiatric morbidity'.[12]

None of the New Zealand researchers indicate whether or not their samples include Maori, or if they do, whether or not there is anything Maori-specific about causality, suicidal behaviour and responses to psychological or psychiatric tests of various kinds. To read the Maori Suicide Review Group and the work of the 'non-Maori' researchers is to read about two different worlds, with only an occasional 'cross-over' about 'psychiatric disorder' which may be painful and diseaseful for Maori, but which hardly requires the conventional 'gatekeepers'.

David Fergusson contends that, although suicide is fascinating for the media, it is not the most serious issue: rather, it is a symptom of the adverse social conditions which give rise to it.[13] He believes in the value of 'early start programs', the sending out of workers into the community to try to change community ways. 'Good' families can become the models for others to emulate. Suicide, he argues, will end when communities achieve a degree of social health, a view which may not be universally accepted. It is, in essence, what Hillman calls the 'interiorisation' of the suicide within the community. However, in Aboriginal societies in New South Wales (and elsewhere), distance, geography, isolation within their domains, and the absence of role models make movement towards 'the middle class' and its (supposed) values not only difficult, but also somewhat impossible.

Some lessons

Much can be gained from studying New Zealand practice, and many of the positive aspects have been referred to, or alluded to, in earlier chapters. In summary, the following should be noted.

Suicide research

There are, in effect, two streams of youth suicide research: one looks through universal (or Western) lenses, the other embraces a Maori perspective. The former is a distinctly medical/psychological model, the latter, a cultural/spiritual one. Neither appears to incorporate earlier or contemporary history, politics, or the consequences of racism (other than to talk about 'social disadvantage'). The Maori perspective seeks liberation from conventional suicidology, and that, I believe, is positive. However, a joining of forces seems the obvious path to follow. Although Aborigines have yet to insist on a 'separate' perspective, such a differentiation between Aboriginal and non-Aboriginal suicide is crucial.

Cultural 'orthodoxy' and a steeping of youth in *Maoritanga* appears not to be prophylaxis enough. Acculturation, re-acculturation, or what Deloria calls revivalism, has many positive consequences, and it may well lower the level of suicidal behaviour. The Yarrabah Museum (near Cairns) certainly appears to have attracted the interest of youth. *Winanga Li*, the first volume in the series 'The Moree Mob', is an attempt to provide genealogies and photographs of the areas known formerly as 'Top Camp', 'Middle Camp' and 'Bottom Camp' when Aborigines were moved from Terry Hie Hie to Moree in the early 1920s. Aborigines in that region have only just begun to find themselves, geographically for a start.

Illiteracy, deafness, grief and cannabis

More Maori suicides leave notes than do Aborigines. At a guess, the general level of Maori literacy is somewhat higher. No one has yet suggested illiteracy as a relevant factor for suicide, but there is at least a high-order proposition that illiteracy, and illiteracy plus deafness, is a key factor in youth disadvantage. In 1988, the Mason inquiry into maximum security and suicide found that 80 per cent of Maori in prison had a hearing problem, and that 20 per cent had a severe hearing problem.[14] Chronic otitis media, 'glue ear', burst eardrums and consequent deafness have been well documented across Aboriginal Australia. These physical/social factors have as much, if not more, validity as the vaguely phrased (mental) 'stress' factors in both countries.

'Five generations of grieving' is the judgement of Dr Erahana Ryan. She believes the youth absorb feelings of racial alienation, emptiness, loss of culture, loss of self and the loss of esteem. 'Stress of loss of who they are' is the key to her therapeutic approach. To this end, she trains Maori health workers, preferably older women who have been 'through the mill'. In the Aboriginal context, there are such Aboriginal women, and several are doing similar work. What they do not have is the benefit of training and supervision, of being mentored, by someone like Dr Ryan.

There is strong anecdotal evidence that many Maori youth suicides have had a cannabis 'problem'. A Maori couple, who lost their son to suicide and who now counsel bereaved families, told me that they know of several youth suicides who were heavily 'into' cannabis: 'They can't afford the hard stuff'. They observe that 'it affects their emotions and they don't hear. They agree with all you say but show no emotional reactions.' This couple suggests a model for Australia: a counselling service by Aborigines for Aborigines.

Mate Frankovich, New Zealand's senior full-time coroner, does not dispute any of the discourse about Maori suicide, but he does point to cases which appear to have nothing to do with the factors discussed thus far, and which appear quite banal. One Maori youth, who used carbon monoxide, left a long note: his message was, to the effect, 'to hell with life, if I can't have pot and I can't find a place to skateboard, I may as well die'. Another 16-year-old male, whose girlfriend looked after his 2-month-old baby, wanted sex; she said no, and he hanged himself. These may well have been the real reasons for the suicides; they may, alternatively, have been the ostensible ones. We must beware the temptation to attribute deeper meanings to all youth suicides.

'Secondary victimisation'

Keri Lawson Te Aho, a consultant psychologist, talks about the legacies of racism and alienation, adding that there is 'a secondary victimisation of Maori youth' in institutions, especially in the mental health system. This is consistent with the views of the Maori Suicide Review Group, who infer that Maori prison inmates are in a 'special' category in the eyes of corrective service personnel: long-term, violent, prone to suicide, and so on. Professor Mason Durie considers that the mental health services for Maori are 'hopeless'.

There is no need to argue the obvious case about such secondary victimisation of Aborigines in Australian institutions. It begins in schools, continues through hospitals, endures in prisons, and sometimes extends even to cemeteries.

Purpose in life

We do not have statistics for Maori suicide in Hamilton, but there is a strong suggestion that the King/Queen Movement community there has a greater sense of cohesion and purpose, and a lower rate of violent behaviour. However, the Maori parents mentioned above lost their son when he was boarding at a Hamilton school. They say that there were at least four suicides among that same school cohort.

Gordon Matenga, New Zealand's only Maori coroner, is a Mormon. He is certain that the extensive participation of Maori in the Queen Movement and the adherence of so many to the Mormon Church account for the low rates of suicide. In Mormonism, the sanctity of human life is paramount. Many New Zealanders from Western Samoa, the Cook Islands and Tokelau are staunch adherents of the Catholic, Methodist and Pacific Island churches. Nevertheless, Samoans have a high rate of suicide: 'It is part of their history', says the Pacific Island coordinator of the New Zealand Research Council. She says that 'there is contempt for people who suicide, and they are buried upside down ... It is worse to lose your face than lose your life'.

By contrast, Dr Rees Tapsell, a Maori psychiatrist, believes that 'a large number of Maori do not have a social glue' which would provide purpose or cohesion. 'They live on the myth of alienation', by which he means that the mere membership of a group on the basis of a common feeling, or reality, of racial alienation is insufficient as a life-sustaining force in the way that nationalism, Mormonism or Black Islam can be a 'glue'.

Sport, as in Australia, is considered by all we interviewed as 'one high spot'. In 1997, the Aranui Sports Academy was established as a way of stopping the drift of Maori and Polynesian boys out of school. Aranui High School switched from rugby league, at which they were champions, to rugby union in order to accommodate these young men. In 1997, they beat St Bedes College in the final, to win the schoolboys' championship. As the *North and South* magazine commented, such a predominantly Maori and Polynesian team victory would hardly arouse attention, but this was 'Christchurch, the most WASPish of all New Zealand cities and until this season, the final bastion of pre-Polynesian rugby'.[15]

The organisers realised 'that one positive thing in many of these young people's lives was sport'. All 33 members of the academy were properly enrolled in the school. The academy's *'take* [purpose] is about changing the kids' attitudes in order to make them more employable, *not* about winning on the sports field'. Students had to complete four years of senior schooling or to have been away from school for a year. In addition to sports activities, classroom work is compulsory. The boys set the agenda, 'no one else'. Needless to say, there was a howl of protest in Christchurch at the academy's victory, with allegations of Aranui's bringing in professional rugby league adults to demolish amateur children in rugby union. The Aranui project could be emulated in any number of New South Wales towns, where the residential divide between East side and West side (as in Christchurch) is as great.

Coroners

Of the 74 coroners in New Zealand, only three are not qualified in law. The independence of coroners from the police is important. Underreporting of suicide and identification of the deceased as Maori are still serious problems, but much less so, in my view, than in Australia. The police form, 'P47 Report for Coroner', makes provision for 'Race', but this does not resolve the biological versus self-identification conundrum. The officer does not always 'get it right' and the coroner is not obliged to distinguish who is or is not Maori. Coronial practice benefits enormously from virtually every larger police station's having an officer designated as inquests officer. Most learn on the job. As few appear to reach the rank of sergeant, there is certainly room in New Zealand and Australia for a professional, career promotion category of inquests officer, or, as in Dallas, a death investigator. Their approach and dedication are impressive, as are their symbiotic relationship with their coroners and their formal 'distance' from other police.

Prevention strategies

In Chapter 10, I will discuss a variety of alleviation strategies in use in the Western world. In addition, there are two projects in New Zealand which were not devised for suicide but which hold promise as effective counters to a preference for death rather than life. 'Going-for-Goal: a Sport-Based Life Skills Program for Adolescents' uses a sporting metaphor to elicit young people's frustrated goals and to assist them to overcome the obstacles to their attainment. Based on an American program, essentially for Afro-American youngsters, it has been trialled by the University of Otago in Dunedin. The other is the 'Smokefree' project run by the Health Sponsorship Council in Wellington. This is very much a peer group pressure exercise in breaking the smoking habit among teenagers. Its methodology could as readily be tried as a way of bringing youth to the point where it is 'cool' to stay alive! It has the singular merit of being run for Maori youth, by Maori youth, who have 'been there and done that'.

Notes

1. Hillman, *Suicide and the Soul*, 49.
2. Goldney, 'Exploring Aboriginal Youth Suicide', 443.
3. Flisher et al, 'Risk-Taking Behaviour', Part II, 474–6.
4. Flisher and Parry, 'Suicide in South Africa', 348–52.
5. Mayekiso, 'Attitude of Black Adolescents toward Suicide', 40–5.
6. American and Alaska Native Mental Health Research Center, *Calling from the Rim*, 7.
7. *Newsweek*, 15 February 1988.
8. American and Alaska Native Mental Health Research Center, *Calling from the Rim*, 75ff.
9. Hezel et al, *Culture, Youth and Suicide in the Pacific*, 123; Rubenstein, in Hezel et al, 89–93; Chen, in Hezel et al, 60.
10. Maori Suicide Review Group, 'Reducing Suicide by Maori Prison Inmates', esp. 19–35.
11. Fergusson and Lynskey, 'Childhood Circumstances, Adolescent Adjustment, and Suicide Attempts', 613.
12. Beautrais, Joyce and Mulder, 'Risk Factors for Serious Suicide Attempts', 1179.
13. Personal communication, Christchurch.
14. Maori Suicide Review Group, 'Reducing Suicide by Maori Prison Inmates'.
15. 'East Side Story', *North and South*, October 1997, 74–80.

10

Towards Alleviation

There are always simple solutions to complex problems. And they're always wrong.

— H.L. Mencken[1]

Existential therapy focuses on death, isolation, meaninglessness and freedom issues, which are easy for American Indians to understand. Death crises occur more often for American Indians at an earlier age and, furthermore, the deaths of their ancestors (which came close to genocide) remains a powerful tribal memory. American Indians are aware of their isolation from mainstream culture. They are both isolated geographically and suffer from racism ... Suicide by the American Indian, for example, may be seen as seeking freedom in death.

— David Lester[2]

By regarding a phenomenon as a psychiatric diagnosis — treating it, reifying it in psychiatric diagnostic manuals, developing instruments to measure it, inventing scales to rate its severity, establishing ways to reimburse the costs of its treatment, encouraging pharmaceutical companies to search for effective drugs, directing patients to support groups, writing about possible causes in journals — psychiatrists may be unwittingly colluding with broader cultural forces to contribute to the spread of a mental disorder.

— Carl Elliott[3]

Suicide 'prevention', especially in North America, is undertaken by doctors — mainly psychiatrists, psychologists and mental health workers who are generally social workers or nurses. In the case of Indians and Alaskan Natives, tribal 'gatekeepers' are sometimes involved in a few programs.[4]

Only three grades of strategy are delineated. Primary 'prevention' focuses on psychiatric disorder, education of the doctors (and then of the children and parents), the provision of 'good general mental health services', psychotherapy for traumatised and sexually abused children, attempts to predict suicide, and a toning down of media hysteria about the subject of suicide. Secondary strategies include establishing suicide prevention centres, medical emergency services and hotline telephone services, and restricting access to lethal weapons. Tertiary strategies can only apply to those who have tried suicide but failed: essentially this involves counselling for those who make 'suicidal gestures'.

In November 2000, the LifeForce Wesley Mission in Sydney conducted a seminar on suicide for the media. The 27-page summary paper, prepared by Randall Pieterse, was excellent in many respects. However, just as it seeks the innovative 'depathologising' of suicide, so it remains entombed in the clichés of mental health. The Mission asks for the continuing 'destigmatisation' of suicide — but then retains its template of 'mental health issues'. It also calls for strong action to increase 'prevention and intervention programs'.

I prefer the words 'alleviation' or 'mitigation' to the conventional 'prevention'. One can only *prevent* what one *knows* is likely to happen, and then only if one can clearly identify a cause which can be ameliorated or mitigated. *We do not know the causes of youth suicide.* 'Prevention' has not diminished youth suicide in Australia, New Zealand, North America, Brazil, the Scandinavian countries, Scotland, Sri Lanka or the Pacific Islands, in each of which the rates of youth suicide have escalated markedly. All we can do is try to slow, or deflect, the development of trends towards attempts at suicide.

More diverse people and professionals than those listed above are needed for successful alleviation. Who I believe they should be will emerge from the following analysis.

I have assembled my conclusions and recommendations under nine headings: philosophies and theories of suicide; research directions; 'prevention' projects; treatment practices; Aboriginal initiatives; Aboriginal and non-Aboriginal cooperative programs; coronial matters; suicide and the role of the police; and practical workshops.

The liberation of suicidology?

Biomedical or ethnic-centred philosophies

'An ethnoscientific or biomedical approach alone will lead us to a lot of mistakes'.[5] This was the considered view of James Shore in summarising the conference on American and Alaskan Native suicide in 1994. His suggestion is simple: to integrate both the biomedical and the ethnic-centred to arrive at a 'balanced and broader biopsychosocial perspective'. However, it is never simple to have new models accepted and implemented.

Were there to be an integration, then the greater accommodation would have to come from those with a biomedical bias. They appear convinced that biomedical research will provide the key to preventing suicide. The thesis that genetic and biochemical causes underlie suicide is, as I argue below, probably the most harmful proposition in suicidology.

Shore writes that most suicide research is descriptive rather than analytical. My view is that it should also be critical. There is a smugness and distancing about the accepted approach to suicidology which concentrates more on 'scientific method', *chi* square correlations and other statistical treatment than on understanding the individual's behaviour. It can also offer a way of avoiding getting involved emotionally with the suicide himself or herself. In my opinion, suicidology needs to be liberated from this domination by statistical method.

Suicide needs all the lenses that can be focused on the phenomenon

Those working in this area need to be steeped in the history of suicide, and in the attitudes to suicide of medicine, religion, law, sociology and psychology; to be exposed to critiques of those attitudes; to be aware of the theories of writers like Hillman, who provide much broader and liberated perspectives; and, above all, they need the portraits of 'indigenous' communities, as provided so succinctly by Lester at the beginning of this chapter, which may induce a different way of thinking about 'indigenous' suicide — because it is different.

Carl Elliott and Ian Hacking have provided us with some important concepts about the significance of cultural and historical rather than psychiatric conditions in defining 'mental disorders'. Consciously or not, they echo Thomas Szasz: that he or she who does the defining thereby creates the victim or sufferer. If you give it a name and a treatment, says Elliott, himself an authority on the philosophy of psychiatry, or give it an explanation rooted in childhood memory, you are on the way to setting up just the kind of conceptual category that makes it a treatable psychiatric disorder. Thus, what used to be called 'weakness, sin, unhappiness, perversity, crime or deviance' are now 'mental disorders'. Both men postulate the likelihood that many of today's 'mental disorders' are, or have, an 'ecological niche', that is, they are transient mental illnesses limited to a certain space and time — such as epidemics of fugue or neurasthenia in nineteenth-century Europe or multiple-personality disorders in America in the late twentieth. 'If the niche disappears, the mental illness disappears along with it' (Elliott 2000).

Suicide is not a niche set in a specific time or place. But calling it a 'mental illness' — as if its roots, causes, symptoms, outcomes, treatments and preventions are universal and immutable — is, simply, silly. We have seen that the link between suicide and madness was a nineteenth-century legal, not medical, fiction, or niche, which was then appropriate for purposes of inheritance law. The time has come, surely, to set aside the *a priori* definitions of mental illness, the mind-set that looks for mental disorders in every case of suicide. If you look hard enough, armed with the long words, if you ask the 'right' questions, if you design the 'we-know-what-we-are-looking-for' tests, as Elliott and others suggest, you will find the disorder — and when the label is applied, sure enough the labelled one will begin to exhibit what it is you expected to find by creating the very construct.

Research directions

Genetic or biochemical 'predisposing' factors

The research into genetic or biochemical factors which predispose people to behave in a certain manner is damaging to the people under scrutiny. There is no evidence of any fruits of such research. This direction is inapplicable to whole populations of people defined, as a stereotyped group, as Maori, Aboriginal, Amerindian or Inuit, where physical and cultural differences within the groups are often greater than their similarities.

There was such an attempt at 'biological determinism' in the Northern Territory in the 1970s. The then Welfare Branch, responsible for Aboriginal affairs, was under strong media and parliamentary pressure about high Aboriginal infant mortality rates which were then between 100 and 150 per 1000 live births, compared with 9 or 10 for non-Aboriginal infants. The Welfare Branch commissioned research into 'the psychological causes of infant mortality' — in effect, asking the chief researcher, a zoologist, to see if there was an 'inherent genetic predisposition' in Aboriginal women to see their babies die! The huge report produced a quite negative conclusion, but the short chapter on the socio-environmental causes of infant mortality — all of which were the responsibility of the Branch — was (literally) excised with a razor blade before being made public.

I do not impute bad motives to those who now suggest research into these areas. However, it must be kept in mind that there are people in biological research who do seek a genetic basis for race and attempt to validate immutable biological determinism, which would then provide the physical proof for their ideologies of both racial difference and racial hierarchy. The current (and energetic) discourse is in the field of sport, where arguments are adduced to show that black athletes have a genetic, or an evolved, metabolism that gives them musculature, speed, a set of reflexive actions and peripheral vision unknown to, or genetically *denied* to, non-blacks. John Hoberman's *Darwin's Athletes* has, I believe, demolished these propositions, at least for serious researchers, even though legions will continue to believe uncritically what the eye perceives.

The flaw lies in a belief in the ability of such genes and resultant biochemistry to emerge in unbelievably short time spans. Thus, 100-metre sprinters are said to win because they have descended from West African slaves: it is contended that they either had to endure great hardship, or escape from slavery, in order to survive. Whatever their circumstances, one must presume that they had to endure or escape over longer distances than 100 or 400 metres.

This model also presumes that they had been slaves for aeons, which is also a false presumption: African slavery in America was a phenomenon of the eighteenth and nineteenth centuries. Since humans walked in Africa some 1.7 million years ago, who or what is responsible for the fast-forwarded, sprinting 'slavery' gene culminating in an 'emancipated' Jesse Owens at the Nazi Olympics in 1936? Iriquois in New York state and Ontario, having lived in lakes and plains country, have become the incomparably best skyscraper girder workers ever known. Seafaring Torres Strait Islanders have become the best layers of railway sleepers and lines in the deserts of Western Australia. Genetics? Or, rather, cultural bent or social aptitude for particular tasks? In similar vein, if there is a genetic basis to Aboriginal youth suicide, why did it lie dormant for 60 millennia and then surface only in the 1960s?

Categorisation

Research is needed into the categories of suicide I suggested in Chapter 6:
- accidental risk-taking suicide
- focal suicide
- 'political' suicide
- 'respect' suicide
- grieving suicide
- 'ambivalently rational' suicide
- 'appealing' suicide
- 'empowerment' suicide
- 'lost' suicide.

While categorisation spells out no solutions, it does go some way towards explanation and may assist in the review of strategies for alleviation.

Research is needed into 'slashing up': these acts may not be self-harm but rather an affirmation of life by seeing warm blood flow or, as the psychiatrist Neil Phillips suggests, a release from tension.

Coronial practice and research need to accommodate the extended tripartite definition of suicide: those beyond reasonable doubt, those which are probable, and those which are possible.

Research should address attempted suicides, seeing them as part of a continuum, not as a separate category of 'the serious ones' and those 'who make gestures'. We know that many who try will try again, and that many who are dead had tried before. It is more logical to treat all who appear to try as being serious about wishing to end their lives.

Research should give more attention to the increasing rates of both parasuicide and suicide among young females. I found that young females are as ready to engage in violent or aggressive behaviour as males, with teenage pregnancy the only prophylaxis against gang membership, petty crime and possibly more serious crime. Girls use tablets in preference to ropes and can often be resuscitated. However, female hanging is beginning, and those who are 'serious' will doubtless come to see the efficacy of that method.

Age ranges

Research needs to abandon the conventional but inconvenient WHO age cohort group of 15–24 years for 'youth'. In the Aboriginal, Maori and American Indian domains, there is every reason to narrow the focus onto an age grouping of 12 to 18 or 19. There is also an urgent need of a special category of child suicide, from 8 to 12.

A separate Aboriginal suicidology

Research in suicide requires a separate Aboriginal suicidology. The Aboriginal and Maori phenomena are not a subset, a footnote or a by-product of 'mainstream' research data. No other cultural group in each of the two countries has the same origins, backgrounds, histories, socialis-ation, cultural milieux, family structures, experiences of racial discrimin-ation, and alienation as do Aborigines and Maori. To persist in the search for 'standard' causality and to assume that a suicide is a suicide regardless of context is to be, at the least, unscientific and simplistic.

'Prevention' approaches

The National Youth Suicide Prevention Strategy

There is both activity and innovation in suicide 'prevention' strategies in Australia.[6] The National Youth Suicide Prevention Strategy, allocated

$31 million between 1995 and 1999 and supplemented in the 1999 federal budget, has four goals: to prevent premature death by suicide; to reduce rates of injury and self-harm; to reduce the incidence of suicidal ideation and behaviour; and to 'enhance resilience, resourcefulness, respect and interconnectedness for young people, their families and communities'. The focus is on the public health model, even though it incorporates 'sensitivity to social and cultural context' by asserting that we need a 'variety of interventions and the involvement of multiple service sectors and government departments'. A variety of professional training programs are under way. The Strategy embraces a 'community development approach', with two areas pinpointed for action: parenting skills programs and school-based 'mental health promotion programs'. The Strategy prefers 'mental health promotion' to the term 'primary prevention'.

The Strategy undertook a *National Stocktake of Youth Suicide Prevention Activities in 1997–98.* Of 919 programs in the stocktake, only 75 were 'identified as belonging to the community development and support approach'. Of those 75, eight (including this study) related to Aborigines and Torres Strait Islanders; only one (presumably my study) emanated from a university. It is important to note that New South Wales had in place, in addition to its 'We Can All Make a Difference: NSW Suicide Prevention Strategy', the development of suicide prevention programs for Aborigines in 1999 and 2000.

A specific Aboriginal emphasis

National and state strategies have to embrace specific Aboriginal 'wings' in all that they do.

A Strategy *Bulletin* quotes a Department of Family and Health Services publication listing of risk factors for suicide: among mental health problems, drug and sexual abuse, homelessness and unemployment appears one other category — 'Aboriginality'![7] The Wesley LifeForce summary also includes 'Aboriginality' alongside 'depression', 'schizophrenia' and 'psychiatric influences' under 'some factors influencing suicide'. In both instances, this may have been shorthand, but it sits badly to have a national suicide body, a key government agency and a dedicated church mission listing race as an inherent cause of its own self-destruction.

What is meant by 'community development strategies' is too broad and ill-defined to apply to specific Aboriginal communities. The geography and demography of the Hunter and others study (1999)—one community which is physically separated from mainstream society and two island communities — cannot apply to the Aborigines in New South Wales. There needs to be a separate Aboriginal strategy and, within that framework, a series of appropriate and region-specific strategies.

What has always bedevilled Aboriginal administration is the search for universal policies and practices. These always fail because of the desire to implement simple and uniform solutions to differing complex problems. Here is an opportunity to avoid repeating past failures and to take the region-by-region, community-by-community approach, which is the long way round, the difficult way round. Such an approach has *never* been attempted by any administrative agency anywhere in Australia.

Treatment practices

In contemporary suicidology concerning Amerindians, there is an expressed desire for euphemisms. Shore (1994) suggests calling prevention programs 'evaluation' programs, being a 'safer' term among people who feel stigmatised by the concept of 'prevention'. 'Fear of stigmatisation', he argues, 'has reinforced the avoidance of research for 20 years'. He presents an intelligent discussion about the hostility of Indians to research: 'In every Navajo *hogan*, there are grandparents, parents, children, maybe great-grandchildren and an anthropologist'. Said in jest, it nevertheless conveys a hostility not much different from that found in Aboriginal Australia. Maori claim they have been 'clip-boarded' and researched beyond endurance. Shore writes that most health professionals who want to undertake research in 'Indian country' encounter these feelings. His point is that, if researchers are not prepared to deal with the hostility, they should not be there.

What does not make sense is Shore's — and Australian bureaucracy's — failure to see that their already euphemistic label, 'mental health', *is the greatest single creator of hostility in Aboriginal communities.*

Mental health makes a great deal of sense, and has an appeal, to the white middle class: we live in an age of medicalised neurosis, one in which suffering of any kind is unhealthy and happiness is deemed an inalienable human right. To be mentally healthy is to be happy. Ergo, to be unhappy (with body or with self) warrants treatment. To Aborigines, the term 'mental health' produces hostility and avoidance: a people who have suffered every conceivable label hardly need the ultimate categorisation of being mentally 'not right'. Optimistic as it may seem to expect a dominant Anglo mainstream to relinquish terms they prefer, there is every reason to demand an appropriate use of language and nomenclatures when the services are intended for Aborigines, whose voluntary acceptance of those services is essential for their success.

The Maori propensity is for 'wellness'. It has the merit of not being an emotionally loaded noun. I have no particular term, acceptable to Aborigines, to offer, but I have no doubt that the sooner that agencies abandon the present terminology, the more likely are those in need of treatment to avail themselves of clinical and support services. An agency or program called 'suicide help' not only doesn't do a violence to language but is one much more likely to attract Aboriginal clientele than 'mental health'.

Aboriginal initiatives

Empowering themselves

What does it mean when researchers and strategy-devisers talk of the need for 'indigenous' communities to 'empower themselves', or to 'engage in self-determination'? For example, a Strategy *Bulletin* states: 'It is crucial that Aboriginal and Torres Strait Islander communities are empowered to develop and implement their own ways of supporting and guiding their young people ... It will be a major challenge to find creative ways of ensuring self-determination for particular communities'.[8] These are shibboleths, mantras and catch-cries, phrases that may sound good but are never accompanied by any specificity as to their meaning in theory or practice. Why, one has to ask, is speaking clearly so avoided and so shunned in Western culture? Why is every bureaucratic verb, especially in the welfare domain, so bloodless, anaemic, even pathetic: 'empowering', 'developing', 'ensuring', 'supporting', 'guiding', 'encouraging', 'focusing', 'convening'? It is as if the bureaucracy shies away from recommending anything specific, but hides behind impenetrable jargon, which can mean all things to themselves and to their political masters.

For 40 years now I have watched, alongside Aborigines, as policy slogans of this kind were invented, barely implemented, and discarded when a different slogan, or euphemism, was suggested. We would do well to revisit Deloria's philosophies of 'leave-us-alone' and self-help, together with a commitment to respond promptly to calls for assistance, but only when asked.

Corporation/incorporation power

By forming corporations or legal associations, Aborigines have a viable power base in mainstream society. The artificial legal *persona* of such bodies is a greater force than the separate legal personalities of the individuals who comprise them. These bodies were originally the agencies through which governments sought to achieve their aims and objectives; however, like Indian corporations in the United States and band councils in Canada, they are capable of proactive, even aggressive assertions of a local will. Land councils, legal aid corporations, housing associations and educational incorporations can band together to innovate, monitor, adjudicate or ameliorate youth behaviour.

'Nothing happens in human affairs without the creation of new power or the redistribution of old power.' Denis Oliver, who helped to establish a National Awareness Campaign to reduce suicide among Western Samoan youth, based this premise on the helper's belief that 'the people in the villages could solve the problem and it was therefore their right and responsibility to dig for the causes and remedies'. The essence of the strategy was to

* inform the people that they had a problem;
* educate them on the facts of the problem;
* create a vacuum for them to move on the problem; and
* facilitate and encourage their action on the problem (Hezel 1994, 74–82).

It was, in large measure, successful.

Aborigines know only too well that they have a problem. Some groups need briefing on ostensible causes and related issues. What they lack — given their struggles for survival on budgets which are forever endangered or cut — is the space, the 'vacuum in which to move'. Corporations have the base not only to bring suicide 'in-house' but also to tackle such matters as institutional racism, discriminatory practices by real estate agents, unilateral dismissal of students from schools. The mechanism for adversarial action, both legal and political, is there: they have to find the best ways to act. In summary, corporations may need some assistance in establishing the monitoring programs, but this has to be on Aboriginal terms.

Domestic violence, sexual assaults and the cannabis problem

Domestic violence has for long been the subject of anguish and attempted resolution in communities. Ernest Hunter believes that suicide is the 'flip-side of domestic violence'.[9] In the period between 1989–90 (when I did my earlier fieldwork in New South Wales) and the 1997–99 field research, I saw an increased willingness of women to report such violence to the police. In response, police promoted awareness of, and the need to report, domestic violence. Reporting is an important first stage: the next battle is to convince the women concerned to testify in court hearings against their abusers, something which all abused women find difficult when the abuser is their husband or partner.

Much has been written, and nothing done, about community justice mechanisms. An outstanding report by the Australian Law Reform Commission on recognising Aboriginal customary laws, chaired initially by the Honourable Justice Michael Kirby and later by Professor James Crawford, dealt with such mechanisms (1986, 133–57). That report has simply been ignored. It needs urgent resurrection, perhaps despite the Prime Minister's rejection of any consideration of a separate 'Aboriginal law'. The New South Wales Law Reform Commission report (in 2000) on 'Sentencing Aboriginal Offenders' contends, despite strong opposition from judges and magistrates, that failure to recognise the role played by customary law can lead to injustice.[10]

It lies within the structural power inherent in the corporation to put an end to the now-rampant sexual abuse of children. These abuses must be reported as police matters, and the consequences borne by both the offender and the affected family; or the behaviour can be dealt with in-house. Traditionally it was, and most severely. Deloria's concept of Indian revivalism could include this scenario.

Cannabis is a relatively new phenomenon in Aboriginal communities. As alcohol is celebrated in the Australian ethos, it can hardly be denied to Aborigines; cannabis is rampant in the non-Aboriginal society and well on the way to being decriminalised. However, 'educating people about the facts' must include a strong message that many Aboriginal youth suicides have had an obsessive association with the substance. There is a difference between 'light recreational party' use and leaving home to live on riverbanks where private plantations can be nurtured. Many of these harmful behaviours, as Hillman would argue, are interior to communities.

Expansion of CDEP occupations

Few Aborigines have an independent source of income. The great majority live on the income generated by social security benefits, paid either directly to the recipients or worked for to the level of the CDEP benefit. The new federal budget allocations in 1999 for Aboriginal employment provided for more CDEP positions. My praise and criticism of CDEP have been given in earlier chapters.

CDEP and suicide

One beneficial aspect of CDEP is that it does allow for important innovation in the context of suicide. Aboriginal corporations which run CDEP have few restrictions on the work undertaken. It ranges from sophisticated landscaping services in Forster, to vegetable-growing in Tingha, to house-building in Woodenbong and Narrabri. CDEP could well create positions, some of which would require special training and guidance, in: remand cell visits; prison visits for those sentenced; and, more importantly, being a 'friend in court', when the youth appears in court.

Parents are often not around: this is possibly an end-of-the-road, had-a-gutful kind of reaction. Too often it is an abdication of parental responsibility. 'Court liaison officer' is an official category now, but only four Aborigines have been appointed in New South Wales. The presence of a friend in court, and friend at the cells, and friend as visitor, is an essential strategy for Aboriginal youth. North American literature reports on the lack of training and on the inability of custodial officers to handle at-risk youth. So, too, with their Australian counterparts.

Incarceration, places and processes

In New South Wales, the majority of police station cells have been decommissioned, even those with an A rating for surveillance. Youth are transported great distances from home to towns with 'super' surveillance systems: cells where it is impossible to attach a cord or cloth; television cameras that run around the clock; often small and narrow perspex cages, located so that desk staff can see the person at all times. These facilities were shown to us, with pride. In many centres, police have been replaced by custody officers from the Department of Corrective Services, who receive some training. It is important to separate policing duties from those of minder or carer. However, the *entire* basis for these procedures is to ensure that there are no deaths in custody. Given the increasing incarceration of Aboriginal youth, even for petty offences, I question the logic of a system which daily increases the rates of arrest while taking more and more evasive action to avoid any further royal commission-type inquiry.

During my fieldwork in the Kimberley in 1990, at Fitzroy Crossing, the then officer-in-charge undertook to drive me around the town. Before leaving the police station, he told a number of young men, and several elders who were sitting in the grounds at tables under shade umbrellas, that they were not to go to town and were to keep away from the local nearby hotel pub. He said he would be back shortly. I asked him who those people were. 'My prisoners', he explained. I asked why they were outdoors and unsupervised (knowing there was absolutely nowhere for anyone to abscond to). 'I'm buggered if any blackfella is going to kill himself in my cells', he replied, as the shadow of the royal commission loomed over everyone. (I endorsed his handling of his prisoners but had a lesser regard for his *motive*.)

The alternatives

Warrakoo is a large property about 85 km west of Wentworth, near the South Australian border. It is a two-hour drive from Mildura, the furthermost northern Victorian town, and is situated near Lake Victoria. Physically, it is a long walk to nowhere and, of the approximately 80 Aboriginal residents there since 1991, only one person has absconded. There are no walls and no restraints.

Warrakoo is an impressive, Aboriginal-run alternative to the juvenile and criminal justice system. When an offender is brought before a magistrate, the legal aid service and/or the medical service can ask that the person be brought before the Warrakoo management board for assessment as to suitability for the 'straightening out' program. Instead of hearing the case or even sentencing, the magistrate can remand for an assessment of suitability for the Warrakoo program. Following rehabilitation, the offender may be considered for release from criminal charge.

The place and the personnel are impressive. There is no sense of incarceration, no shadow of warders. The manager commands loyalty and respect. The chairman of the board is an Aborigine. On her assessing board is the former Dareton police sergeant who is committed to alternative systems of rehabilitation, particularly for those who appear to be at high risk of suicide. A recent assessment, in 1999, included a Wilcannia prisoner facing a long sentence in Geelong, Victoria. He believed that he had turned a corner and was assessed, by television link-up with the Warrakoo board, which recommended his acceptance. He may now be able to complete part of his sentence in this program.

Warrakoo has enabled many youth, mostly in their 20s, to rehabilitate and to give up alcohol. The board sees alcohol, not drugs, as the key issue. Almost all of their residents have been sexually abused in childhood. The Victorian institutions have been willing supporters of the program, but not the New South Wales Police. Most of the residents are South Australian and Victorian. A second large property, in northern Victoria, is being purchased, to be run as a cultural revival centre for, among others, Aboriginal youth at risk.

In earlier research, I observed similar schemes, especially the Wildman River camp in Arnhem Land in the Northern Territory, an open but much less free arrangement than Warrakoo. There had been a short-lived experiment in Western Australia in which youth were sent to their tribal elders in the Port Hedland region. Many of the youth emerged as 'changed people'. There are two new facilities for Aboriginal males in New South Wales: the Warrakirri Centre at Ivanhoe and the Yetta Dhinnakkal Centre at Brewarrina. The former, which is for inmates serving their remaining six months and who are considered non-violent, allows them to work on local community projects. Inmates are placed as close as possible to their families. The Brewarrina facility tries to incorporate Aboriginal culture and customs in its programs. Unlike Warrakoo, both are rehabilitative facilities *after* conviction; Warrakoo aims at rehabilitation *without* conviction. News reports suggest a healthy interest in acquiring skills, such as bulldozer operating, and, more importantly, in life.

The reality is that, unless bureaucrats in police and corrective services begin to use, or even help to establish, such Aboriginal-run exercises, increasing numbers of Aboriginal youth will crowd the jails, uprisings will take place, as in Casuarina in Western Australia, and increasing suicides in custody will bedevil those in charge. There were 17 deaths in custody in that institution in 2000, 14 of them Aboriginal.

The need for alternatives was brought into sharp focus early in 2000 when a 17-year-old Aborigine committed suicide in custody in Darwin. He was incarcerated under the now-notorious Northern Territory law which prescribes prison for a third property offence, no matter how minor. This lad had stolen Texta pens. Mandatory sentencing, which removes any and all discretion from a magistrate, operates in both the Territory and Western Australia. The death of 'Johnno' led to a major national (and international) outcry over the severity of such laws, aimed — despite protestations of egalitarianism — at Aboriginal youth. A Coalition backbench revolt appeared likely, with several MPs threatening to cross the floor to vote for a federal parliamentary over-riding of the Territory law. The Prime Minister 'compromised' with the Chief Minister of the Territory: $5 million in federal funds would be given to provide alternatives to mandatory sentencing (while leaving the law intact). By mid-2001, no such scheme was in operation. It will be interesting to observe what kind of alternatives, if any, are instituted and how many are based on a Warrakoo-like philosophy.

Painting

The North Queensland study by Hunter and others (1999) includes nine examples of symbolic representations of suicide by hanging. While they may well be symptomatic of grief, or the pervasiveness of suicide 'ideation' in the three communities in their study, there could well be value in the deliberate encouragement of painting and sculpture as 'purgation' of suicidal feelings. The painting below is an example of such art. In Nowra, health workers have been reasonably successful in suicide education by showing the paintings (including this one), or photographs of them, to young people at risk. Community organisations could consider a 'paint-your-feelings' program.

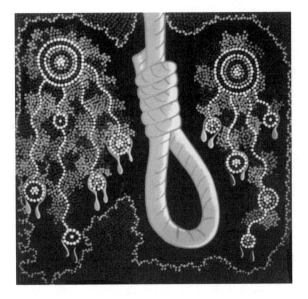

Sport

Enough has been said to date about the role and value of sport in giving young people a sense of belonging, coherence, loyalty — and purpose in life. What remains is for Aboriginal communities to make strong representations to sporting associations, and to national and state sport and recreation bodies, to allow Aborigines into competitions; to provide sports administrators in each community; and to fund teams for equipment and travel.

In other written pieces, I have shown that the Australian Sports Commission and the New South Wales Department of Sport and Recreation are overly concerned with sport at the elite level. No attention is paid to sport as therapy or as a physical or mental focus for youth, as a substitute for group cohesion, as 'medication' for circulatory and metabolic disease (such as diabetes), as an answer to what Peter Toohey calls 'the deleterious worm of boredom',[11] as leisure and therefore as a possible alternative to the togetherness of the pub. Of all 'group therapies' available, sport is the most logical in our armoury, and the one, I believe, most likely to succeed.

Where Aborigines have been expelled, rejected or frozen out of competitions, or teams disbanded — as at Coomealla and Moree in the first instances, and Wilcannia and Menindee in the latter — corporations need to use their power to fight for inclusion, mediation of disputes, funds to travel and buy equipment; and capital grants to enhance what few playing fields they have, such as the grassing of ovals and the installation of lights.

In 2000, the Australian Institute of Criminology established a round table, of which I was a member, on the relationship between sport and crime prevention. The subsequent *Trends and Issues* publication made some strong recommendations, including:

Sport and physical activity can combine with other interventions to reduce crime in particular groups and communities.

It appears that sport and physical activity can reduce crime by providing accessible, appropriate activities in a supportive social context. In other words, sport and physical activity must be connected positively within the social fabric of groups and communities.[12]

Since we were dealing with *crime*, we refrained from an open discussion of suicide. However, much of what was said is as relevant to suicide as it is to the other behaviours we were seeking to mitigate.

In November 2000, a photographic exhibition of 72 members of the Aboriginal and Islander Sports Hall of Fame ended after four months showing at the Museum of Contemporary Art in Sydney. Prior to closing, a group of young Aboriginal inmates from Silverwater and Long Bay were given a day release to attend the exhibition, followed by discussion with former champion boxer George Bracken, rugby Wallaby Gary Ella and me. Hardly a research experiment, it was nevertheless a goal-oriented occasion, one which described the obstacles — child removal, segregation, discrimination, forcible denial of Aboriginality, and so on — which these sports heroes had had to overcome. Atmospheres and architectures such as this seem to me appropriate places in which to use sport as a motivator about life. We took pains to explain that not everyone can become a Mal Meninga, but that sport offers a variety of participations: as referees, touch judges, competition organisers, fund-raisers, club administrators, trainers of juniors, fan club organisers, newsletter-producers, and the like. If most Aboriginal prisoners cannot be brought to such exhibitions, such exhibitions could assuredly be taken, with champions in tow, to the prisons.

Mentors and enlightened witnesses

Throughout this research, discussion with Aborigines focused on the need for 'gurus', 'respect' figures, mentors, tutors, guides in the community, individuals to turn to when life betrays them. The American literature makes constant references to 'gatekeepers', almost always assuming they will be the tribal elders (of yore). Ideally, there should be someone within

the community group who becomes a first port of call for the youth at risk. There are different roles for those assuming real responsibility:
- a guru figure, seen as a voice of wisdom;
- a mentor, such as a sporting hero or role model;
- an enlightened witness, one who gives verity to what the individual has experienced and suffered and cannot talk about, thus enabling victims to retain some belief in themselves.

There are no training courses for such figures. It is a matter of personality, repute, what the Maori call *mana*. However, a starting-point for consideration is that Aboriginal (and Maori) men and women do train as grief counsellors. If they can be seen to mediate grief, they may well come to be seen as people who can counsel, or be able to refer the victim to more specialised personnel.

Aboriginal Community Liaison Officers (ACLOs) come closer than anyone else to performing this function, but their association with the police is often a barrier. However, ACLO training, to date informal and learned on the job, would benefit from a formal approach, including some specialised youth work, and an understanding of the whole suicide canvas.

Programs to assist Aborigines

I discuss below ten programs which have the potential to alleviate suicide. All require input from non-Aboriginal sources. Two may require that Aboriginal community members visit New Zealand, or that New Zealand personnel tour Aboriginal communities.

Aboriginal suicide 'AA'

In the United States, there are growing numbers of groups formed by relatives and friends of suicides. The 'survivors of suicide' hold promise for the possibility of some alleviation. Suicide avoidance can be modelled on Alcoholics Anonymous and Gambling Anonymous programs. Our limited observation (perhaps a dozen large group meetings) was that, within a group, individuals were keen to talk about their suicide attempts: it was a kind of revelation time. Regular 'suicide AA' meetings, in their own domains, may draw youth. The capacity for such a strategy is already there. In the initial period, external assistance may be needed for establishing protocols of do's and don'ts, handling such matters as anonymity and confidentiality.

Needless to say, the naming of such an initiative must not be euphonious or euphemistic. At a Wide Bay Indigenous Youth Life Promotion Unit conference in Hervey Bay, Queensland, in 2000, I addressed a group of some 80 or 90 *Murri* people. My topic was the thrust of this book. There were at least 20 youth present, aged from about 8 to 16. I suggested they be asked to leave. The Torres Islander organiser suggested they stay. At question time, every sensible question came from the youth, especially those at the younger end. Suicide (of their cohort) was put on the table, baldly, starkly: they didn't flinch, and I learned not to. Suicide rather than 'life promotion' was what they wanted to discuss.

In September 1999, I conducted a one-day workshop for staff of the New South Wales Department of Corrective Services. Like all such agencies, they have an acute sensitivity about deaths in custody. A dozen or so recommendations emerged and have since been acted upon. One that needs further pursuit, in all prisons and detention centres in all jurisdictions, is confrontation of the suicide issue with inmates: not from a lecturer behind a lectern, but as a seminar around a table. Some professional personnel may need to be present to answer some questions, or to proffer some advice, if sought. But the thrust of these exercises is to bring suicide out of the dark corners of everybody's minds.

Smoke free/suicide free?

The Health Sponsorship Council in Wellington, New Zealand, has been quite successful in seeking sponsorships for sport, youth and Maori programs from other than tobacco companies. The Council provides, or raises, funds to replace tobacco sponsorship. One of many programs is SMOKEFREE, with a Maori subset called 'Smokefree Maori', aiming at abandoning the habit. It is not the usual 'quit smoking' campaign, accompanied by terrifying pictures of damaged lungs. Rather, a reverse psychology is used: that it is 'cool' and 'with it' not to smoke. 'Cool' activities include dances, with large attendances. The non-smokers gather en masse; smokers are asked to smoke away from the group, at a distant, segregated space. The peer group pressure of the 'cool' ones seems to be prevailing.

Throughout, the accent is on positive change to a healthy lifestyle. Youth are asked to consider taking this experience to their homes and workplaces and, above all, to the *marae*, 'the last bastion of Maoritanga and lifestyle'. And the slogan is to stop smoking for the benefit of all Maori: to do it for your people. In a sense, this is replacement rather than displacement innovation. It is learning to do something new, and it is the germ of an important idea: that 'cool' kids don't commit suicide.

'Going-for-Goal' (GOAL)

Ken Hodge at the University of Otago in New Zealand and Steve Danish at Virginia Commonwealth University in the United States have established both pilot and ongoing life-skills programs, 'basic skills needed to achieve *across* [different] environments'. The project authors believe that sport provides an excellent metaphor for this message. Adolescents aged 10 to 14 are taught to

- identify positive life goals;
- focus on the process (not the outcome) of goal attainment;
- use a general problem-solving model;
- identify health-compromising behaviours which can facilitate goal attainment;
- seek and create social support; and
- transfer these skills from one life context to another, for example sport to classroom, school to career.

The pilot study in Dunedin has been promising, especially given that New Zealand youth are so sports-conscious. GOAL has been established in 25 places in the United States. There is every reason to believe that GOAL can not only be taught in Aboriginal societies but also that its premises, aims and methods are appropriate to suicide prevention or, rather, life-positive outlooks. Dr Ken Hodge should be brought to Australia to teach us the GOAL system, particularly for 'audiences' in institutions.

Parenting and conflict resolution skills

Duclos and others examined suicidal behaviour among American Indian adolescents in detention (1994, 198). Factors involved were alcohol abuse and dependency, frequent run-ins with police, frequent interpersonal conflicts, chronic family instability and, above all, 'prolonged, unresolved grieving' and 'continued deprivation of parental caring', resulting in 'difficulties with the law'. The authors could as well have been writing about Aboriginal youth.

Parenting styles vary across cultures. There are many who deplore what they see as a laxity in Aboriginal child-rearing practices, at least in non-traditional domains. Certainly there is a difference in the degree of anxiety about life's dangers. Aboriginal parents often allow their children to see and experience risks, believing that 'once-burned-twice-shy' will teach the young. The virtues of cultural systems are not in question in this context. A significant problem to be faced is why some Aborigines are today failing as parents.

In all cultures, there is, at bottom, a 'being there' for one's children: loving and nurturing, guiding them through emotional and intellectual difficulties, setting boundaries for behaviour, disciplining when appropriate, assisting in decision making, and the all-embracing obligation to provide food, shelter and clothing. There are many reasons why these skills can be missing, including child removal, parental absorption in grief, and family breakdown — all leading to the absence of role models. However, even where these skills are lacking, they can be taught — and learned.

If we are serious about reducing suicide, then we have to travel to the problem, not wait for the problem to come to the consulting room, by appointment. This applies to all the strategies suggested in this chapter. In the main, Aboriginal parents will not leave home to attend classes or workshops in a city, or in the next large town. They will not travel to environments in which they feel ill at ease, as in a university or TAFE (unless for pleasure, or escape from the kitchen, as is now common with painting classes). They avoid 'mental health units' at hospitals. Internets or websites are inappropriate tools, and Aborigines are unlikely to watch instructional video material.

In sum, classes will have to be facilitated by invitation, at Aboriginal places, and essentially on their terms. Even the most 'culturally sensitive' institutions in Australia are unaware of their assimilationist and 'euro' or 'class-centric' values. Teaching parenting skills and grief counselling are, I believe, the most important skills in initiating any alleviation.

Conflict resolution is another invaluable tool for defusing explosive situations. It also gives an insight into the individual's pain, frustration and needs and how to express them without self-harm. It can be learned in a few sessions, and courses can be tailored to the needs of different groups: young men, young women, mothers, grandmothers, aunties, and so on.

Grief counselling

No other cultural group in Australia is so exposed to death so frequently, especially early death. For many, grief is prolonged, constant and unresolved. Grief counselling is essential if the cycle is to be broken. I am told that for anyone to become a counsellor, they must have a degree in psychology, preferably an Honours year, followed by specialised training. Possession of a BA Hons (Psych) does not necessarily guarantee a good counsellor: specific short-term training could. There is a need to explore the idea of bringing professional counsellors to Aboriginal centres for introductory lessons on what to do, or what not to do, in the immediacy of death, especially by suicide. Even if these 'trainees' learn only how to recognise and refer to specialised professionals, that would be a start. I have every confidence in suitable Aborigines' fulfilling the role of grief counsellors. Those with a nursing or other health work background could be immediate candidates.

Removed children

Every family we met during this research had a strong or direct connection with the removal system, and its effects spill over across the entire Aboriginal population. Grief counselling is usually conducted one-on-one or in a small group. Larger group sessions could address the issue of a whole community in grief. Children and kin of the stolen generations need special attention.

There is another kind of child removal: the large movement of Aboriginal youth to juvenile detention facilities. Most families have one or more children either in such a facility or who have recently been there. The removal is temporary and visits to them are possible. But the family member is absent and missed. It is a complex problem, but counselling could begin to address issues where they affect entire family structures. It is worth noting that in Western Australia, parental visiting is, in many instances, out of the question. Youth from the Kimberley are mostly incarcerated in Perth, between 2000 and 2500 km distant.

School programs

The United States and Canada consider school programs on suicide a virtue. For Canadian Indians, the issue is important because the discredited system of removing children to boarding schools still prevails, therefore special programs need to be included in the school syllabus.

There is American evidence that some programs have been effective. Four high schools established programs for Amerindian girls at high risk of suicide (Lester 1997, 171–2). The girls were paid an hourly wage for attending two group meetings for one-and-a-half hours each week. The curriculum included parenting skills, the psychology of sexuality, decision making, drug and alcohol matters, unwed pregnancies and even suicide, 'presented by medicine men'. The program lasted two years, with dropouts and replacements. The outcome was: 10 per cent of the girls became pregnant, as opposed to the earlier figure of 30 per cent; grades improved slightly; there was no police trouble in the group; and 90 per cent of the drinkers had cut down their intake. Only three of the girls attempted suicide. A similar program on a Zuni reservation also produced lowered scores on a measure of suicide potential as compared to a control group who did not take the program. A contradictory North American report opposes these programs, suggesting that they 'enhance' the notion of suicide and give youth ideas they may not have entertained before.

Aboriginal youth at the suicide risk age — from 12 upwards — could not benefit from any school-based programs unless they were, indeed, still attending school: the programs would simply not reach them. There is much more likelihood of success if classes were conducted by Aborigines, and by other respected helpers, outside of school hours, at Aboriginal medical services, legal services or on land council premises. It may be many years before Australian education authorities rise to the challenge of discussing youth suicide openly. All personnel I have met believe that silence will assist the problem to go away, at least from their school.

Sport

The Australian Sports Commission and the New South Wales Departments of Sport and Recreation and of Health should initiate programs to bring rural and remote Aboriginal sporting facilities closer to a 'level playing field'. More pertinent, they should help Aborigines to participate on any kind of playing field.

The GOAL program could be integrated into these initiatives. This is not merely a recommendation about money for travel, equipment and improved facilities; rather, it is that these agencies develop and implement sports policies which focus on life skills, early starts, suicidal and risk-taking behaviours, aggression, leisure in its true sense, recreation, techniques for coping with boredom, and specific activities of therapeutic benefit for diabetics.

Police and Community Youth Clubs (PCYCs)

The New South Wales Police Service should rethink its role in Aboriginal life. Community policing is, or was, for long the ideal of the service. Even if 'frontline policing' has replaced that policy, the community aspect remains a much-needed aspect of good policing. Policemen and policewomen interact with Aboriginal youth more than do any other non-Aborigines. They see and hear more than anyone else. They are present when everyone else is off duty. PCYC officers are in an even more advantageous position to be police who *assist* rather than police who *arrest*. They offer Aboriginal people what no one else can: space, an outlet for energy, a meeting place, sport, computers, computer games, pool, preparation for driving licences, food, possibly an enlightened witness, and a respite from home life. In the great majority of towns, including the towns which want curfews, caged shop windows, alcohol-free zones, boot camps and the like, these officers are the youth workers. The potential for suicide monitoring, and suicide and life-skills education, is nowhere better than in refurbished premises, with enthusiastic and better-trained PCYC personnel.

Ann Morrice's literacy program

Three to six hours of training is all that is required to train teachers to teach literacy to children. There is something of a 'magic bullet' available in Ann Morrice's language/literacy program, which has already been demonstrated as being highly effective in at least 300 schools in Australia, including Aboriginal schools in South Australia and Western Australia. The technique is also effective with English-as-a-second-language students.

The philosophy is based on oral language development, linked to meaningful content and to the child's visual world. Speaking, listening, reading and writing are linked in meaningful contexts. Skill-based learning is included, and the written product is the focal point towards which lessons are directed. The process includes all the conventions of writing: phonemic awareness, phonics, conventional spelling, grammar, punctuation, syntax, reading skills, and comprehension. The technique can be taught at any venue and is not based on school attendance. A key to the program is that it builds on the positives which exist for the child in his or her own environment. Ernabella, a remote South Australian Aboriginal community, has shown remarkable results from an approach that places a positive value on the children's own environment.

At the sixth national conference on Suicide Prevention Australia in Melbourne in March 1999, Ms Morrice demonstrated her technique. (Demonstration is more effective than trying to describe the method.) Subsequently, several Aboriginal community representatives invited her to visit and train local people. The cost of her programs is minimal. The efficacy is beyond any doubt. (The web version of my original report shows examples of Aboriginal literacy developing under her techniques.) The responses of Aboriginal youth border on the miraculous, especially in view of the disposition of conventional teachers to dismiss Aboriginal educability in general, or to cease bothering with children once they reach a certain age.

The federal government's pledge to implement a literacy program is to be applauded. But, for reasons discussed throughout this book, much of the ensuing activity will not reach Aboriginal children. We cannot wait for standard school procedures, including special literacy projects, to become attractive to Aboriginal children. We can, however, teach them literacy, in a remarkably short time, outside of school, with the hope, or belief, that literacy skills will give them both the confidence and the incentive to return to, or to stay at, school.

The coronial system

In Chapter 4, I discussed at length the definitional problems of coroners' deciding who is Aboriginal, what is youth and what is suicide. It is also clear, as shown in Chapter 9, that coronial under-reporting of suicide is common in New Zealand, the United States, Canada and elsewhere. I am disinclined, for example, to accept that the extremely low rates of male youth suicide reported in Spain, Portugal, Chile and Italy are due solely to Catholic inoculation against the behaviour.

It must be repeated that coronial bias is not deliberately obstructive. On the contrary, as I have explained, kindness, a concern for the avoidance of stigma and chagrin, and care for the families of the bereaved are notable features of small-town life. However, if we are to focus on a specific problem of age, race, class or gender-related suicides, our coroners have to demarcate those categories, allowing for acceptable 'margins of error', to enable a greater understanding of the many factors behind any individual's contemplation of suicide and its implementation.

The movement towards a national database on youth suicide is laudable. But it will be flawed if we perpetuate a system which allows or produces serious under-reporting. There is an urgent need to reintroduce the concept of a national, uniform coronial system, with minimal standards of education and professional training, especially in rural and remote areas. There is a need for in-service courses and 'refresher' seminars for those currently in office, including such topics as the goals and approaches of national and state suicide strategy bodies; the problems posed by youth suicide in general; youth suicide in other countries; and the pressing matter of Aboriginal youth suicide.

There is a need to reconsider the prevailing dictum which excludes any presumption of suicide. Britain, according to an Australian High Court decision in June 1999, is now 'a foreign power'. British tradition about suicide verdicts may well have outworn its applicability in Australia in the new millennium. Coroners should be allowed the latitude of the three-verdict model: definite suicide, probable suicide and possible suicide, even if that classificatory system were not made public (to avoid undue distress) but were available as a guide to those engaged in research and planning strategy.

In addition to the making of physical findings at autopsy, there is an urgent need for a national system of 'socially profiling' suicide. Recording the social features surrounding a suicidal act is preferable to trying to conduct a psychiatric analysis post-mortem.

Police investigators have a special and important role in the Coroner's Office in Glebe. But there are no specialist police officers in rural towns. In all domains, there is a need for a team of assessors to work with the police to establish such social profiles. Assessors need to be appropriately trained: they don't have to be psychiatrists or forensic anthropologists, but the latter should be included in any such teams.

The police and suicide

All police training procedures should include at least a ten-hour block of material on the phenomenon of suicide, including attention to Aboriginal suicide. Although suicide is no longer a criminal act, the police are the first or, after a medical visit, the second to attend a body. The police investigate the circumstances and report to a coroner. The police are the custodians of the youth who threaten, or succeed in, suicide in detention. Clearly they are ill equipped to deal with such matters. Caging a detainee — often flattened, butterfly-style, inside a perspex box — and looking at a television screen is hardly a 'treatment'. At best, it is preventing a media or investigative process into yet another death in custody. The police presumption, for the most part, is that custody itself gives rise to the suicide: yet police are given no insight into the events occurring outside of custody which lead to the suicide while in custody. Given the extra-ordinary role that the police have had, and still have, in Aboriginal lives, there is every reason to have trainee and working police exposed to those aspects of Aboriginal life which promote thoughts of suicide.

Police regional commands should emulate the model established at Hornsby Police Station, where a senior constable is the youth school liaison officer, giving lectures on suicide at schools and youth centres. The New South Wales Education Department should consider allowing people from outside the school system, such as these police liaison officers, to conduct lectures or, preferably, workshops for older high school pupils.

The Aboriginal Community Liaison Officers (ACLOs) are in the forefront of practically every facet of Aboriginal life. They warrant being formed into a professional category in the police service, with higher salaries, overtime (not paid in their 'package'), an ACLO union, their own vehicles, and in-service training, especially in suicide. And more Aborigines should be encouraged to join the police service.

Workshops

The easiest path to new knowledge is to listen to attractively delivered material, preferably at times and places which suit the listener's professional or personal lifestyle. Reading and studying tend to be dismissed once one has graduated, trained, or is on the job. Short, sharp workshops *in situ* have educational advantages: they can be styled as in-service training, advanced studies, professional training, and even certificated training. They also build on the capacities of the people attending: Aborigines, police, coroners, lawyers, mental health workers, and so on. The materials can be framed as new, supplementary or complementary, rather than suggesting 'a whole new ball game'. Several such workshops can be arranged, with minimal difficulty and within reasonable costs, by the organisations concerned. Almost every agency has a component of in-service training and hence funding is not required. In most instances, the costs will be in terms of weekend rostering, travel to an equidistant, suitable venue, and the travel and/or fee costs of the presenters.

Pharmacists

The medical and pharmaceutical professions are rightly concerned about 'non-compliance', that is, patients who are not taking what is prescribed for them. A New South Wales pharmacist, who specialises in 'compliant packaging systems', informs me that non-compliance is not merely a problem with the aged and the confused, but with 'normal' people.

Throughout this study, we observed the standard dispensing of pharmaceutical drugs to people who cannot read the labels, the instructions and the manufacturer's micro-printed inserts describing adverse effects or contra-indications. During the research, I approached the New South Wales branch of the Pharmaceutical Society of Australia about seminars for regional pharmacists, with a view to their dispensing medication to introducing medication-under-observation — as is the practice with methadone or programs for the treatment of tuberculosis in several countries. Several lectures and seminars were given to country town pharmacists: the responses have been very positive in that Aborigines in a few locales are now taking to the use of blister and directive packs. This needs state-wide implementation.

There is evidence of patients visiting several different doctors or clinics and emerging with contra-indicated, and even toxic, antidepressants. One would like to believe that every general practitioner and hospital doctor is versed in antidepressant pharmacology. They may consult the abbreviated bi-monthly pharmacology 'bible', *MIMS*, but few would routinely consult the enormous *MIMS Annual*, a detailed source on contra-indications and adverse effects, or check an on-line authority. There is a need for regional workshops by staff from such bodies as the Pharmaceutical Society and medical educational bodies.

Such instruction is as much about Aborigines taking medication for their diabetes, heart and kidney disease as it is about minimising the availability of lethal means of suicide, or attempted suicide. Blister-packing or, better still, 'daily-dosage' packing could well mean that the young girl from Brewarrina, discussed in Chapter 5, would not have had the 50 Digesic tablets on which she fatally overdosed.

Police

Regional workshops can be conducted with little effort. Several of the police officers whom we interviewed, who had attended an in-service course on Aboriginal history and culture, were enamoured of the materials given to them. All claimed a better appreciation of their clients. The only caveat is that history and culture need to be directed as much to the present as to the past. There is a danger in many of these 'Aboriginal Studies' courses of the painting of an historic, romanticised and idealised picture of a people who, in the listener's experience, have no relationship whatever to the people they deal with in their daily lives. Often, these 'traditional' courses produce an antithetical effect: they make the contemporary population appear altogether removed from, or even 'deviant' from, their 'attractive' ancestors.

There is no shortage of Aboriginal and non-Aboriginal personnel to conduct such workshops. The focus, however, must be on suicidal behaviour, its possible causes, the warning signs (if any), the movements towards suicide, ways of deflecting choices that look like taking a destructive path, and so on.

Coroners

We interviewed 31 New South Wales coroners in this study. Some are extremely competent and confident. Others are unsure in matters of suicide, and many are not *au fait* with Aboriginal societies. Several feel isolated, even though there is regular, helpful advice and service from the State Coroner and his staff.

Most were positive about wanting to attend a regional workshop on all coronial matters, including the suicide issue, at least once, if not twice, yearly. They see the coroners' association meetings as being for the 'real coroners' in Sydney and Melbourne. A few felt that they could not take off any time to attend training, as there was no locum and because they also acted as clerks of the court. I have no doubt that most would be willing to attend a workshop on, for example, the contents of this book.

Custody officers

I have not inquired into the training of those officers who now form custodial units in rural police stations; nor do I know what training is given to corrective service officers in prisons in New South Wales. However, it would be surprising if the situation were markedly different from Canada and the United States, where the general conclusion is that such personnel are under-trained regarding prisoners at risk of suicide. The New South Wales Corrective Services system does have psychologists who prepare screening tests to detect suicidal tendencies. But screening on admission is not the same as knowledge on the part of the custodian as to what to look for, how to look for it, and what to do about it if something untoward manifests. Immediate referral to a prison hospital is neither the sole nor the whole answer.

Workshops should be conducted, in police stations and jails, to familiarise officers with the dimensions and possible causal ingredients of the problem.

Mental health workers, local doctors and nurses

Health personnel in every region would benefit from refresher workshops. My experience is that they are always interested in how they are faring, new inputs, how other jurisdictions function, what makes Aborigines 'tick', what the latest ideas on suicide are. The most commonly expressed 'complaint' is that they 'don't know how to get through to Aborigines'. That, at the least, is true. The fault is not personal: research in North America has shown that mental health jargon is a barrier to patient–therapist communication and understanding, and therefore to therapy of any kind.

Such workshops would need to tackle the history of an Aboriginal experience which has resulted in an antipathy to government institutions of the 'welfare' type. We all need to face the reality of this history, and in facing it assist in a breakthrough to less hostile attitudes.

Psychiatrists and psychiatrists-in-training

In 1999, a group of 47 psychiatrists-in-training at Sydney hospitals asked Ernest Hunter and me, among others, to address them. At a Hunter Valley two-day workshop — ironically, given my views, sponsored by the makers of Aropax — they claimed that they lacked confidence in handling youth suicide and asked if there were any special tools for handling Aboriginal youth. The Otago Medical School curriculum, discussed earlier, ensures that every graduate is taught whatever knowledge, however limited or speculative, is available about Maori suicide. The National University Curriculum Project, established by the Hunter Institute of Mental Health in Newcastle, is currently preparing what can be called a 'suicide syllabus' for use in Australian university curricula for, among others, doctors and nurses.

Informal or formal university and/or hospital workshops for psychiatry registrars would provide an ideal opportunity to correlate and integrate the various approaches to youth suicide. It is not a matter of persuading them to choose one or other of only two alternative approaches. Rather, it is to overcome what appears to be a fear of intervening, or trespassing, into an 'Aboriginal territory' for which they have no invitation, no training and no culturally appropriate qualification.

The agenda for these workshops need to be discussed with the professions and people listed here. However, a starting-point could be their analysis of the Hunter et al study of suicide in North Queensland communities, the Maori Suicide Review Group report, and this book. Above all, it is essential to appreciate that Aboriginal youth suicide has to be understood as emanating from complex social factors, rather than simply being an expression of mental illness.

Reflections

I didn't begin this project with any hypotheses. I had no preconceived notions about the nature or causes of suicide, nor any moral or theological position on the act of self-destruction. As I travelled, I listened, watched, discussed, read, searched, researched, wept at times, and read some more. I didn't know, at the outset, what a 'public health model' was; nor did I have any of the vocabulary of 'mental disorders' or 'mental health problems'. I have discussed my observations and ideas with medical friends, including some psychiatrists. I had, and still have, no animus towards psychiatrists or towards any of the health-care professions. My wish is to help them to widen their horizons.

Some four years later, I find that I have had the temerity to enter a field called suicidology. I don't have a licence to practise as a suicidologist, but nor has anyone else. This book is not intended as a polemic, as an argument for the sake thereof, nor as a challenge to the current ideologies or methodologies of any of the concerned professions. But it does have one concerted and, I hope, coherent thrust: that the suicide portrait of young Aborigines, Maori, American and Canadian Indians, among others, is not simply different from, but is radically different from, youth suicide in the respective mainstream societies in these countries. Suicidologists, and those involved in 'prevention' and 'intervention', must stretch their disciplines, their conceptualisation and their imagination. There is no 'best possible practice' or 'best possible technology' in suicide studies. But there must be room for the widest possible exchange of ideas available to our varied disciplines. There is no room for dogma, let alone for any scientific approach which assumes an underlying uniformity of motivation, in this most fascinating, remarkable and inherently gut-wrenching of all human behaviours.

Notes

1. A renowned American essayist, critic, satirist and lexicographer. I do not recall the source for this quotation.
2. Lester, *Suicide in American Indians*, 174. My emphasis.
3. Elliott, 'A New Way To Be Mad'.
4. Ibid., ch. 9, 153–82.
5. Shore, 'Synopsis'.
6. See, for example, *Youth Suicide Prevention Bulletin*, no. 1, September 1998, and no. 3, May 1999.
7. Ibid., September 1998, 14.
8. Ibid., 18.
9. Personal communication.
10. *Sydney Morning Herald*, 23–25 December 2000.
11. Spectrum, *Sydney Morning Herald*, 23–25 December 2000.
12. Australian Institute of Criminology, 'Crime Prevention through Sport and Physical Activity', 1.

Appendix
Communities and Sites Visited

New South Wales

Region 1

Bennelongs Haven (via Kempsey)
Bowraville
Casino
Coffs Harbour
Corindi Beach
Dungog
Forster
Grafton
Greenhills (via Kempsey)
Kempsey
Lismore
Macksville
Nambucca Heads
Port Macquarie
Purfleet (via Taree)
Taree
Tweed Heads
Woodenbong/Urbenville

Region 2

Batemans Bay/Bingi Point
Bega
Canberra
Eden/Twofold Farm
Jervis Bay/Wreck Bay
Narooma
Nowra
Queanbeyan
Wallaga Lake

Region 3

Bathurst
Condobolin
Coonabarabran
Cowra
Dubbo
Lake Cargelligo
Lithgow
Murrin Bridge
Orange
Parkes
Wellington

Region 4

Armidale
Boggabilla/Toomelah
Gunnedah
Inverell/Tingha
Moree
Narrabri
Tamworth
Wee Waa

Region 5

Bourke
Brewarrina
Broken Hill
Cobar
Dareton/Wentworth
Menindee
Warrakoo (via Dareton)
Wilcannia
New Zealand

Auckland
Carterton
Christchurch
Dunedin
Hamilton
Manukau
Wellington

Region 6
La Perouse
Wollongong*
Newcastle*

*consultation of coroners files only

Bibliography

Aboriginal Education Foundation and Flinders University of South Australia 1990 *Taking Control: A Joint Study of Aboriginal Health in Adelaide with Particular Reference to Stress and Destructive Behaviour 1988–89*, Flinders University Monograph no. 7.

Alvarez, A. 1974 *The Savage God: A Study of Suicide*, Penguin Books, London.

American and Alaska Native Mental Health Research Center 1994 *Calling from the Rim: Suicidal Behavior among American Indian and Alaska Native Adolescents*, Monograph Series, vol. 4, *Journal of the National Center*, University of Colorado Press, Niwot, CO.

AOWWK 2002 *Acting on What We Know: Preventing Youth Suicide in First Nations*, Report of Advisory Group on Suicide Prevention, Ottawa.

Atkinson, Judy 1988 Violence in Aboriginal Australia, draft paper for the National Committee on Violence, Canberra.

Australian Bureau of Statistics (ABS) 1994 *Suicides Australia 1982–1992*, cat. no. 3309.0, Commonwealth of Australia.

—— 1997 *Population Distribution: Indigenous Australians*, cat. no. 4705.0, Commonwealth of Australia.

—— 1999 *Causes of Death: Australia 1997*, cat. no. 3303.0, Commonwealth of Australia.

Australian Institute of Criminology 2000 Crime Prevention through Sport and Physical Activity (Margaret Cameron and Colin McDougall), *Trends and Issues*, no. 165, September.

Australian Institute of Family Studies 1998 *Youth Suicide Prevention: Programs and Activities, National Stocktake*, March, Melbourne.

Australian Law Reform Commission 1986 *The Recognition of Aboriginal Customary Laws*, Report no. 31.

Australian Psychological Society 1999 *Suicide: An Australian Psychological Society Discussion Paper*, Carlton, Victoria, September.

Bachman, Ronet 1992 *Death and Violence on the Reservation: Homicide, Family Violence, and Suicide in American Indian Populations*, Auburn House, New York.

Barber, James, J. Punt and J. Albers 1988 Alcohol and Power on Palm Island, *Australian Journal of Social Issues* 23(2), 87–101.

Baume, P.J.M., C.H. Cantor and P.G. McTaggart 1997 *Suicides in Queensland: A Comprehensive Study 1990–1995*, Australian Institute for Suicide Research and Prevention, Griffith University, Brisbane.

Beautrais, A.L., C.A. Coggan, D.M. Fergusson and L. Rivers 1997 *The Prevention, Recognition and Management of Young People at Risk of Suicide: Development of Guidelines for Schools,* National Health Committee, NZ Ministry of Education, Wellington.

Beautrais, Annette, Peter Joyce, Roger Mulder, D.M. Fergusson, B.J. Deavoll and S.K. Nightingale 1996a Prevalence and Comorbidity of Mental Disorders in Persons Making Serious Suicide Attempts: A Case-Control Study, *American Journal of Psychiatry* 153(8), 1009–14.

Beautrais, Annette, Peter Joyce and Roger Mulder 1996b Access to Firearms and the Risk of Suicide: A Case Study Control, *Australian and New Zealand Journal of Psychiatry* 30, 741–8.

—— 1996c Risk Factors for Serious Suicide Attempts among Youths Aged 13 through 24 Years, *Journal of the American Academy of Child and Adolescent Psychiatry* 35(9), 1174–82.

Bell, Gail. 2005 The Worried Well: the Depression Epidemic and the Medicalisation of Our Sorrows, *Quarterly Essay* 18, Black Inc., Melbourne.

Biskup, M. (ed.) 1992 *Suicide: Opposing Viewpoints*, Greenhaven Press, San Diego.

Blum, R.W. and P.M. Rinehart 1997 *Reducing the Risk: Connections That Make a Difference in the Lives of Youth*, Division of General Pediatrics and Adolescent Health, University of Minnesota.

Bowles, John 1985 Suicide and Attempted Suicide in Contemporary Western Samoa. In Hezel et al (eds),*Culture, Youth and Suicide in the Pacific*, 15–35.

Brett, Cate 1997 East Side Boys, *North and South*, Auckland, October.

Burvill, P.W. 1975 Attempted Suicide in the Perth Statistical Division 1971–1972, *Australian and New Zealand Journal of Psychiatry* 9(4), 273–9.

Callaghan, Bruce & Associates 1998 Proactive Youth Policing — the NSW PCYC Initiative: Report of the NSW Ministerial Inquiry into Police & Community Youth Clubs in NSW, unpublished.

Cavanagh, Robert, Roderic Pitty and Gregory Woods 1997 *Too Much Wrong: Report on the Death of Edward James Murray*, Northern New South Wales Aboriginal Community Legal Service, Newcastle.

Cawte, John et al 1968 Arafura, Aboriginal Town: The Medico-Sociological Expedition to Arnhem Land in 1968, unpublished typescript, restricted use, call number MS 483, AIATSIS, Canberra.

Chen, Lincoln, A. Kleinman and Norma Ware 1994 *Health and Social Change in International Perspective*, Harvard School of Public Health, Boston.

Cheng, Andrew 1995 Mental Illness and Suicide: a Case-Control Study in East Taiwan, *Archives of General Psychiatry*, 52, 594–603.

Coggan, Carolyn and Robyn Norton 1994a Reducing Self-Directed Harm (Suicide and Attempted-Suicide) among Young People: A Public Health Approach?, *Community Mental Health in New Zealand* 8(2), 26–31.

—— 1994b Suicide and Attempted Suicide among Young People Aged 15–24 years in the Northern Health Region: An Area Analysis, Report 1173–1443, August, Injury Prevention, School of Medicine, Auckland.

Commonwealth of Australia 2000 *Reconciliation — Australia's Challenge*, Final Report of the Council for Aboriginal Reconciliation to the Prime Minister and the Commonwealth Parliament, December.

Commonwealth Department of Human Services and Health 1997 *Youth Suicide: a Background Monograph*, 2nd edn, Australian Government Publishing Service, Canberra.

Cornwell, John 1996 *The Power To Harm: Mind, Medicine and Murder on Trial*, Viking, London.

Coulthard, Glen 1999 Colonization, Indian Policy, Suicide, and Aboriginal Peoples, The School of Native Studies, University of Alberta, http://www.ualberta.ca/~pimothe/suicide.html

Deavoll, B.J., R.T. Mulder, A.L. Beautrais and P.R. Joyce 1993 One Hundred Years of Suicide in New Zealand, *Acta Psychiatrica Scandinavica* 87, 81–5.

Deloria, Vine Jr 1988 *Custer Died for Your Sins — an Indian Manifesto*, University of Oklahoma Press, Norman.

Department of Health 1992 *Healthy Start*, Maternal and Child Health Branch, Hawai'i.

Dietrich, Uta and Anne Kempton 1996 Prevention of Deliberate Self Harm 1992–1996, North Coast Public Health Unit, New South Wales Health Department.

Dizmang, Larry et al 1974 Adolescent Suicide at an Indian Reservation, *American Journal of Orthopsychiatry* 44(1), January, 43–7.

DSM-IV-TR 2000 *Diagnostic and Statistical Manual for Mental Disorders*, American Physchiatric Association, 4th edn, Washington DC.

Duclos, Christin, Warren Le Beau and Gail Elias 1994 American Indian Adolescent Suicidal Behavior in Detention Environments. In American and Alaska Native Mental Health Research Center, 1994 *Calling from the Rim*, 189–214.

Dudley, Michael et al 1992 Youth Suicide in New South Wales: Urban–Rural Trends, *Medical Journal of Australia* 156, 20 January, 83–8.

—— 1997 Suicide among Young Rural Australians 1964–1993: A Comparison with Metropolitan Trends, *Social Psychiatry and Psychiatric Epidemiology* 32, 251–60.

—— 1998a Coroners' Records of Rural and Non-Rural Cases of Youth Suicide in New South Wales, *Australian and New Zealand Journal of Psychiatry* 32, 242–51.

—— 1998b Suicide among Young Australians, 1964–1993: An Interstate Comparison of Metropolitan and Rural Trends, *Medical Journal of Australia* 169, July, 77–80.

—— 2004 Addressing Indigenous Suicide: a Special Case? A Response to Colin Tatz, *Australian Aboriginal Studies* 2, 26–33.

Durkheim, Emile 1968 *Suicide: A Study in Sociology*, Routledge & Kegan Paul, London.

Eastwell, Harry 1988 The Low Risk of Suicide among the Yolgnu of the Northern Territory: The Traditional Aboriginal Pattern, *Medical Journal of Australia* 148(7), 338–40.

Eddleston, Michael et al 1998 Deliberate Self Harm in Sri Lanka: An Overlooked Tragedy in the Developing World, *British Medical Journal* 317, 11 July, 133–5.

Elliott, Carl 2000 A New Way To Be Mad, *Atlantic Monthly*, December; online at <www.theatlantic.com/issues/2000/12/elliott>.

Elliott-Farrelly, Terri 2004 Australian Aboriginal Suicide: The Need for an Aboriginal Suicidology?, *Australian e-Journal for the Advancement of Aboriginal Health (AeJAMH)*, 3(3), 1–7.

Feinberg, Joel 1970 *Doing and Deserving: Essays in the Theory of Responsibility*, Princeton University Press, Princeton.

Fergusson, David and Michael Lynskey 1995a Childhood Circumstances, Adolescent Adjustment, and Suicide Attempts in a New Zealand Birth Cohort, *Journal of the American Academy of Child and Adolescent Psychiatry* 34(5), May, 612–22.

—— 1995b Suicide Attempts and Suicidal Ideation in a Birth Cohort of 16-Year-Old New Zealanders, *Journal of the American Academy of Child and Adolescent Psychiatry* 34(10), October, 1308–17.

Filc, D. 2004 The Medical Text: Between Biomedicine and Hegemony, *Social Science and Medicine* 59.

Firestone, Robert W. 1997 *Suicide and the Inner Voice*, Sage Publications, Thousands Oaks, CA.

Flisher, A.J. et al 1992 Mortality from External Causes in South African Adolescents, 1984–1986, *South African Medical Journal* 81, January, 77–80.

—— 1993 Risk-Taking Behaviour of Cape Peninsula High-School Students, *South African Medical Journal* 83, July, 474–6.

Flisher, A.J. and C.D.H. Parry 1994 Suicide in South Africa, *Acta Psychiatrica Scandinavica* 90, 348–53.

Flisher, Alan and Derek Chalton 1995 High-School Dropouts in a Working-Class South African Community: Selected Characteristics and Risk-Taking Behaviour, *Journal of Adolescence* 18, 105–21.

Flisher, Alan et al 1997 Seasonal Variation of Suicide in South Africa, *Psychiatry Research* 66, 13–22.

Frankl, Viktor 1984 (ed.) *Man's Search for Meaning*, Washington Square Press, New York.

Goffman, Erving 1961 *Asylums*, Penguin, London.

Goldney, Robert 2000 Exploring Aboriginal Youth Suicide, *Medical Journal of Australia* 172(9), 1 May, 443.

—— 2002 Is Aboriginal Suicide Different? A Commentary on the Work of Colin Tatz, *Psychiatry, Psychology and Law* 9 (2), 257–59.

Grattan, Michelle (ed.) 2000 *Reconciliation: Essays on Australian Reconciliation*, Black Inc., Melbourne.

Hacking, Ian 1995 *Rewriting the Soul*, Princeton University Press, Princeton, NJ.

—— 1998 *Mad Travelers: Reflections on the Reality of Transient Mental Illnesses*, University of Virginia Press, Charlottesville.

Hafen, Bruce and Jonathon Hafen 1996 Abandoning Children to Their Autonomy: The United Nations Convention on the Rights of the Child, *Harvard International Law Journal* 37(2), Spring, 449–91.

Harrison, James et al 1997 Youth Suicide and Self-Injury — Australia, *Australian Injury Prevention Bulletin*, Issue 15, Australian Institute for Health and Welfare, Canberra.

Hassan, Riaz 1995 *Suicide Explained: The Australian Experience*, Melbourne University Press, Melbourne.

—— 1996 *Social Factors in Suicide in Australia*, 52, Australian Institute of Criminology, Canberra.

—— 1998 One Hundred Years of Emile Durkheim's Suicide: A Study in Sociology, *Australian and New Zealand Journal of Psychiatry* 32, 168–71.

Healey, Kaye (ed.) 1997 *Suicide: Issues in the Nineties*, Spinney Press, Sydney.

Hezel, Francis 1994 What Can We Do To Prevent Suicide in the Pacific?, *Pacific Health Dialog* 1(1), March, 74–82.

Hezel, Francis, Donald Rubenstein and Geoffrey White (eds) 1985 *Culture, Youth and Suicide in the Pacific: Papers from an East-West Center Conference*, University of Hawai'i at Manoa.

Hicks, Jack 2005 *Statistics on Deaths by Suicide in Nunavut (and Other Inuit Regions in Canada) 1975 to 2004*, jack@jackhicks.com

Hillman, James 1997 *Suicide and the Soul*, 2nd edn, Spring Publications, Woodstock, Connecticut.

Hoberman, John 1997 *Darwin's Athletes: How Sport Has Damaged Black America and Preserved the Myth of Race*, Houghton Mifflin, Boston.

Horton, David (gen. ed.) 1994 *The Encyclopaedia of Aboriginal Australia*, AIATSIS, Canberra.

House of Representatives Standing Committee on Family and Community Affairs 1997 *Aspects of Youth Suicide: Summary Report*, Australian Government Publishing Service, Canberra.

Human Rights and Equal Opportunity Commission (HREOC) 1997 *Bringing Them Home: Report of the National Inquiry into Separation of Aboriginal and Torres Strait Islander Children from Their Families*, Sydney.

Hunter, Ernest 1988a Aboriginal Suicides in Custody: A View from the Kimberley, *Australian and New Zealand Journal of Psychiatry* 22(3), 273–82.

—— 1988b On Gordian Knots and Nooses: Aboriginal Suicide in the Kimberley, *Australian and New Zealand Journal of Psychiatry* 22, 264–71.

—— 1989 Changing Aboriginal Mortality Patterns in the Kimberley Region of Western Australia 1957–86: The Impacts of Deaths from External Causes, *Aboriginal Health Information Bulletin II*, May, 27–32.

—— 1990 A Question of Power: Contemporary Self-Mutilation among Aborigines in the Kimberley, *Australian Journal of Social Issues* 25(4), 261–78.

—— 1993 *Aboriginal Health and History: Power and Prejudice in Remote Australia*, Cambridge University Press, Cambridge.

Hunter, Ernest, Joseph Reser, Mercy Bairda and Paul Reser 1999 An Analysis of Suicide in Indigenous Communities of North Queensland: The Historical, Cultural and Symbolic Landscape, unpublished report, May, 120pp.

Isaacs, S et al 1998 Suicide in the Northwest Territories: a Descriptive Overview, May, unpublished paper for a manuscript entitled 'Suicide in the Northwest Territories', Copy held by Colin Tatz.

Jarrett, Ada, Penny Driver and Fleur Herscovitch Toomelah: Community Profile 1991, unpublished.

Jones, Ivor 1973 Psychiatric Disorders among Desert and Kimberley People, *Australian Institute of Aboriginal Studies Newsletter* 3(6), 17–20.

Khalidi, Noor Ahmad 1996 Hopeless Youth in the Lucky Country, unpublished report for Office of Indigenous Affairs, Department of Prime Minister and Cabinet.

Kidson, Malcolm and I. Jones 1968 Psychiatric Disorders among Aborigines of the Australian Western Desert, unpublished typescript, call number PMS 918, AIATSIS, Canberra.

Kirmayer, Laurence et al (eds.) 2000 *The Mental Health of Indigenous Peoples: Proceedings of the Advanced Study Institute, May 29–31 2000*, Institute of Community and Family Psychiatry, Sir Mortimer B. David – Jewish General Hospital & Division of Social and Transcultural Psychiatry, McGill University.

Kosky, Robert 1998 Suicide: Rational or Irrational?, *Australian Psychiatry* (6)6, December, 289–91; see also correspondence following his paper, *Australian Psychiatry* (7)1, 1999, 35–6.

Kral, Michael 2003 *Unikkaartuit: Meanings of Well-Being, Sadness, Suicide, and Change in Two Inuit Communities*, Final Report to the National Health Research and Development Programs, Health Canada, Project #6606-6231-002. (Draft for Nunavut Version).

Kreitman, Norman 1988 Definition of Suicide, *British Journal of Psychiatry* 153(6), 343.

—— 1990 Research Issues in the Epidemiological and Public Health Aspects of Parasuicide and Suicide. In D. Goldberg and D. Tantum (eds), *The Public Health Impact of Mental Disorders*, Hogrefe & Huber, Lewiston, NY, 73–82.

Kwiet, Konrad 1984 The Ultimate Refuge: Suicide in the Jewish Community under the Nazis, *Year Book XXIX*, Leo Baeck Institute, New York, 136–67.

Lester, David 1987 *Suicide as a Learned Behavior*, Charles Thomas, Springfield.

—— 1988 *Suicide from a Psychological Perspective*, Charles Thomas, Springfield.

—— 1989 *Suicide from a Sociological Perspective*, Charles Thomas, Springfield.

—— 1993 *The Cruelest Death: The Enigma of Adolescent Suicide*, The Charles Press, Philadelphia.

—— 1997 *Suicide in American Indians*, Nova Science Publishers Inc., New York.

LifeForce Wesley Mission 2000 Suicide in Australia, a Dying Shame, summary paper for Suicide and the Media Workshop, Wesley Mission, Sydney, 6 November.

Malchy, Brian et al 1997 Suicide among Manitoba's Aboriginal People, 1988 to 1994, *Canadian Medical Association Journal* 156(8), 1133–8.

Maley, Barry 1994 Youth Suicide and Youth Unemployment, in-house publication, Centre for Independent Studies, Sydney.

Maori Suicide Review Group 1996 Reducing Suicide by Maori Prison Inmates, unpublished report, NZ Department of Corrections and Te Puni Kokori.

Marx, Emanuel 1976 *The Social Context of Violent Behaviour: A Social Anthropological Study in an Israeli Immigrant Town*, Routledge & Kegan Paul, London.

May, Phillip 1995 Adolescent Suicide in the West, paper to Second Bi-Regional Adolescent Suicide Prevention Conference, Salt Lake City, December, US Department of Health and Human Services.

Mayekiso, T. [date uncertain] Attitude of Black Adolescents toward Suicide, *Southern Africa Journal of Psychiatry* 7(1), 40–5.

McIlvanie, Christine 1982 The Responsibility of People, BA Honours dissertation, Politics Department, University of New England, Armidale.

Mental Health Foundation of New Zealand 1997 *Young People and Depression*, Auckland.

Miller, Alice 1990 *Banished Knowledge*, Virago Press, London.

Millward, Alan 1997 Research and Evaluate Strategies To Reduce Incidents of Anti-Social Behaviour in the Lower Clarence, unpublished dissertation, Police College, New South Wales.

Ministry of Health 1996 *Youth Mental Health Promotion, Including Suicide Prevention: The Public Health Issues 1995–1996*, Wellington, NZ.

—— 1997a *Youth Suicide Statistics for the Period 1991–95*, NZ Health Information Service, Wellington.

—— 1997b *Suicide Trends in New Zealand 1974–94*, NZ Health Information Service, Wellington.

NACCHO (National Aboriginal Community Controlled Health Organisations) 2993 *A Way Through? The Minefield of Measuring Aboriginal Mental Health: Community and Post-Colonial Perspectives on 'Emotional and Social Well-Being' –related , population Inquiry Methods and Strategy Development*, Review and Discussion Paper, NACCHO, Canberra.

National Mental Health Strategy 2000 *Promotion, Prevention and Early Intervention for Mental Health — A Monograph*, Commonwealth of Australia, Canberra.

Neame, Peter 1997 *Suicide and Mental Health in Australia and New Zealand*, Neame, Brisbane.

Peck, M., Norman Farberow and R. Litman 1985 *Youth Suicide*, Springer Publishing Co., New York.

Pinto, C. and T.D. Koelmeyer 1991 Self Inflicted Deaths in Auckland: A Study of 1057 Cases, *New Zealand Medical Journal* 4(907), 88–9.

Pounder, D.J. 1991 Changing Patterns of Male Suicide in Scotland, *Forensic Science International* 51, 79–87.

RCAP 1995 Royal Commission on the Aboriginal People, Choosing Life: Special Report on Suicide Among Aboriginal People, Canada Communication Group Publishing, Ottawa.

Read, Peter 1983 *The Stolen Generations: The Removal of Aboriginal Children in New South Wales, 1883 to 1969*, Occasional Paper no. 1, NSW Ministry of Aboriginal Affairs, Sydney.

Reser, Joseph 1991 Aboriginal Mental Health: Conflicting Cultural Perspectives. In J. Reid and P. Trompf (eds), *The Health of Aboriginal Australia*, Harcourt Brace Jovanovich, Sydney.

—— 2004 What Does it Mean to Say that Aboriginal Suicide is Different? Differing Cultures, Accounts and Idioms of Distress in the Context of Indigenous Youth Suicide, *Australian Aboriginal Studies* 2, 34–53.

Royal Commission into Aboriginal Deaths in Custody (RCIADIC) 1991 Commissioner Elliott Johnston QC, *National Report*, 5 vols, Australian Government Publishing Service, Canberra.

Seligman, Martin 1995 *The Optimistic Child*, Random House, Sydney.

Senate Legal and Constitutional References Committee 2000 *Healing: A Legacy of Generations*. The Report of the Inquiry into the Federal Government's Implementation of Recommendations Made by the Human Rights and Equal Opportunity Commission in *Bringing Them Home*, November. (There is a dissenting report by Senators Payne and Coonan, both government senators.)

Shneidman, Edwin 1996 *The Suicidal Mind*, Oxford University Press, New York.

Shore, James 1994 Synopsis. In American and Alaska Native Mental Health Research Center, *Calling from the Rim*, 250–63.

Skegg, K., B. Cox and J. Broughton 1995 Suicide among New Zealand Maori: Is History Repeating Itself?, *Acta Psychiatrica Scandinavica* 92, 453–9.

Stengel, Erwin 1964 *Suicide and Attempted Suicide*, Penguin Books, Melbourne.

Szasz, Thomas 1974 *The Second Sin*, Anchor Books, New York.

—— 1979 *The Theology of Medicine: The Political–Philosophical Foundations of Medical Ethics*, Oxford University Press, Oxford.

Tatz, Colin 1964 Aboriginal Administration in the Northern Territory of Australia, PhD thesis, Australian National University.

—— 1972 *Four Kinds of Dominion*, University of New England, Armidale.

—— 1979, *Race Politics in Australia: Aborigines, Politics and Law*, University of New England, Armidale.

—— 1983 Aborigines and the Age of Atonement, *Australian Quarterly* 55(3), Spring.

—— 1990 Aboriginal Violence: A Return to Pessimism, *Australian Journal of Social Issues* 25(4), November, 245–60.

—— 1994a A Question of Rights and Wrongs. In Oliver Mendelsohn and Upendra Baxi (eds), *The Rights of Subordinated Peoples*, Oxford University Press, Delhi, 159–77.

—— 1994b Aborigines: Sport, Violence and Survival, CRC Project 18/1989, Criminology Research Council, Canberra, April.

—— 1995 *Obstacle Race: Aborigines in Sport*, University of New South Wales Press, Sydney.

—— 1997 Immortality and Black Youth Suicide, *Sydney Morning Herald*, 20 December.

—— 1998 Race Relations in the 21st Century, *Sydney Institute Quarterly* 2(3), 3–11.

—— 1999 *Genocide in Australia*, Research Discussion Paper 8/99, AIATSIS, Canberra.

—— 1999 Aboriginal Suicide is Different: Aboriginal Youth Suicide in New South Wales, the Australian Capital Territory and New Zealand: Towards a Model of Explanation and Alleviation, Criminology Research Grant 25/96–7, found at www.aic.gov.au/crc/reports/tatz/index.html

—— 2001 *Aboriginal Suicide is Different: a Portrait of Life and Self-Destruction*, Aboriginal Studies Press, Canberra.

—— 2002 Rejoinder to Is Aboriginal Suicide Different? A Commentary on the work of Colin Tatz, *Psychiatry, Psychology and Law*, 9(2), 260–261.

—— 2004 Aboriginal, Maori and Inuit Youth Suicide: Avenues to Alleviation?, *Australian Aboriginal Studies 2004* 2, 15–25.

Tatz, Colin and Paul Tatz 2000 *Black Gold: The Aboriginal and Islander Sports Hall of Fame*, Aboriginal Studies Press, Canberra.

Te Ropu Rangahau Hauora a Eru Pomare 1995 *Hauora: Maori Standards of Health III, A Study of the Years 1970–1991*, Huia Publishers, Wellington, NZ.

Thompson, Richard 1998 *The Challenge of Racism: A Discussion Document*, Peacemaker Press, Christchurch.

Tully, James 1995 *Strange Multiplicity: Constitutionalism in an Age of Diversity*, Cambridge University Press, Cambridge.

Turnbull, Colin 1972 *The Mountain People*, Simon & Schuster, New York.

University of Minnesota Adolescent Health Program 1992 *The State of Native American Youth Health*, Minnesota.

Vijayakumar, V & S Rajkymar 1999 Are Risk Factors for Suicide Universal? A Case-Control Study in India, *Alta Psychiatrica Scandinavica*, 99, 407–411.

Waldram, James 1997 The Aboriginal Peoples of Canada: Colonialism and Mental Health. In Ihsan Al-Issa and Michael Tousignant (eds), *Ethnicity, Immigration and Psychopathology*, Plenum Press, New York.

Waldren, Murray 2001 *Moran v. Moran*, HarperCollins, Sydney.

Waller, Kevin 1994 *Coronial Law and Practice in New South Wales*, Butterworths, Sydney (1973 edn, Law Book Company, Sydney).

Weber, Max 1970 *From Max Weber: Essays in Sociology* (eds. H. H. Gerth and C. Wright Mills), Routledge & Kegan Paul, London.

Wekstein, Louis 1979 *Handbook of Suicidology: Principles, Problems and Practice*, Brunner/Mazel, New York.

Williams, Mark 1997 *Cry of Pain: Understanding Suicide and Self-Harm*, Penguin, London.

Zilboorg, Gregory 1936 Suicide among Civilized and Primitive Races, *American Journal of Psychiatry*, vol. 92.

Index